Advanced Energy
Design Guide
for
K-12 School Buildings

This publication was prepared under the auspices of ASHRAE Special Project 134 and was supported with funding from DOE through PNNL contract #137545.

PROJECT COMMITTEE

Shanti Pless
Chair

Merle McBride	Ozgem Ornektekin
Vice-Chair	*USGBC Representative*
Mike Nicklas	Pete Jefferson
AIA Representative	*Member at Large*
John Murphy	Mark Ryles
ASHRAE Representative	*Member at Large*
Ken Seibert	Eric Bonnema
ASHRAE Representative	*Analysis Support*
Craig Kohring	Matt Leach
IES Representative	*Analysis Support*
Chad McSpadden	Lilas Pratt
IES Representative	*Staff Liaison*
Robert Kobet	Bert Etheredge
USGBC Representative	*ASHRAE Staff Support*

STEERING COMMITTEE

Don Colliver
Chair

Bill Worthen	Jeremy Williams
AIA Representative	*DOE Representative*
Rita Harrold	Mick Schwedler
IES Representative	*ASHRAE SSPC 90.1 Liaison*
Brendan Owens	Adrienne Thomle
USGBC Representative	*ASHRAE TC 7.6 Liaison*
Tom Watson	Lilas Pratt
ASHRAE Representative	*ASHRAE Staff Liaison*

Any updates/errata to this publication will be posted on the ASHRAE Web site at www.ashrae.org/publicationupdates.

Advanced Energy Design Guide for K-12 School Buildings

Achieving 50% Energy Savings Toward a Net Zero Energy Building

American Society of Heating, Refrigerating and Air-Conditioning Engineers
The American Institute of Architects
Illuminating Engineering Society of North America
U.S. Green Building Council
U.S. Department of Energy

ISBN 978-1-936504-13-8

© 2011 American Society of Heating, Refrigerating
and Air-Conditioning Engineers, Inc.
1791 Tullie Circle, N.E.
Atlanta, GA 30329
www.ashrae.org

Printed in the United States of America

Printed on 10% post-consumer waste using soy-based inks.

Cover design and illustrations by Emily Luce, Designer.
Cover photograph by Andres Alonso, courtesy of RRMM Architects.

Library of Congress Cataloging-in-Publication Data

Advanced energy design guide for K-12 school buildings : achieving 50% energy savings toward a net zero energy building / American Society of Heating, Refrigerating and Air-Conditioning Engineers, Inc. ... [et al.] ; project committee Shanti Pless, chair ... [et al.].
    p. cm.
  Includes bibliographical references.
  ISBN 978-1-936504-13-8 (softcover : alk. paper) 1. Elementary school buildings--Energy conservation--United States. 2. Sustainable buildings--Design and construction--Standards--United States. I. Pless, Shanti D. II. American Society of Heating, Refrigerating and Air-Conditioning Engineers.
  TJ163.5.U5A3825 2011
  727'.10472--dc23
            2011031194

ASHRAE Staff

SPECIAL PUBLICATIONS

Mark Owen
*Editor/Group Manager
of Handbook and Special Publications*

Cindy Sheffield Michaels
Managing Editor

James Madison Walker
Associate Editor

Elisabeth Parrish
Assistant Editor

Meaghan O'Neil
Editorial Assistant

Michshell Phillips
Editorial Coordinator

PUBLISHING SERVICES

David Soltis
*Group Manager of Publishing Services
and Electronic Communications*

Jayne Jackson
Publication Traffic Administrator

PUBLISHER

W. Stephen Comstock

Contents

Sidebars—
Case Studies and
Technical Examples

Acknowledgments

The *Advanced Energy Design Guide for K-12 School Buildings* is the second in a series of Advanced Energy Design Guide (AEDG) publications designed to provide strategies and recommendations for achieving 50% energy savings over the minimum code requirements of ANSI/ASHRAE/IESNA Standard 90.1-2004, *Energy Standard for Buildings Except Low-Rise Residential Buildings*. The 50% AEDG series addresses building types that represent major energy users in the commercial building stock. This Guide is the result of the dedicated, collective efforts of many professionals who devoted countless hours to help K-12 school facilities use less energy.

The primary authors were the 11 members of the ASHRAE Special Project 134 Committee (SP-134) who represented the participating organizations—primarily the American Society of Heating, Refrigerating and Air-Conditioning Engineers, Inc. (ASHRAE); the American Institute of Architects (AIA); the U.S. Green Building Council (USGBC); the Illuminating Engineering Society of North America (IES); and the U.S. Department of Energy (DOE).

The chair would like to personally thank all the members of the project committee for their diligence, creativity, persistence, and willingness to take the time to support this Guide. They worked extremely hard to pull together practical, technically sound information covering all aspects of low-energy-use K-12 school building design. They provided guidance in the areas of lighting and daylighting and on many types of HVAC systems and envelope considerations. Their expertise and differing views greatly enriched this Guide. The authors brought many years of experience and good practices in design, construction, commissioning, and operation of K-12 school buildings to achieve significant energy savings.

The project would not have been possible without DOE's financial support for project committee expenses, Guide development, National Renewable Energy Laboratory energy modeling analysis, and committee leadership. The Chair would also personally like to thank Jeremiah Williams, the DOE technology development manager in the Building Technologies Program.

The project committee met four times and held eight conference calls in ten months. Each face-to-face meeting required two nights in a hotel; thus, the chair would also like to express his appreciation to the authors' families for their patience. In addition, the chair acknowledges the support of the project committee members' employers, including Innovative Design; H.E. Williams Inc.; MDA Engineering Inc.; New York City Department of Education; CMTA; M.E. Group; M+G Architects; The Ohio Valley Educational Cooperative;

Owens Corning; Trane, a business of Ingersoll Rand; the University of Kentucky; Kobet Collaborative; and the National Renewable Energy Laboratory.

The project committee's efforts were guided by the AEDG Steering Committee, composed of members from the partner organizations—ASHRAE, AIA, USGBC, and IES—and by DOE. Its members provided direction and guidance to complete the Guide within 12 months. The Steering Committee assembled an expert team of authors and defined a scope that kept the project committee's task manageable and focused. The representatives from these organizations brought a collegial and constructive spirit to the task of setting policy.

In addition to the voting members of the project committee, a number of individuals played key roles in the Guide's success. Specifically, thanks to Lilas Pratt and Bert Etheredge for serving as gracious hosts at their facilities, to Paul Hutton of Hutton Architecture Studio and Stu Reeves of Poudre School District for providing valuable insight on their work in high performance schools, and to Vern Smith for his focus on commercial kitchens in schools and his direct contributions to Chapter 5. Many thanks also to Brent Griffith of the National Renewable Energy Laboratory for providing invaluable EnergyPlus modeling and debugging assistance.

Twenty-five people participated in two peer reviews, providing more than 660 remarks that helped strengthen and clarify the Guide. Their thoughtful input is much appreciated, and the chair hopes they see the impacts of their recommendations in the finished text.

A huge debt of gratitude is extended to the authors of the previously published 30% Energy Savings AEDGs, for they paved the way and defined basic structure, content, and format, as well as reporting and review procedures. Following in their footsteps has resulted in consistency among the AEDGs and has been a tremendous time saver. Building on their success enabled the project committee to finish its work in a timely manner.

Additional thanks to the ASHRAE staff, including Lilas Pratt and Bert Etheredge, whose direction and guidance were invaluable and whose organizational skills and dedication helped keep the project committee on track. The ASHRAE staff managed an enormous number of documents, coordinated with all authors with great competence and efficiency, and helped turn the documents into a first-rate publication. This Guide could not have been developed without their contributions.

Finally, the committee greatly appreciates Eric Bonnema and Matt Leach of the National Renewable Energy Laboratory for providing detailed simulation and analysis support.

Shanti Pless
Chair, Special Project 134

June 2011

Abbreviations and Acronyms

ACCA	Air Conditioning Contractors of America
AEDG-K12	*Advanced Energy Design Guide for K-12 School Buildings*
AFF	above finished floor
AIA	American Institute of Architects
ASHRAE	American Society of Heating, Refrigerating and Air-Conditioning Engineers
ASTM	ASTM International
ANSI	American National Standards Institute
BEF	ballast efficacy factor
BF	ballast factor
BoD	Basis of Design
Btu	British thermal unit
C	thermal conductance, $Btu/h \cdot ft^2 \cdot °F$
c.i.	continuous insulation
Cx	commissioning
CxA	commissioning authority
CCT	corrected color temperature
CDD	cooling degree day
CFL	compact fluorescent lights
CFM	cubic feet per minute
CMH	ceramic metal halide
COP	coefficient of performance, dimensionless
CRI	Color Rendering Index
CRRC	Cool Roof Rating Council
d	diameter, ft
DCV	demand-controlled ventilation
DFR	daylighting fenestration-to-floor area ratio
DL	Advanced Energy Design Guide code for *daylighting*
DOAS	dedicated outdoor air system
DOE	Department of Energy
DX	direct expansion
E_c	efficiency, combustion, dimensionless
ECM	energy conservation measure *or* electronically commutated motors

E_t	efficiency, thermal, dimensionless
EER	energy efficiency ratio, Btu/W·h
EF	energy factor
EL	Advanced Energy Design Guide Code for *electric lighting*
EN	Advanced Energy Design Guide Code for *envelope*
EUI	energy use intensity
EX	Advanced Energy Design Guide Code for *exterior lighting*
F	slab edge heat loss coefficient per foot of perimeter, Btu/h·ft·°F
FC	filled cavity
fc	foot candle
GSHP	ground-source heat pump
Guide	*Advanced Energy Design Guide for K-12 School Buildings*
HC	heat capacity, Btu/(ft^2·°F)
HDD	heating degree day
HID	high-intensity discharge
HV	Advanced Energy Design Guide code for *HVAC systems and equipment*
HVAC	heating, ventilating, and air conditioning
IAQ	indoor air quality
IES	Illuminating Engineering Society of North America
IESNA	Illuminating Engineering Society of North America (no longer used)
in.	inch
IPLV	integrated part load value, dimensionless
KBtu	thousands of British thermal units
kW	kilowatt
LBNL	Lawrence Berkeley National Laboratory
LCCA	life-cycle cost analysis
LED	light-emitting diode
LPD	lighting power density, W/ft^2
Ls	liner systems
N/A	not applicable
M&V	measurement and verification
MLPW	mean lumens per watt
NEMA	National Electrical Manufacturers Association
NFRC	National Fenestration Rating Council
NREL	National Energy Renewable Laboratory
O&M	operation and maintenance
OA	outdoor air
OPR	Owner's Project Requirements
PF	projection factor, dimensionless
PL	Advanced Energy Design Guide code for *plug loads*
ppm	parts per million
PSC	permanent-split capacitor
PV	photovoltaic
QA	quality assurance
R	thermal resistance, h·ft^2·°F/Btu
R - in.	R-value followed by the depth of insulation in inches
RFP	Request for Proposal
ROI	return on investment
SAT	supply air temperature
SHGC	solar heat gain coefficient, dimensionless
SP	special project
SRI	solar reflectance index, dimensionless
SSPC	standing standards project committee
SWH	service water heating
TAB	test and balance

TC	technical committee
U	thermal transmittance, $Btu/h \cdot ft^2 \cdot {}^\circ F$
USGBC	U.S. Green Building Council
VAV	variable air volume
VFD	variable-frequency drive
VFR	view window-to-floor area ratio
VT	visible transmittance
W	watts
WH	Advanced Energy Design Guide code for *service water heating*
WSHP	water-source heat pump

Foreword:
A Message for School Boards
and Administrators

If you are thinking a year ahead, sow a seed.
If you are thinking ten years ahead, plant a tree.
If you are thinking one hundred years ahead, educate the people.

—Chinese proverb

Among the most pressing issues facing our modern world are improving environmental stewardship and conserving our natural resources. As populations grow, and finite raw materials are consumed in ever greater numbers, we must find better ways to manage our planet's resources and to preserve its ecosystems. In the process, we must develop methods of instructing future generations about energy conservation.

Strategies to reduce the negative impact of human activity on the natural world begin with education. School leaders can be instrumental in expanding public awareness of sustainability by providing students positive examples of the cohabitation of natural and built environments. Energy-efficient school buildings can serve as models and laboratories for teaching conservation principles through integrated, project-based curriculum.

The health and education of our children are also important issues. High-performance school buildings provide safer and healthier learning spaces and improve student attendance. They also provide an opportunity to use the building as a teaching tool and to facilitate students' interaction with the environment. Finally, but not least of all, they can significantly lower operational and life-cycle costs.

IMPROVED LEARNING ENVIRONMENT

Significant research demonstrates that the quality of the physical environment affects student performance (Earthman 2002). An environment that includes appropriate lighting, sound, temperature, humidity, cleanliness, color, and air quality can help students learn better. In many cases, improving these attributes can also reduce energy use.

Quality lighting systems include a combination of daylighting and energy-efficient electric lighting systems. Together, these elements reduce visual strain and provide better lighting quality. Daylighting is a key strategy for achieving energy savings, as it requires little or no electrical lighting, which can reduce cooling loads.

Advanced energy-efficient heating and cooling systems produce quieter, more comfortable, and more productive spaces. In addition, they promote cleaner, healthier indoor environ-

xvi | Advanced Energy Design Guide for K-12 School Buildings

ments that can lower student and staff absentee rates and improve teacher retention, which can translate to higher test scores and lower staff costs.

ENHANCED ENVIROMENTAL CURRICULUM

Schools that incorporate energy efficiency and renewable energy technologies make a strong statement about the importance of protecting the environment. Buildings can be teaching tools that demonstrate scientific and philosophical best practices. They can help students understand a variety of disciplines, including architecture, engineering, mathematics, physics, statistics, biology, data analysis, language skills, social sciences, and literature. School building design and construction processes also provide opportunities for school leaders to grow their leadership capacity and, by applying sustainable design features, demonstrate the importance of education's connection to the natural environment. In addition, the spaces in the facility—including efficient classrooms with the latest technology, state of the art laboratories, special education units, music and art classrooms, interactive media centers, and staff rooms that enforce integration and teamwork—also support curriculum programs and improve the quality of teaching and learning.

REDUCED OPERATING COSTS

Many schools spend more money on energy each year than on school supplies. By using energy efficiently and lowering a school's energy bills, millions of dollars each year can be redirected toward improving facilities, increasing teachers' salaries, or providing educational resources. Strategic up-front investments in energy efficiency provide significant long-term savings. Smart use of a site's climatic resources, and more efficient envelope design, are keys to reducing a building's overall energy requirements. Efficient equipment and energy management programs help meet those requirements more cost effectively. Energy-efficient schools reduce facility operating costs and vulnerability to volatile energy pricing and can help to stabilize school budgets. The price of energy continues to trend upward; using less energy contributes to a more secure future for our country and our communities.

LOWER CONSTRUCTION COSTS/FASTER PAYBACK

We have been trained to think that energy efficiency must cost more; however, thoughtfully designed, energy-efficient schools can cost less to build than normal schools. For example, optimizing the envelope to match the climate can substantially reduce the size of the mechanical systems. A school with properly designed north-south glazing will have lower mechanical costs than one with the same amount of glazing on an east-west orientation and will cost less to build. More efficient lighting means fewer lighting fixtures are needed. Better insulation and windows mean heating systems can be downsized. Likewise, cooling systems can often be downsized with a properly designed daylighting system and a better-insulated envelope. Some energy-efficient design strategies may cost more up front, but the money saved on energy makes up the difference within a few years. Lower total costs, including lower operations expenses, and cost transfers also signify responsible stewardship of public funds. This translates into greater community support for school construction financing, whether through local district bonds or state legislative action.

ACHIEVING THE 50% ENERGY SAVINGS GOAL

Building a new school to meet a goal of at least 50% energy savings is not difficult, but it does take thought and determination. Foremost, the school system must commit to the goal; a commitment that is incorporated in district policy is helpful. An individual from the school with decision-making power must champion the project. The design team must be willing and able

Sidebar

Energy

MY SCHOOL MY PLANET

Lighting accounts for about one-third of the electricity used in the United States each year. People are coming up with more ways to use less electricity for lighting in order to save energy.

Bright Ideas:

New York City classrooms have big windows. In this school, the lights near the windows are controlled by **daylight sensors** that turn off the lights when there is a lot of sunshine.

Motion sensors in this school turn on the lights if people are in a room and turn them off when it is unoccupied.

A **central computer system** is used to turn off the lights in the whole school or in parts of the school when they are not needed.

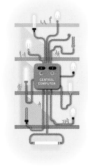

Using less electricity for lighting means:

• Fewer power blackouts

• Less pollution—because when the city uses less electricity its power plants pollute less to produce a design that meets the target energy savings. It must also ensure that the building is constructed as designed and that school system staff are trained to operate the energy systems properly.

A building can have the best possible design for achieving energy savings, but unless it is constructed and operated as designed, it will not realize energy savings. Make sure that the energy- and water-saving methods and devices selected by the design team are incorporated into the building plans and specifications; that everything is built and tested accordingly; and that school personnel, including those occupying the building, are provided the necessary documentation and training to operate the building properly. Operations and maintenance personnel and teachers must be trained in the proper operation of a school's energy systems. Initial training should be backed up by a long-term commitment to maintain an informed staff, including administrative, instructional, and facilities personnel, and to fund proper upkeep over the life of the installed systems.

A GOAL WITHIN REACH

The *Advanced Energy Design Guide for K-12 School Buildings* (AEDG-K12) was developed by a diverse group of industry experts to provide innovative and proven concepts for energy-efficient buildings, while concentrating on best business practices and reasonable construction costs.

The Guide is intended to be used by school leaders and design professionals in the construction of new schools that are 50% more energy efficient than the minimum code requirements of ASHRAE/IESNA Standard 90.1-2004. Recommendations focus on achieving at least 50% better energy performance than conventional schools while improving the learning environment and providing teachable models of energy-efficiency principles. Used correctly, the AEDG-K12 will guide the design and construction of schools that produce energy savings that offset the addition of renewable energy systems over the life of the building.

The energy savings outlined in this Guide are within the reach of any school district. Following the path to energy savings outlined will provide opportunities for school buildings to reduce our dependence on fossil fuels, lessen the impact on our domestic energy infrastructure, reduce operational and life-cycle costs, and provide environmental stewardship through lower carbon emissions and enhanced educational opportunities to advance student achievement.

REFERENCES

Earthman, G.I. 2002. School facility conditions and student academic achievement. Document WWS-RR008-1002, University of California Los Angeles Institute for Democracy, Education, and Access.

Schneider, M. 2002. Do school facilities affect academic outcomes? National Clearinghouse of Educational Facilities, National Institute of Building Sciences, Washington, D.C.

Note: Graphics are educational signage examples from the NYC School Construction Authority. Reprinted with permission.

Energy

MY SCHOOL MY PLANET

The position of the sun changes throughout the day and throughout the year. Morning and afternoon sun is lower than mid-day sun, which can cause glare. Because we live north of the equator, the southern faces of buildings get more of the sun's heat and light.

For thousands of years people have designed buildings to take advantage of, or to control, the heat and light from the sun.

Here's how it works at this school:

EAST
Light-colored brick reflects light to the playground.

NORTH
Fewer windows on the colder side of the building means reduced heat loss.

The neighboring apartment building helps protect classrooms from morning glare.

WEST
Special reflective coatings and deep vertical fins shield windows from the low afternoon sun.

SOUTH
Few windows mean low solar heat gain. The solar panels face south to maximize the amount of sunlight they receive.

Designing based on solar orientation saves energy and makes a building a nicer place to be!

Introduction

1

The *Advanced Energy Design Guide for K-12 School Buildings* (AEDG-K12; the Guide) provides user-friendly, how-to design guidance and efficiency recommendations for elementary, middle, and high school buildings. Correctly following the recommendations in the Guide will result in school facilities that consume 50% less energy than conventional schools (as defined by the minimum requirements set forth in ANSI/ASHRAE/IESNA Standard 90.1-2004, *Energy Standard for Buildings Except Low-Rise Residential Buildings* [ASHRAE 2004]).This document contains voluntary recommendations for designing low-energy-use buildings and is intended to supplement existing codes and standards but not to replace, supersede, or circumvent them. Even though several design packages are provided in the document, this Guide represents *a way*, but *not the only way*, to build energy-efficient small to medium office buildings with 50% energy savings.

The intended audience of this Guide includes, but is not limited to, building owners, architects, design engineers, energy modelers, general contractors, facility managers, and building operations staff. Specifically, Chapter 2 is written for a target audience of all design team members, whether they are design professionals, construction experts, owner representatives, or other stakeholders. Chapters 3 through 5 orient more towards design professionals to pursue sound design advice and identify interdisciplinary opportunities for significant energy reduction. The focus of this Guide is to identify proven concepts that are feasible to implement, and to benchmark necessary energy performance criteria for 50% energy savings. The Guide requires school leaders and design professionals to be intentional about the goals of their project and possibly to think differently about their processes and operations.

The mission of K-12 school buildings is to facilitate the education of young people. The performance requirements of these buildings will be the driving force behind most design decisions, and the benefits of some energy-saving measures could compromise the fundamental goal of facilitating education. The energy-saving measures in this Guide are intended to complement, or at least to avoid compromising, the delivery of educational services in these buildings

The energy savings projections of this Guide are based on site energy consumption rather than on source energy. *Site energy* refers to the number of units of energy consumed on the site and typically metered at the property line. *Source energy* takes into account the efficiency with which raw materials are converted into energy and transmitted to the site and refers to the total amount of energy originally embodied in the raw materials. For example, it is generally accepted that site electrical energy is 100% efficient, but in fact it takes approximately 3 kWh of total energy to produce and deliver 1 kWh to the customer because the production and distribution of electrical energy is roughly 33% efficient.

The Guide was developed by a project committee that represents a diverse group of professionals and practitioners. Guidance and support was provided through a collaboration of the American Society of Heating, Refrigerating and Air-Conditioning Engineers (ASHRAE), the American Institute of Architects (AIA), the Illuminating Engineering Society (IES), the U.S. Green Building Council (USGBC), and the U.S. Department of Energy (DOE).

In essence, this Guide provides design teams a methodology for energy-savings goals that are financially feasible, operationally workable, and otherwise readily achievable. Because technology to conserve and generate energy is advancing rapidly, it is clear that innovation is an important ingredient to the success of reducing energy consumption in school facilities. It is the hope of the authors that this publication exposes other existing best practices and leads to new concepts in high-performance building design.

GOAL OF THIS GUIDE

The Guide strives to provide direction and recommendations to reduce total site energy use by at least 50% in K-12 school buildings, using ASHRAE/IESNA Standard 90.1-2004 as the basis for minimum code-compliant baseline building. The energy saving goal is to be achieved in each climate location rather than an aggregated national average. The 50% savings is determined based on whole-building site energy savings, which includes plug and process loads.

SCOPE

This Guide applies to all sizes and classifications (elementary, middle, and high) of K-12 school buildings. Space types covered by the Guide include administrative and office areas, classrooms, hallways, restrooms, gymnasiums with locker rooms and showers, assembly spaces with either flat or tiered seating, libraries, and food preparation and dining areas. The Guide does not cover atypical spaces, such as indoor swimming pools, wet labs (e.g., chemistry), dirty dry labs (e.g., woodworking and auto shops), or other unique spaces with extraordinary heat or pollution generation.

The primary focus of this Guide is new construction, but recommendations may be equally applicable to schools undergoing complete or partial renovation, such as addition, remodeling, and modernization projects (including changes to one or more systems in existing buildings).

Included in the Guide are recommendations for the design of the building opaque envelope; fenestration; lighting systems (including electrical interior and exterior lights and daylighting); heating, ventilation, and air-conditioning (HVAC) systems; building automation and controls; outdoor air (OA) requirements; service water heating (SWH); and plug and process loads, including kitchen equipment. Additional savings recommendations that are included but not necessary for 50% savings are discussed in the "Additional Bonus Savings" section of Chapter 5.

The recommendation tables do not include all of the components listed in ASHRAE/IESNA Standard 90.1-2004. Though this Guide focuses only on the primary energy systems within a building, the underlying energy analysis assumes that all other components and systems comply with the minimum design criteria in ASHRAE/IESNA Standard 90.1-2004 and ANSI/ASHRAE Standard 62.1, *Ventilation for Acceptable Indoor Air Quality* (ASHRAE 2010b).

In addition, the Guide is not intended as a substitute for rating systems or references that address sustainability in the full range of areas related to school design, such as acoustics, productivity, indoor air quality (IAQ), water efficiency, landscaping, and transportation, except as they relate to energy use. Nor is this a design text. The Guide presumes good design skills and expertise in school-building design.

ENERGY MODELING ANALYSIS

To provide a baseline and quantify the energy savings for this Guide, two prototypical schools were developed and analyzed using hourly building simulations. These building models include a 74,000 ft² primary school and a 211,000 ft² secondary school, each of which was carefully assembled to be representative of construction for K-12 school buildings of its class. Information was drawn from a number of sources, including CBECS, Dodge Construction Data, and various K-12 school templates from around the country. The space types included in each prototype design are shown in Table 1-1.

Two sets of hourly simulations were run for each prototype. The first set meets the minimum requirements of ASHRAE/IESNA Standard 90.1-2004, and the second uses the recommendations in this Guide. Each set of prototypes was simulated in eight climate zones adopted by the International Energy Code Council (IECC) and ASHRAE in development of the prevailing energy codes and standards. The climate zones were further divided into moist and dry regions, represented by 16 climate locations. All materials and equipment used in the simulations are commercially available from two or more manufacturers.

Energy savings for the recommendations vary depending on climate zones, daylighting options, HVAC system type, and school type, but in all cases are at least 50% when compared to ASHRAE/IESNA Standard 90.1-2004, ranging from 51% to 65%. Calculations based on DOE determinations also project energy savings of approximately 47% when compared to ASHRAE/IESNA Standard 90.1-2007 and 28% when compared to ASHRAE/IES Standard 90.1-2010. It is estimated that the energy savings from using this Guide are 55% when compared to ASHRAE/IESNA Standard 90.1-1999, the baseline standard of the 30% AEDG series. Energy saving analysis approach, methodologies, and complete results of the prototype building simulations are documented in a technical report published by the National Renewable Energy Laboratory (Bonnema et al. 2011).

Table 5-1 Prototype Design Space Types

Space Types	Primary School	Secondary School
Auditorium		×
Art room	×	×
Cafeteria	×	×
Classroom	×	×
Corridor	×	×
Gymnasium		×
Kitchen	×	×
Library		×
Lobby	×	×
Mechanical/Electrical/Telecomm Room	×	×
Media Center	×	
Multipurpose Room	×	
Office	×	×
Restroom	×	×

ACHIEVING 50% ENERGY SAVINGS

Meeting the 50% energy-savings goal is challenging and requires more than doing business as usual. Here are the essentials.

1. *Obtain building owner buy-in.* There must be strong buy-in from the owner/operator and facility staff. The more they know about and participate in the planning and design process, the better they will be able to help achieve the 50% goal after the school becomes operational. The building owner must decide on the goals and provide the leadership to make the goals reality.

2. *Assemble an experienced, innovative design team.* Interest and experience in designing energy-efficient buildings, innovative thinking, and the ability to work together as a team are all critical to meeting the 50% goal. The team achieves this goal by creating a building that maximizes daylighting; minimizes process, heating, and cooling loads; and has highly efficient lighting and HVAC systems. Energy goals should be communicated in the request for proposal and design team selection, based in part on the team's ability to meet the goals. The design team implements the goals for the owner.

3. *Adopt an integrated design process.* Cost-effective, energy-efficient design requires trade-offs among potential energy-saving features. This requires an integrated approach to school design. A highly efficient lighting system, for instance, may cost more than a conventional one, but because it produces less heat, the building's cooling system can often be downsized. The greater the energy savings are, the more complicated the trade-offs become and the more design team members must work together to determine the optimal mix of energy-saving features. Because many options are available, the design team will have wide latitude in making energy-saving trade-offs.

4. *Consider a daylighting consultant.* Daylighting is an important strategy for achieving the 50% energy-savings goal; however, it requires good technical daylighting design. If the design team does not have experience with a well-balanced daylighting design, it may need to add a daylighting consultant.

5. *Consider energy modeling.* This Guide provides a few design packages to help achieve energy savings of 50% without energy modeling, but whole-building energy modeling programs can provide more flexibility to evaluate the energy-efficient measures for an individual project. These simulation programs have learning curves of varying difficulty, but energy modeling for school design is highly encouraged and is considered necessary for achieving energy savings of 50%. See DOE's Building Energy Software Tools Directory at the Department of Energy, Energy Efficiency and Renewable Energy website for links to energy modeling programs (DOE 2011). Part of the key to energy savings is using the simulations to make envelope decisions first and then evaluating heating, cooling, and lighting systems. Developing HVAC load calculations is not energy modeling nor is it a substitute.

6. *Use building commissioning.* Studies verify that building systems, no matter how carefully designed, are often improperly installed or set up and do not operate as efficiently as expected. The 50% goal can best be achieved through building commissioning (Cx), a systematic process of ensuring that all building systems—including envelope, lighting, and HVAC systems—perform as intended. The Cx process works because it integrates the traditionally separate functions of building design; system selection; equipment start-up; system control calibration; testing, adjusting, and balancing; documentation; and staff training. The more comprehensive the commissioning process, the greater the likelihood of energy savings. A commissioning authority should be appointed at the beginning of the project and work with the design team throughout the project. Solving problems in the design phase is more effective and less expensive than making changes or fixes during construction. The perceived value of the Cx process is that it is an extension of the quality control processes of the designer and contractor. See the section "Using Integrated Design

to Maximize Energy Efficiency" in Chapter 2, the section "Quality Assurance" in Chapters 3 and 5, and Appendix C of this Guide for more information.

7. *Train building users and operations staff.* Staff training can be part of the building Cx process, but a plan must be in place to train staff for the life of the building to meet energy-savings goals. The building's designers and contractors normally are not responsible for the school after it becomes operational, so the building owner must establish a continuous training program that helps occupants and operations and maintenance staff maintain and operate the building for maximum energy efficiency. This training should include information about the impact of plug loads on energy use and the importance of using energy-efficient equipment and appliances.

8. *Monitor the building*: A monitoring plan is necessary to ensure that energy goals are met over the life of the building. Even simple plans, such as recording and plotting monthly utility bills, can help ensure that the energy goals are met. Buildings that do not meet the design goals often have operational issues that should be corrected.

CONDITIONS TO PROMOTE HEALTH AND COMFORT

Throughout the project, the design team should continuously discuss how energy-saving measures will impact comfort, IAQ, and acoustics. The design and construction of a high-performance school building requires an integrated approach where these factors remain a priority and are not adversely affected when striving for energy reduction.

For specific guidance regarding the interrelation of thermal comfort, IAQ, sound and vibration, and other factors, refer to ASHRAE Guideline 10, *Interactions Affecting the Achievement of Acceptable Indoor Environments* (ASHRAE 2011).

INDOOR AIR QUALITY (IAQ)

ASHRAE Standard 62.1-2010 defines minimum requirements for the design, installation, operation, and maintenance of ventilation systems, but IAQ encompasses more than just ventilation. For more information, refer ASHRAE'S *Indoor Air Quality Guide: Best Practices for Design, Construction, and Commissioning* (ASHRAE 2009), which provides specific guidance for achieving the following key objectives:

- Manage the design and construction process to achieve good IAQ.
- Control moisture in building assemblies.
- Limit entry of outdoor contaminants.
- Control moisture and contaminants related to mechanical systems.
- Limit contaminants from indoor sources.
- Capture and exhaust contaminants from building equipment and activities.
- Reduce contaminant concentrations through ventilation, filtration, and air cleaning.
- Apply more advanced ventilation approaches.

THERMAL COMFORT

ANSI/ASHRAE Standard 55-2010, *Thermal Environmental Conditions for Human Occupancy* (ASHRAE 2010a), defines the combinations of indoor thermal environmental factors and personal factors that produce conditions acceptable to a majority of occupants.

According to ASHRAE Standard 55, six primary factors must be addressed when defining conditions for thermal comfort: metabolic rate, clothing insulation, air temperature, radiant temperature, air speed, and humidity. For example, appropriate levels of clothing, the cooling effect of air motion, and radiant cooling or heating systems can increase occupant comfort efficiently.

All parties should consider allowing a wide deadband for occupied mode setpoints as a measure to reduce energy use (as compared to the minimum deadband range stated in energy codes). However, these expanded temperature ranges should not be so extreme as to compromise occupant productivity.

VISUAL COMFORT

If designed and integrated properly, daylighting and electric lighting will maximize visual comfort in the space. Electric lighting should be designed to meet Illuminating Engineering Society of North America (IES) recommended levels. Providing light levels that are too high or too low can cause eye strain and loss of productivity. Direct sun penetration should be minimized in work areas because the resulting high contrast ratio may cause discomfort.

Optimizing student orientation to windows is also important in minimizing discomfort. Computer screens should never be orientated facing the window (student with back to window) or facing directly away from the window (student facing window). Both of these alignments produce high-contrast ratios that cause eye strain. Locate the computer screen and student facing perpendicular to the window wall to minimize visual discomfort.

Further recommendations for visual comfort can be found in the *IESNA Lighting Handbook* (IESNA 2000), specifically in Chapter 2 "Vision: Eye and Brain" and Chapter 4 "Perception and Performance."

ACOUSTIC COMFORT

In the classroom, communication is essential to learning. Proper acoustics is especially important for children, because their ability to hear and listen differs from that of adults. Providing good acoustics reduces barriers to education for people with non-native language skills, learning disabilities, and/or impaired hearing. The need for clear communication in classrooms has been recognized for many years and is addressed by the Acoustical Society of America (ASA) in ANSI/ASA S12.60-2010, *Acoustical Performance Criteria, Design Requirements, and Guidelines for Schools*.

Proper acoustics must be a priority in all design decisions and not adversely affected by energy reduction measures. Addressing acoustics during the design phase of a project, rather than attempting to fix problems after construction, likely will minimize costs.

HOW TO USE THIS GUIDE

- Review Chapter 2 to learn how an integrated design process is used to maximize energy efficiency. Checklists are included to help establish and maintain the energy-savings target throughout the project. Review the integrated design strategies for design professionals, including information on architectural design features and energy conservation measures by climate zone.
- Review Chapter 3 to understand how to benchmark and set energy goals for your specific project. These exercises are especially important when designing a unique project on a specific site, the characteristics of which do not match this Guide's analyzed baseline building in shape, orientation, and glazing. Case studies in this chapter provide perspective into how other schools have designed and built energy-efficient buildings.
- Use Chapter 4 to review climate-specific design strategies and select specific energy-saving measures by climate zone. This chapter provides prescriptive packages that do not require modeling for energy savings. These measures also can be used to earn credits for Leadership in Energy and Environmental Design (LEED) Green Building Rating System™ and other building rating systems.
- Use Chapter 5 to apply the energy-saving measures in Chapter 4. This chapter suggests best design practices, how to avoid problems, and how to achieve additional savings with energy-efficient appliances, plug-in equipment, and other energy-saving measures.
- Refer to the appendices for additional information:
    - Appendix A—Envelope Thermal Performance Factors

- • Appendix B—International Climate Zone Definitions
- • Appendix C—Commissioning Information and Examples
- • Note that this Guide is presented in inch-pound (I-P) units only; it is up to the individual user to convert values to the International System (SI) as required.

REFERENCES AND RESOURCES

ASA. 2010. ANSI/ASA S12.60-2010, *Acoustical Performance Criteria, Design Requirements, and Guidelines for Schools*. Melville, NY: Acoustical Society of America.

ASHRAE. 1999. ANSI/ASHRAE/IESNA Standard 90.1-1999, *Energy Standard for Buildings Except Low-Rise Residential Buildings*. Atlanta: American Society of Heating, Refrigerating and Air-Conditioning.

ASHRAE. 2004. ANSI/ASHRAE/IESNA Standard 90.1-2004, *Energy Standard for Buildings Except Low-Rise Residential Buildings*. Atlanta: American Society of Heating, Refrigerating and Air-Conditioning Engineers.

ASHRAE. 2007. ANSI/ASHRAE/IESNA Standard 90.1-2007, *Energy Standard for Buildings Except Low-Rise Residential Buildings*. Atlanta: American Society of Heating, Refrigerating and Air-Conditioning Engineers.

ASHRAE. 2009. *Indoor Air Quality Guide: Best Practices for Design, Construction, and Commissioning*. Atlanta: American Society of Heating, Refrigerating and Air-Conditioning.

ASHRAE. 2010b. ANSI/ASHRAE Standard 62.1-2004, *Ventilation for Acceptable Indoor Air Quality*. Atlanta: American Society of Heating, Refrigerating and Air-Conditioning Engineers.

ASHRAE. 2010a. ANSI/ASHRAE Standard 55-2010, *Thermal Environmental Conditions for Human Occupancy*. Atlanta: American Society of Heating, Refrigerating and Air-Conditioning.

ASHRAE. 2010c. ANSI/ASHRAE/IES Standard 90.1-2010, *Energy Standard for Buildings Except Low-Rise Residential Buildings*. Atlanta: American Society of Heating, Refrigerating and Air-Conditioning.

ASHRAE. 2011. ASHRAE Guideline 10-2011, *Interactions Affecting the Achievement of Acceptable Indoor Environments*. Atlanta: American Society of Heating, Refrigerating and Air-Conditioning.

Bonnema, E., M. Leach, and S. Pless. 2011. Technical support document: Development of the *Advanced Energy Design Guide for K-12 Schools: 50% Energy Savings*. NREL/TP-5500-51437, National Renewable Energy Laboratory, Golden, CO. www.nrel.gov/docs/fy11osti/51437.pdf.

DOE. 2011. Building energy software tools directory. U.S. Department of Energy, Washington, D.C. http://www.eere.energy.gov/buildings/tools_directory.

IESNA. 2000. *IESNA Lighting Handbook*, 9th Edition. New York: Illuminating Engineering Society of North America.

Integrated Design Process

2

PRINCIPLES OF INTEGRATED DESIGN

Integrated design is a method of design and construction that uses an interactive team approach for all phases of a project's management. Integrated design in some form is necessary to achieve at least 50% energy savings over the minimum code requirements of ASHRAE/IESNA Standard 90.1-2004 (ASHRAE 2004). In an integrated design, all parties work together through all phases of design and construction to maximize efficiency of the project and to yield coordinated, constructible, and cost effective results. This approach increases project productivity, provides higher performing buildings, and protects construction budgets by reducing unnecessary change orders.

Integrated design in school projects fosters unique opportunities to build connections between the school community, the school facility, and the school curriculum and to provide connection between the built environment and student achievement. School districts may take advantage of the design and construction process as a student learning experience. When construction is complete, the building can serve as a teaching tool for environmental awareness and energy conservation as part of an integrated project-based curriculum. If thoughtfully applied, an integrated design process can help cultivate improved school leadership and an enhanced school environment to improve student performance.

The efficiency and quality of the design and construction is obtained through the following team interactions and processes:

- Issue a Request for Proposal (RFP) to
    - define energy design and performance goals and expectations;
    - define education programming to connect the facility to operations, school core curriculum, design and construction processes, and the community; and
    - identify the project team and stakeholders (especially school district leadership, administration, faculty, facilities staff, and students).
- Establish early involvement of all design and construction team members. Include operations and maintenance staff as part of the owner's team.
- Establish initially agreed upon and documented common goals, including operational base line performance benchmarks.
- Use the building as a teaching tool.

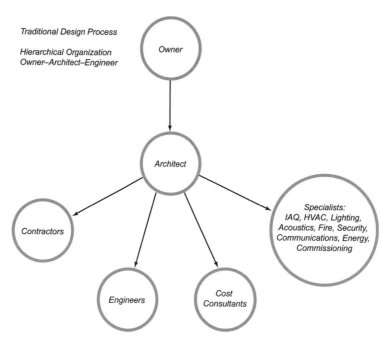

Figure 2-1   Traditional Project Design Team
Adapted from ASHRAE (2009)

- Consider new and different methodologies in the building design, and use the project as an innovation incubator.

- Establish open communication, with early input on project strategies from all parties. Conduct Owner's Project Requirements workshops and a project kickoff meeting to discuss goals and facilitate mutual cooperation.

- Provide life-cycle costing to determine the feasibility of project systems, taking into account future organization and staffing levels expected once the school is built.

A key difference between integrated design and conventional design and construction methods is the consideration of life-cycle costs in making project decisions. This requires a holistic approach at the beginning of the project to input relevant programming, design, construction, and operations information to the extent possible. Owners, architects, engineers, contractors, commissioning agents, community partners, operations personnel, teachers, and other integrated design team members must work together from the outset of a project to accumulate the information necessary to make data-driven decisions. Since key design choices will be based on operational savings, it is essential that the project team continually review strategies with the owner's operations and maintenance staff to ensure there is adequate capacity for the number of people, as well as required energy management skills for the desired results.In design-bid-build project deliveries that are common in school projects, contractors will need to be consulted for needed construction information that would be available in a design-build or construction management delivery.

It follows that the integrated process requires the formation of the project team as early in the project as possible. Early collaborative goals and performance metrics; appropriate budget; and open, inclusive participation contribute to trust among team members and to the project's overall success. Inclusion of all project team members benefits the project by allowing all participants to provide their expertise throughout the process.

Figures 2-1 and 2-2 illustrate interaction in traditional design team and integrated design team structures, respectively.

Figure 2-2 Integrated Project Design Team
Adapted from ASHRAE (2009)

Operating as an Integrated Design Team

When the Spring Independent School District built the Gloria Marshall Elementary School, they realized that in order to break away from tradition and conventional design, they would need to assemble a cohesive design team composed of three distinct participants: a visionary architect, an owner's champion to sell the unorthodox design to the school board, and an engineering firm with the design experience and data to support new system technologies.

As the architectural firm completed conceptual drawings and began looking at energy conservation strategies and the building envelope, it became apparent that the architectural influences on the energy usage of the building would use energy was limited to building orientation, wall and roof construction and insulation, window glazing type, window placement, and the ability to bring daylight into the building. The architect determined that the engineering systems within the building could have a greater influence on energy use. An engineering firm with the expertise, knowledge, and data available to prove high-performing building concepts was identified, and an architecture and engineering team was formed.

During the design process, the design team relationship between the architect and the engineering firm operated differently than the architectural firm's historical relationships consulting mechanical, electrical, and plumbing (MEP) firms. Compromise was required between the architect's efforts to reduce energy consumption through a reduction in the cubic feet of the building space and the engineer's efforts to expand the cubic feet to take advantage of natural daylighting and daylight harvesting through open bay areas and high ceilings in classrooms. Compromise also occurred between the electrical engineer and the interior designer on the color and reflectiveness of the classroom carpet and walls along with their ability to contribute to the available foot candles.

Learn more about the Gloria Marshall Elementary School project in the Chapter 3 case study section.

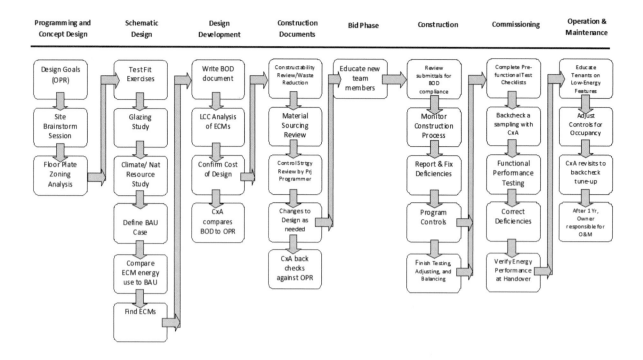

Figure 2-3   Integrated Project Design Team

Additional details on how to set up and deliver a project using an integrated design process can be found in AIA's *Integrated Project Delivery: A Guide* (AIA 2007). A copy of the full guide can be downloaded from the contract documents section of the AIA website at www.aia.org/contractdocs/AIAS077630.

USING INTEGRATED DESIGN BY PROJECT PHASE

Integrated design establishes key collaboration agreements to remove barriers between parties and encourage early contributions of wisdom and experience. This section provides best practice guidance to achieve at least 50% energy efficiency in building design. Figure 2-3 gives a snapshot of the key steps in each phase leading toward energy-efficient solutions.

PROJECT KICKOFF

The project kickoff meeting is the most important meeting because it establishes the final Owner's Project Requirements (OPR). This exercise may be led by the architect or the commissioning agent (CxA) and allows the owner's personnel and other stakeholders to define what a successful project means, including a review of the educational objectives. Establishing a well-defined OPR and Basis of Design (BoD) at the beginning of the project will help ensure that energy goals are integrated into the design and considered throughout the project. Inclusion of the stakeholders (e.g., school and district leaders, students, teachers, parents, facility operators, and community members) will produce more creative and integrated solutions and lead to community investment, which are keys to a project's success. Aligning design goals with teaching and learning objectives will provide real-world learning opportunities for students. An OPR can cover construction costs, serviceability, operating costs, required spaces and adjacencies, functional aspects, specific maintenance or system preferences, sequence of operations and minimum maximum setpoints for equipment use, frequency of use, education goals, facility-integrated curriculum, using the building as a teaching tool, and other owner priorities. It is strongly recommended that the traditional OPR from the commissioning process be further augmented to include the following information:

- Energy rating systems (LEED® Green Building Rating System, Green Globes, ENERGY STAR™, etc.)
- Life-cycle costing of systems and cost transfer analysis
- Ownership/leasing arrangements, including renewable energy credits, utility back-charging, or metering
- Prioritization of the goals and requirements in each of the categories listed in the preceding paragraph to guide future fund allocation decisions
- The owner's chain of (decision making) command and communication, including adjustments of OPR or BoD requests, and expenditure approvals
- Funding that is designated to achieve a specific goal (i.e., departmental contributions or a named donor)
- Constraints imposed by the site, code, or planning agreements with the city, pre-existing standards (if any), corporate sustainability policy statements, etc.
- Site-based measurements (submetering) of actual plug-load usage of existing equipment or similar equipment at another owner facility
- Educational student curriculum and staff training objectives

OPR information is necessary to ensure that all parties on the design and construction team are equally aware of the owner's priorities. While there may be multiple systems that can meet the required specifications, system selection can be narrowed or specific systems identified that meet the overall project criteria (including the Owner's operational capacity) at this early part of the project. This lowers risk for all parties and provides a reference document for the future to guide decisions when budget pressures may challenge system selection. It is acknowledged that during the course of the project the OPR may grow (or change) to accommodate owner preferences and to take advantage of new technology or opportunities. Nevertheless, it is good practice to consolidate all of the owner's goals, intentions, and requirements into a single OPR document in order to keep track of all the information and keep the project team focused.

PROGRAMMING AND CONCEPT DESIGN

During the programming and concept design phase, the project inputs are compiled and organized. A series of collaboration sessions are conducted to assist the integrated design team in reviewing the OPR for site-specific opportunities and risks. Collaborative sessions are conceptual exercises that are key to elaborating on concepts envisioned by the design. They usually include a series of holistic site investigation and building massing studies to determine which strategy best addresses the following issues:

- Educational program and project-based curriculum for experiential learning for higher student achievement
- Site conditions (existing shading from adjacent buildings or landscaping, outdoor air quality, outdoor ambient noise environment, site surface material)
- Orientation and availability of natural resources (sun, wind, geothermal, climate, bodies of water)
- Local material availability or reuse opportunity
- Storm water runoff scheme, wetlands impact, utilities available
- Status of surrounding buildings and review of code/planning regulations that may create obstructions to natural resources in the future or otherwise limit the design
- Hardscaping or landscaping potential to reduce heat island effect or provide natural shading
- Security concerns
- Accessibility to public transportation or alternative transportation options
- Other sustainability opportunities such as acoustics, indoor air quality, water efficiency, etc.
- Environmental risks or challenges

The goal of the programming and collaborative concept sessions is to review a number of schemes and to identify appropriate strategies and resources for use by the integrated design team. It may be difficult to correctly estimate final costs for each model or to determine final systems, but the integrated design team should be able to rank schemes qualitatively against the OPR based on past experience. The result of the exercise should be a consensus on the major site parameters, confirmation of the building program (including space types, associated areas, and adjacencies), and identification of the major design strategies for meeting the OPR.

A proper building orientation and envelope are critical to achieving at least 50% energy savings. At this stage, most program information will be in verbal or diagrammatic form, but building orientation and envelope strategies and drawings should emerge early in the process. The integrated design team should review potential building massing and orientation strategies revealed in the program concept sessions to determine whether low-energy solutions are possible and what building strategies may be necessary to ensure comfort and performance. Variables to consider in this exercise include the following:

• Daylighting potential versus glare versus solar heat gain
• Reflectivity of other surfaces
• Natural ventilation potential for cooling
• Glazing types, shading devices, and fenestration size
• Operable window sizes (if allowed)
• Perimeter occupant comfort
• Projected heat loss/heat gain and impact on annual HVAC energy use
• Daylight harvesting and impact on potential energy savings due to orientation
• Landscaping potential for natural shading
• Indoor air quality (ASHRAE 2009, 2010c)
• Solar heating ventilation air

At this point in the project, the project team should reach a consensus on program design concepts and parameters, including but not limited to those expressed in the OPR and educational program, as well as parameters related to the site, building envelope, orientation, daylighting, possible systems, etc. The owner must confirm the basic strategies for a positive and productive work-place environment, including the extent of visual connection with the outdoors.

SCHEMATIC DESIGN

In the schematic design phase, programming ideas and concepts are developed into diagrammatic plans. As a test exercise, the architectural team members identify where in the building the various program occupancies will be. Typical approaches generally favor natural light in all instructional areas and most other areas that are student inhabited. School design best practice also favors a visual outdoor connection in addition to the natural light requirements, especially in instructional areas. Interior spaces without access to natural light should be utilized as much as possible for mechanical equipment, storage, and restrooms.

The schematic design plan and proposed building massing provide opportunities to study and identify envelope strategies for fenestration and opaque surfaces that further program parameters and enhance the indoor environment for occupants.

At this point, detailed sun-path computer projections can be generated to explore the exposure of intended glazing locations and the resulting penetration of solar rays into the building. It is strongly suggested, at this early stage, that the design team perform a review of proposed glazing areas and overall envelope thermal performance against the ASHRAE/IES Standard 90.1 (ASHRAE 2010a) prescriptive requirements and the recommendations of this Guide for the relevant climate zone. These steps will help establish appropriate glazing schemes for achieving programmed daylighting and outside visual connections, while also meeting energy efficiency goals. Establishing a proper energy model of the building envelope (including the glazing scheme) early in the design process is essential to meeting a goal of at least 50%

energy savings. Unnecessary costs can be avoided or transferred to improve glazing or overall building envelope performance in order to further reduce energy use.

Similarly, a more detailed weather/climate/natural resource analysis usually quantifies true frequency-of-occurrence potential for the following:

- Natural ventilation for cooling
- Free heating/cooling through HVAC systems
- Daylighting
- Night-time heat purge of thermal mass
- Heat recovery
- Use of radiant surfaces

All of this additional analysis informs the design team as to which mechanical and electrical systems should be considered in order to provide a comfortable indoor environment. Typical mechanical and electrical plant room sizes, riser locations, and ceiling cross-sectional depths should be generated for the most traditional services approach to serve as a baseline for initial and life-cycle cost comparisons in subsequent phases.

Once a baseline building is created, its costs are estimated and compared to the OPR's to ensure that even the most "standard" of the available designs meets the first-cost and program requirements. If these requirements are met, it is often useful to perform a preliminary energy analysis by zone, including an analysis of approximate annual operating costs. This usually involves analyzing energy for the primary space types (classrooms, gyms, offices, etc.) and projecting energy usage per square foot. During schematic design, this level of calculation is usually adequate to confirm trends in energy savings associated with design decisions.

The last task necessary in the schematic design phase is to identify energy conservation measures (ECMs) that might be applied to the baseline case. This is the point at which it is necessary to thoroughly discuss and document trade offs and cost transfers. Typical exploratory interdisciplinary discussions during this phase include the following:

- Selection of structural material and its relative use as thermal mass or thermal insulation
- Selection of internal wall finish type and its potential obstruction of thermal mass heat transfer performance
- Selection of floor material type and finish and its potential use as an air-distribution, heating, or cooling device
- Selection of façade type and orientation and each face's relative proportion and performance of glazing and opaque wall insulation
- Selection of glazing visual light transmittance versus solar heat gain coefficient to allow daylighting without overheating
- Configuration of roofing shape/slope/direction and applicability of cool-roofing materials, clerestory skylights, and/or installation of photovoltaic or solar hot-water panels.
- Selection of electric lighting approach and zoning compatibility to accommodate ambient-versus-task lighting, occupancy sensors, daylight harvesting, and time-of-day controls
- Commitment to ENERGY STAR equipment for plug-load use reduction
- Review of plug-load use intensity by the owner's personnel
- Once all the building loads are all identified, review of alternate HVAC and comfort cooling systems

As a conclusion to the discussions, the design team usually identifies a certain number of optimal energy conservation measures that they wish to include in the base case. Through a life-cycle cost analysis, a more complete energy model is created to test the initial cost of the ECMs against their relative operating costs savings. A matrix of options is developed to assess each ECM against a common set of criteria, including but not limited to the following:

- Additional first-costs investment
- Anticipated annual energy costs savings
- Anticipated annual maintenance and operations costs savings

- Simple payback period (construction costs divided by annual savings)
- Return on investment
- $kBtu/ft^2 \cdot yr$ reduction
- Annual carbon emissions savings, including the decay overtime
- Additional percent savings as compared to the applicable version of ASHRAE/IES Standard 90.1
- Potential additional USGBC LEED® points for Energy and Atmosphere (EA) Credit 1 or other categories
- Range of indoor thermal comfort achieved throughout the year
- Range of lighting levels achieved throughout the year

There may be other project-specific OPR that should be incorporated into the matrix. The key point is that it is essential for all parties to understand the whole view of any ECM application, so that a balanced decision can be made that considers all of the impacts on the desired goals of the project, including operations. The goal is to pick a selection of ECMs to pursue during the design development phase. These decisions are crucial and must be completed before design work and calculations begin.

DESIGN DEVELOPMENT

The design development phase establishes the final scope of ECMs incorporated into the project's architectural, structural, HVAC, electrical, plumbing, and commissioning design documents (specifications and drawings). The final energy models are usually submitted to code authorities to show compliance with the applicable version of ASHRAE/IES Standard 90.1 (or with the local code, whichever is more stringent) and may be used for submissions for LEED certification. Development of the final project scope includes further design, calculation, and documentation of the building envelope and structural, lighting, electrical, and mechanical/plumbing services that are regulated by code, as well as owner-agreed limits on plug-load densities and the sequence of operations for HVAC systems. Additionally, there is often a financial investment/life-cycle cost analysis (LCCA) of the ECM components in conjunction with cost estimates. Estimates are more detailed at this phase and help the design team to decide which ECMs to maintain as goals in the next phase of design. During design development, the design intent is documented through the BoD report, which is compared to the OPR to ensure that the owner's goals will be met.

Design development is the phase of the project in which the original OPR is confirmed via the project's scope. The LCCA provides the basis for value engineering and for decisions regarding first costs and estimates.

CONSTRUCTION DOCUMENTS

In the construction documents phase, final details are determined for all systems, including provisions for sustainability features and ECMs. Mechanical, electrical, and plumbing systems incorporate system drawings, specifications, BoD reports, controls drawings, controls points lists, and sequences of operation. The CxA reviews all of the documents and the updated BoD for compliance with the OPR.

At this point, it is important for the project team to review and confirm the following:

- Project constructability
- Cost-optimization and waste-reduction techniques
- Necessary documentation and acquisition of material to meet the performance requirements for each of the energy conservation measures
- Control strategies
- Design intent of specifications

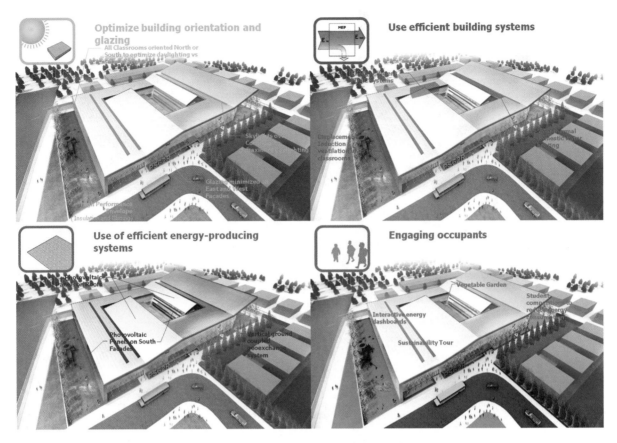

Figure 2-4   Example Diagrams Showing Energy Efficiency Measures
Source: New York City School Construction Authority

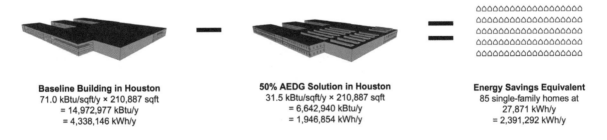

Baseline Building in Houston	50% AEDG Solution in Houston	Energy Savings Equivalent
71.0 kBtu/sqft/y × 210,887 sqft	31.5 kBtu/sqft/y × 210,887 sqft	85 single-family homes at
= 14,972,977 kBtu/y	= 6,642,940 kBtu/y	27,871 kWh/y
= 4,338,146 kWh/y	= 1,946,854 kWh/y	= 2,391,292 kWh/y

Figure 2-5   Graphic Example Showing Comprehensible Scale of Energy Savings

The development of a simplified, user-friendly school energy education document by the design team is strongly recommended at this phase, before the key designers demobilize and the bidding and construction phases begin. The document should be provided in a format that can be modified over the life of the building and should include the following:

- Sample introductory content for the owner or building operator that explains why energy efficiency is important to the school
- A simple diagram representing the energy efficiency features of the building (Figure 2-4)
- A comparative estimate of maximum possible energy savings in familiar terms (Figure 2-5)
- A "What You Can Do to Help" section that lists the desired occupant behaviors

Energy Goals By Design Phase Checklist

A checklist of the energy design goals for each of the project phases discussed in this chapter may be a helpful tool for the design team.

Programming and Concept Design

Activities	Responsibilities	✓
Select the core team • Include energy goals in the RFP • Designers—including project architect, engineer, and other design consultants • Commissioning authority • Construction manager	Owner (school board members and administrators)	
Adopt energy goals	Owner and designers	
Assess the site • Evaluate centrality to the community • Evaluate access to public transportation • Identify on-site energy opportunities • Identify best building orientation	Owner, designers, construction manager	
Define functional and spatial requirements	Owner and designers	
Define energy efficiency and budget benchmarks	Owner, designers, construction manager, estimator	
Prepare the design and construction schedule	Owner, designers, construction manager	
Determine building—envelope and systems preferences	Owner, designers, construction manager	
Perform cost/benefit analysis for energy strategies	Owner and designers	
Identify applicable energy code requirements	Owner and designers	

Schematic Design

Activities	Responsibilities	✓
Identify energy conservation measures (ECMs)	Owner, designers, construction manager, CxA	
First costs investment calculation	Cost estimator	
Base case life-cycle cost assessment	Cost estimator	
First costs and LCCA comparison to OPR cost budget	Cost estimator, designers	
Anticipated annual energy costs savings	Designers	
Anticipated annual maintenance costs savings	Owner and CxA	
Simple payback period	Designers	
Return on Investment	Owner, cost estimator, designer	
kBtu/sf/yr reduction	Designer	
Carbon emissions savings	Designer	
Additional% savings compared to Standard 90.1	Designer, CxA	
Potential additional USGBC LEED points not limited to Energy and Atmosphere Credit 1	Sustainability consultant	
Range of indoor thermal comfort achieved throughout the year	Designer	
Range of lighting levels achieved throughout the year	Designer	

Design Development

Activities	Responsibilities	✓
Prepare diagrammatic building plans that satisfy functional program requirements	Designers	
Develop specific energy strategies	Owner, designers, construction manager, CxA	
Develop the site plan to make best use of building orientation and daylighting strategies	Designers	
Select building systems, taking into account their desired energy efficiency	Owner, designers, construction manager	
Develop building plans, sections, and details incorporating the above strategies	Designers	
Develop architectural and lighting details; for example, lighting, fenestration, exterior sun control, taking into account their energy implications	Designers	
Refine the design; for example, refine the building elevations to reflect the appropriate location and size of windows	Designers	
Perform design reviews at each phase of the project to verify that the project meets functional and energy goals	Owner, designers, construction manager, CxA	
Calculate building HVAC loads and run energy models to optimize design at each design stage (schematic, design development, and construction drawings) to ensure that energy goals are being met; use recommended loads for lighting power density from this Guide	Designers	
Match capacity of HVAC systems to design loads to avoid costly overdesign; specify equipment efficiency as recommended by this Guide	Designers	
Perform final coordination and integration of architectural, mechanical, and electrical systems	Designers	
Prepare specifications for all systems	Designers	
Integrate commissioning specifications into project manual	Designers and CxA	
Prepare cost estimates at each phase of design	Construction manager, CxA, estimator	
Review and revise final design documents	Owner, designers, CxA	

Bid Phase

Activities	Responsibilities	✓
At the pre-bid conference, emphasize energy efficiency measures and the commissioning process	Owner, designers, construction manager, CxA	

Energy Goals By Design Phase Checklist *(Continued)*

A checklist of the energy design goals for each of the project phases discussed in this chapter may be a helpful tool for the design team.

Construction

Activities	Responsibilities	✓
At all job meetings, review energy efficiency measures and commissioning procedures	Owner, designers, construction manager, CxA	
Verify that building envelope construction carefully follow the drawings and specifications	Designers, CxA	
Verify that HVAC, plumbing, and electrical systems meet specifications	Designers, CxA	

Commissioning

Activities	Responsibilities	✓
Prepare pre-occupancy punch list	Owner, designers, construction manager, CxA	
Conduct system functional performance tests	Designers, construction manager, CxA, general contractor, subcontractor	
Submit completed operations and maintenance manuals	CxA, general contractor, subcontractor	
Provide operations and maintenance training for school facilities staff	CxA, general contractor, subcontractor	

Operations & Maintenance

Activities	Responsibilities	✓
Establish building operations and maintenance program	CxA, general contractor, subcontractor, owner, facility staff	
Resolve any remaining commissioning issues identified during the construction or occupancy phase	Owner, construction manager, CxA, general contractor, subcontractor	
Certify building as substantially complete	Owner, facilities staff, designers, construction manager, CxA	
Purchase computers and other energy using appliances that meet Energy Star efficiency to reduce plug loads	Owner, administrators, facility staff)	
Monitor post-occupancy performance for one year	Owner, administrators, facility staff	
Create post-occupancy punch list	Owner, administrators, facility staff	
Grant final acceptance	Owner, designers, construction manager, CxA	

Post Occupancy

Activities	Responsibilities	✓
Purchase computers and other energy using appliances that meet ENERGY STAR efficiency to reduce plug loads	Owner, facility staff	
Monitor post-occupancy performance for one year	CxA, facility staff	
Create post-occupancy punch list	CxA, facility staff	
Grant final acceptance	Owner, designers, construction manager, CxA	

- Opportunities for project-based curriculum using the building features
- Training for key system and equipment operations (DOE 2011a)

BID PHASE

Most school projects will use a design-bid-build delivery method. Projects using other delivery methods may bypass the bid phase. For projects that include a bid phase, the following measures must be taken by the design team to achieve at least 50% energy savings:

- Acquire timely and appropriate construction information and expertise in the early phases of the project to ensure effective scheduling; constructability; availability of equipment, materials, and necessary skilled labor; and quality, accurate estimating and cost control.
- Conduct a thorough pre-bid conference to review the desired owner goals, including ECMs, the commissioning process, and contract documents.
- Consider adding general performance specification requirements, including requirement of contractor experience on high performance buildings, to ensure that owner goals are achieved.
- Review documents with the owner to verify adequacy of operations and maintenance (O&M) requirements, including training, sequence of operations, preventive maintenance, commissioning procedures, and building energy management controls (software and hardware).

CONSTRUCTION

During the construction phase, the CxA and the design professionals on the integrated design team will review submittals and construction performance to ensure compliance with the contract documents. This allows the integrated design team to ensure that construction meets all regulatory requirements and is in compliance with the manufacturer's performance and warranty standards. Design and construction professionals on the integrated design team are responsible for reviewing construction, reporting any deficiencies of installed work, and requiring remedial efforts to correct work as necessary. Any deviation from the construction documents must be approved by the integrated design team and documented to prove that the substitution will not adversely affect energy efficiency (among other things). It is recommended that (to a reasonable extent) the owner's O&M staff attend construction progress meetings, make routine site visits, review shop drawings, and become familiar with the equipment and systems being installed (especially their scheduled maintenance requirements).

After all equipment is installed and the building is enclosed, equipment manufacturers will perform testing procedures during start-up to confirm that equipment is operating correctly, and the commissioning agent will provide functional testing (also included in the contract documents). A testing and balancing contractor will adjust the settings on the equipment to achieve correct water flow and airflow, as required in the contract construction documents, to ensure smooth interface of mechanical operations and controls.

The contracting team and the manufacturer's representatives are responsible for producing a set of O&M manuals and performing a specified number of hours of training for the owner's personnel. If possible, provide preventive maintenance charts for each major piece of equipment, preferably physically located on the equipment. It is recommended that the training sessions be taped and posted on the school intranet for current and future operators' reference. It is further recommended that key technical facility operators overlap with contractor operations at least a month before the final inspection, and that checklists are started to familiarize operators with the equipment and design intent. When final inspection begins, building operators should accompany the contractor and design team during testing and commissioning of the equipment.

COMMISSIONING

The commissioning process is the last performance testing applied to most projects. The CxA will have written checklists based on the equipment submittals reviewed during the construction administration phase. The CxA will turn over the checklists for the construction team to complete based on the manufacturer's startup reports and other collected information (including warranty and wiring information). Once the checklists are complete, the CxA will perform an on-site random sampling to check results and confirm that the reported findings are true and repeatable. After confirmation, the CxA will release the functional test procedures, written in response to the contractor's detailed sequence of operations. The CxA will supervise the controls contractor running the equipment through its operations to prove adequate automatic reaction of the system to artificially applied inputs. The inputs simulate a variety of extreme, transition, emergency, or normal conditions. When testing is completed to the satisfaction of the CxA, a report is written for the owner confirming that the performance goals of the project have been met. At this time, the owner can take overbuilding operations from the contractor with confidence that the building is operating as intended and meets the goal of at least 50% energy savings. Once the building is transferred, proper and ongoing O&M (including measurement and verification) will be necessary to ensure continued 50% energy savings, as well as operational paybacks established in the life-cycle costing.

The CxA should assist with the supervision of the formal training of the owner's operations personnel. The training should ensure that operators can operate the systems properly and can take corrective actions should systems deviate from their commissioned state. It is useful to run and monitor key aspects of the building for a one-month period just before contractor transfer to verify energy-related performance and to confirm the final setpoint configurations in the O&M documents. This will allow the owner to return the systems to the original commissioned state (assuming good maintenance) at a future point, with comparative results.

Additionally, prior to transfer of the building to the owner, it is recommended that the project team provide a seminar on the school energy education document to school leaders, building staff, students, parents, community, and other stakeholders. As with the training of building operators, it is recommended that this seminar be taped for future occupants and posted online. The integrated design process began with these same stakeholders. Now, partly for the building's performance, and partly for education and curriculum, it is best practice to review the goals of the project, including energy conservation and occupant behavior.

OPERATIONS AND MAINTENANCE

Operations and maintenance (O&M) and measurement and verification (M&V) of the equipment after the contractor's transfer of the building to the owner are crucial to the energy efficiency over the life of the building and essential to achieving at least 50% energy savings. It is recommended that building operators secure certification as a Certified Energy Manager. Depending on the school district size and recommendations from the integrated design team, direct digital controls can be utilized to program HVAC operations to match the occupancy of the school. It is often the case that the first year of occupancy reveals a more accurate picture of how the building will perform. Actual occupancy patterns may be different from the original design assumptions in the energy model. Initially, it is best practice to monitor the facility on a monthly basis to confirm benchmark performance. Additional information on M&V benchmarking can be found in Chapter 5 (QA14 and QA16)

Often, a service extension will be approved to allow the CxA to review the status of operations 11–18 months after the building has been transferred to the owner. The CxA may recommend adjustments to system setpoints to optimize operations. Occasionally, a second measurement and verification exercise is performed at this time to benchmark the energy use of each piece of equipment. If there are extreme seasonal climatic differences, the second set of benchmarks may be established in an alternate season.

Maintenance is the second owner-controlled aspect of operational efficiency. The O&M manuals will contain information regarding preventative and periodic maintenance activities that should be performed to keep the equipment running in order to achieve 50% energy savings. Some examples of necessary preventative maintenance activities are as follows:

- Keep HVAC filters clean to minimize pressure drops.
- Inspect and replace broken sensors to maintain proper feedback from the controls system to HVAC equipment.
- Inspect and repair broken actuators to maintain proper demand control ventilation and/or air-side economizer cycles.
- Inspect and maintain good water quality to ensure proper performance of heat exchangers and clean inner surfaces of piping.
- Inspect and maintain condensate pans to ensure air quality and reduce microbial growth.
- Inspect, clean, and possibly replace light bulbs that are not maintaining proper light levels.
- Inspect and calibrate supply air HVAC sensors to ensure comfort and air quality.
- Inspect pumps and fans to make sure motors are oiled and operating properly.

POST OCCUPANCY OPERATIONS: THE BUILDING AS A TEACHING TOOL

In school buildings designed for low energy use, it is important to remember that occupant behavior and building operation is crucial to achieving at least 50% energy savings. When people understand the goals of the building and the impact of occupant behavior on energy conservation, they can substantially reduce energy use. School leaders, especially local boards of education, the superintendent, and administrative staff, must build support for energy-efficiency initiatives at the district level. With that foundation, principals, teachers, school staff, and students can change the culture of sustainability at the school level.

A school energy education document can be instrumental in the development of a school culture where occupant behavior is seen as integral to the education climate and the operation and performance of the school. School energy education document training should start at the beginning of the project so that desired culture is established during the design and construction process. Schools can use lunch presentations, staff meetings, and appropriate model class lessons to integrate school energy education concepts into school curriculum and practices. They may even develop games, student and staff competitions, and incentives to help facilitate a culture of environmental awareness and energy conservation.

The design and construction team can benefit from hosting a seminar for the initial occupants (taped, if possible, for future occupants and posted online) to describe the building's design intent and sustainability features. This is an ideal way to introduce occupants to school energy education guidelines and to allow local school leadership to state their support for energy-efficiency initiatives within the school. It is important to caution occupants that low-energy buildings sometimes require a period of operation to reach their optimized control strategy. All occupants are invited to submit and share energy-performance comments as additional input for improving operations. This type of personal engagement will encourage behaviors by the school staff and students that have a positive impact on the operation of the building. In addition, first adopters can act as efficiency coaches for future staff and students.

INTEGRATED DESIGN BEST PRACTICES

BUILDING SITE AND DESIGN INFLUENCES

Climate Characterizations

Several major climatic variables, including temperature, wind, solar, and moisture, impact the energy performance of buildings. These variables continuously change and can be characterized by annual or seasonal metrics.

- An indicator of the intensity and length of the heating season is represented by heating degree-days, as shown in Figure 2-6.

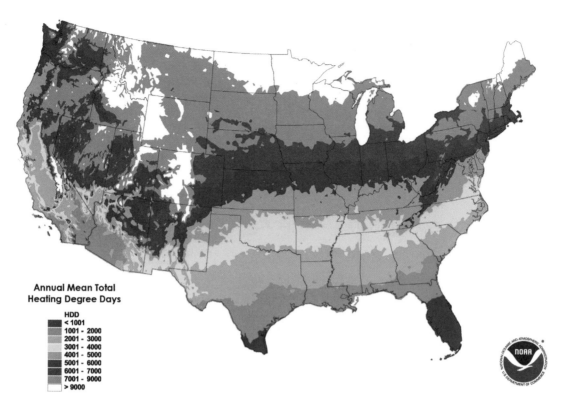

Figure 2-6   Heating Degree-Days
Source: NOAA (2005)

- An indicator of the intensity and length of the cooling season is represented by cooling degree-days, as shown in Figure 2-7.

- An indicator of the consistent intensity of the sun's energy is represented by the annual solar radiation, as shown in Figure 2-8.

- An indicator of the worst case for removal of airborne moisture (i.e., dehumidification) is represented by the design dew point, as shown in Figure 2-9.

- An indicator of the ability of the air to engage in evaporative cooling is represented by the design wet bulb, as shown in Figure 2-10.

In combination, these variables show that distinct patterns emerge with regard to climate types, each of which has particular energy impacts on building design and operation. The U.S. is divided into eight primary climate zones for the specification of design criteria in the major energy codes, such as the International Energy Conservation Codes and ASHRAE/IESNA Standard 90.1 and ASHRAE/USGBC/IES Standard 189.1 (ASHRAE 2010b). Figure 2-11 shows these climate zones as compared to cooling degree-days (CDDs) and heating degree-days (HDDs).

The characterization of these climate zones is based on seasonal performance metrics, not on peak or design values. Each climate zone is clustered by HDD65 for the heating and CDD50 for the cooling and further subdivided by moisture levels as humid (A), dry (B), and marine (C) to characterize their seasonal values. Sixteen cities have been identified as sufficient to represent all of the climate zones, as shown in Table 2-1.

It is important that the design team determine the particular unique characteristics of the climate closest to the site. Annual hourly climate data is usually used for energy modeling and is available from federal government sources (DOE 2011b). In addition to the acquisition of

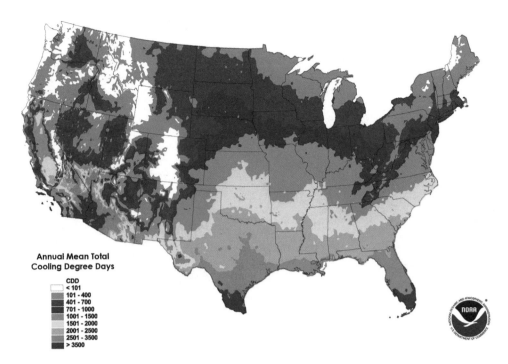

Figure 2-7   Cooling Degree-Days
Source: NOAA (2005)

Global Horizontal Solar Radiation - Annual

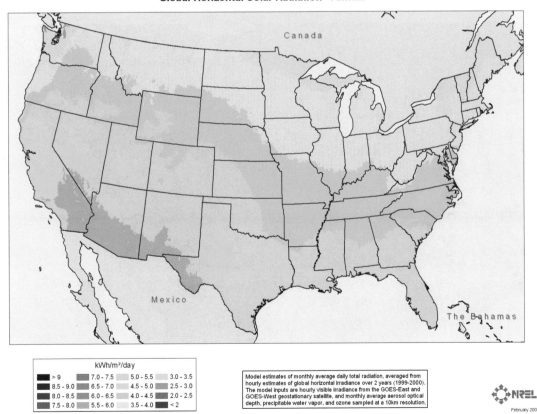

Figure 2-8   Annual Solar Radiation
Source: NREL (2005)

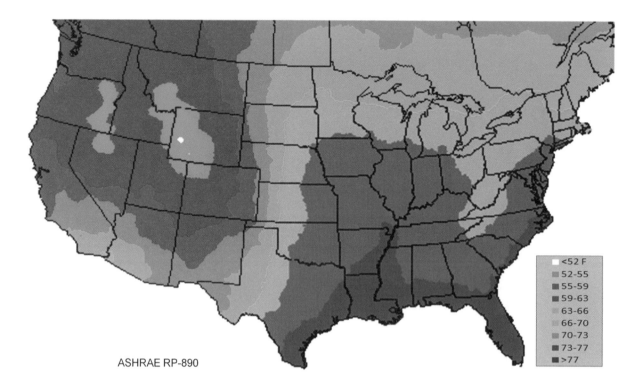

Figure 2-9   Design Dew-Point Temperatures
Source: Colliver et al. (1997)

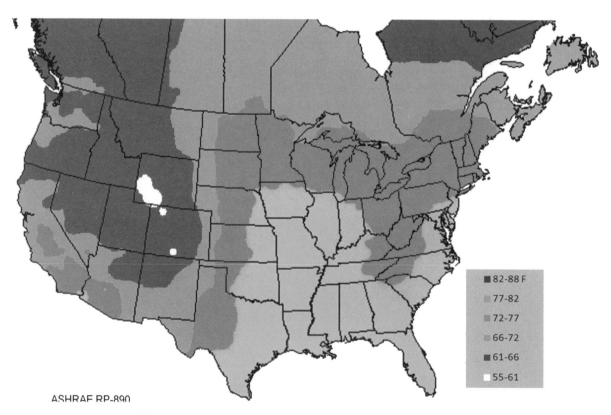

Figure 2-10   Design Wet-Bulb Temperatures
Source: Colliver et al. (1997)

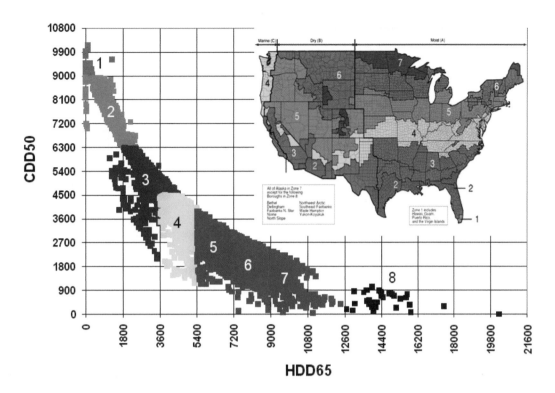

Figure 2-11   U.S. Climate Zone Map

Table 2-1   Cities Characterized by Climate Combinations

Climate	Hot	Mild	Cold	Very Cold	Extremely Cold
Marine		San Francisco-3C Seattle-4C			
Humid	Miami-1A Houston-2A Atlanta-3A	Baltimore-4A	Chicago-5A Minneapolis-6A		
Dry	Phoenix-2B Los Angeles-3B (coastal) Las Vegas-3B (others)	Albuquerque-4B	Denver-5B Helena-6B	Duluth-7	Fairbanks-8

local data, it is necessary to assess any local topography or adjacent properties that would cause reduction in access to sunlight and passive solar heating.

Climate Dependence

Multiple combinations of climate conditions influence the energy performance of a building. Comparisons of the energy used for heating, cooling, interior and exterior lights and equipment, fans, pumps, service water heating, and refrigeration in a primary school with ground-source heat pump heating and cooling systems are shown in Figure 2-12.

A review of the graph shows distinct trends. In climates below 3000 HDD65, the cooling energy is greater than the heating energy. In climates above 5000 HDD65, heating energy use

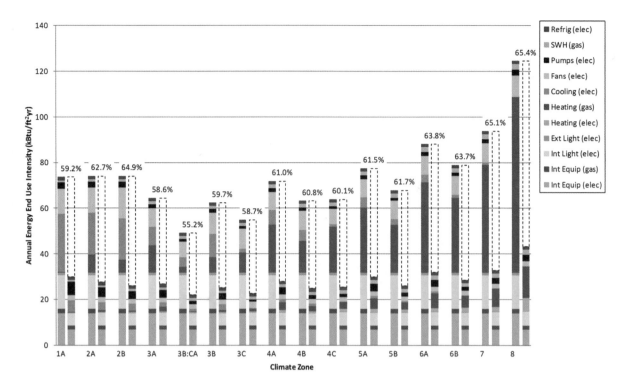

Figure 2-12 Primary School with Ground Source Heat Pumps
Source: Bonnema et al. (2011)

dominates cooling energy use. In all climates, energy use is essentially constant for interior and exterior lights and equipment, fans, pumps, service water heating, and refrigeration. These relationships are similar for a primary school with fan-coil units for the heating and cooling system (Figure 2-13).

The heat released by the interior lights, plug loads, and fans add to the cooling load and diminish the heating load, which highlights the importance of addressing these loads in conjunction with envelope construction.

Fundamentally, the following can be seen in the Figures 2-12 and 2-13:

- Lighting, plug, and fan loads are constant inputs and therefore consistent values in the energy-use intensity (EUI) budget. Indeed, the only fluctuation most likely occurs from fan energy reacting to ON/OFF controls in response to climate.
- Heating EUI contribution increases with HDDs, as expected, but the scatter in the plot has to do with passive heating arising from solar contributions, depending on the sunniness profile of the particular city. This becomes particularly obvious when looking at the pairs of heating and cooling contributions for a given HDD value—high heating goes with low cooling, which means that there is limited solar free heating. Similarly, high cooling goes with low heating, which means there is a lot of solar heat to manage and the design team must note whether the savings in heating sufficiently offset the penalties in cooling energy.

Building Shape

The basic shape of the building has a fundamental impact on its daylighting potential, energy transfer characteristics, and overall energy usage.

Building plans that are circular, square, or rectangular result in more compact building forms. These buildings tend to have deep floor plates that the potential of sidelighting a significant percentage of occupiable space. Building plans that resemble letters of the alphabet, such as

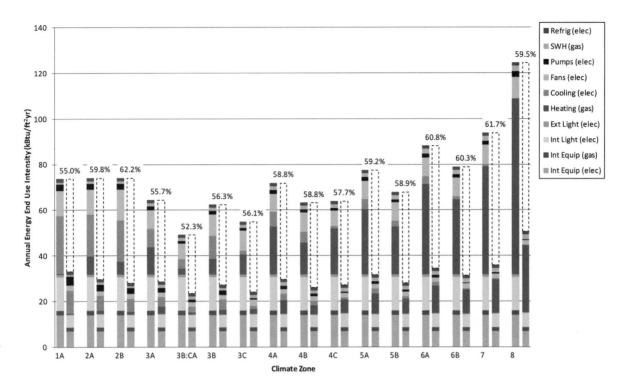

Figure 2-13   Primary School with Fan Coil Units
Source: Bonnema et al. (2011)

H, L and U, or that have protruding sections and surfaces at angles other than ninety degrees relative to adjacent building surfaces, tend to have shallow floor plates where sidelighting strategies result in a higher percentage of daylighted floor area. (Atriums and other core lighting strategies may also be introduced into more compact building forms to achieve a similar effect.)

Less compact forms increase a building's daylighting potential, but they also may magnify the influence of outdoor climate fluctuations. Greater surface-to-volume ratios increase conductive and convective heat transfer through the building envelope. Therefore, it is critical to assess the daylighting characteristics of the building form in combination with the heat transfer characteristics of the building envelope in order to optimize overall building energy performance.

The shape of the building also defines the window area and orientations that are available. Windows allow solar gains to enter the building, which are beneficial during the heating season but increase the cooling energy. The building shape needs to be designed so that the solar loading is properly managed. The solar management strategy changes according to local climate characteristics, as solar intensity and cloudiness differ. Additionally, the shape of the building will determine how wind impinges on the outdoor surfaces to assist natural ventilation or creates outdoor microclimates. In addition, attention must be paid to the effect of wind passing through openings in the façade (e.g., windows, louvers, trickle vents, cracks), as this can drive unforeseen and/or uncontrollable infiltration.

Building Size

The size of the building impacts energy use. Analysis of a 74,000 ft^2 one-story primary school building and a 211,000 ft^2 two-story secondary school building clearly demonstrates the differences. Figure 2-14 presents the baseline site energy use intensities for these two buildings for compliance with ASHRAE/IESNA Standard 90.1-2004.

The size of the building also impacts what energy conservation measures are possible. For example, a small 5000 ft^2 alternative school could be residential construction with wood-framed

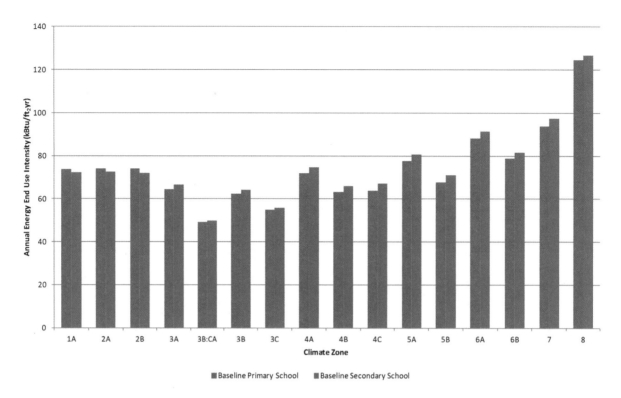

Figure 2-14 Energy End-Use Intensity for K-12 Schools
Source: Bonnema et al. (2011)

walls and ceilings as well as residential HVAC equipment in which the minimum efficiencies are set by the National Appliance Energy Conservation Act of 1987. In these cases, there are limited options for obtaining more energy-efficient HVAC equipment.

Building size and especially depth of floorplate can have significant impacts on the feasibility of daylighting and natural ventilation.

Number of Stories

As the number of stories in a school increases from one to two or three, some aspects of design become more complicated. For instance, requirements for structural performance and durability/design life may affect choice of envelope components, the viability of exposed thermal mass, and the amount of area that may be used for fenestration. All of these may influence energy performance.

Typically, schools with more than one story have less skin area, which leads to lower construction costs, preservation of more of the site for other uses, and potential energy savings due to less envelope loss. However, these schools run the risk of trapping a large block of space as purely internal and without connection to the outdoors. It is more difficult to daylight (especially toplight) a school with more than one story, so great care must be taken to give desired spaces access to daylight. If an increased amount of space with access to natural daylight or ventilation is preferred, the designer of a multiple story school can introduce toplight using skylights, clerestories, monitors, sawtooths, atria, etc. Horizontal glazing captures high-angle sun and may be difficult to shade. Exterior louvers, translucent glazing, vertical glazing, and other means should be considered to distribute toplight evenly into an interior space.

Building Orientation

The orientation of the school building has a direct impact on energy performance primarily due to the orientation of the fenestration. The annual solar radiation impinging on a surface varies by orientation and latitude.

The north solar flux (south solar flux for the southern hemisphere) receives the least solar radiation for any location; however, north daylighting is preferred due to a lack of control requirements for glare from direct sun penetration (reflections from adjacent buildings may require blinds on north windows for glare control). The east and west solar fluxes are essentially the same. The west exposure needs to be critically evaluated since it contributes to the peak or design cooling load. Southern facing orientations in the northern hemisphere have the second largest solar intensity and the greatest variation in sun angle. Great care must be applied when designing external shading for this orientation, as attention must be paid to heat gain, glare, and the possibility of passive solar heating in cold climates. The horizontal solar flux receives the largest amount of solar radiation and must be carefully evaluated if flat skylights on the roof are being considered. Clerestories on the roof facing north are a preferred option.

Building orientation and the placement of fenestration can significantly affect a design's ability to provide useful daylight to perimeter zones. Using caution when performing simultaneous building configuration studies and internal space planning can maximize the amount of normally occupied space that can use daylighting for ambient light.

MULTIDISCIPLINARY COORDINATION FOR ENERGY EFFICIENCY

Integrated design strategies require significant multilateral agreement on design intent from a variety of stakeholders. The following tips are provided to identify a series of items for which a direction and agreement must be achieved. Truly holistic low-energy design solutions are not achieved solely through the optimization of each component, but rather by exploiting the mutually-beneficial synergies between otherwise independent design strategies.

Define Business as Usual and Baseline Buildings

One of the very first things the design team must define is the "business as usual" (BAU) design solution—this is a model building that represents typical design and operational practices without energy efficiency considerations. It is often a minimally prescriptive ASHRAE/IESNA Standard 90.1-equivalent simple structure that virtually fills the site with as low a profile as possible. The energy use of this building typically represents the high end of allowable limits and sets the comparative standard against which absolute savings are achieved on the road to net-zero energy use. As each energy conservation measure (ECM) is applied, the design team should keep track of all incremental victories achieved at each step. The comparison to the BAU is a real measure of success reflective of all design decisions.

The second key item that the design team must define is what the "baseline" design solution will be once the preferred building configuration's design is completed. The baseline design is very different from the BAU design because the current ASHRAE/IES Standard 90.1 requires that all proposed and baseline energy models have identical shapes, footprints, and occupancies. Thus, the baseline does not reward fundamental building configuration decisions for their positive effect on energy use.

It is important for the design team to agree to move away from both the BAU and the baseline in making proactive design decisions. It is also important that the benchmark for success does not shift.

Benchmarking

While the BAU represents the highest allowable energy use intensity on site by calculation methods, there are a number of other energy-use benchmarks that represent the existing building stock in the United States, such as the following:

Cost Control Strategies and Best Practices

This guide provides information for achieving high-performance building design in K-12 school projects. Owners should not expect energy-efficient schools to cost more. They can cost more, but they shouldn't have to. These designs can be accomplished without a serious cost premium. The following strategies and best practices detail approaches for controlling costs in high performance K-12 school projects.

Integrated Design

- Align program, budget, and energy goal at the beginning of the project.
- Have a good understanding of cost before significant design work has been done.
- Analyze costs as energy decisions are being made.
- At a minimum, integrate in cost estimators and design engineers at the 50% schematic design phase.
- Coordinate system placement (structural, mechanical, electrical, etc.) to reduce building volume costs.
- Plan for future integration of renewable energy by designing to be renewable-ready. Examples include the following:
  - Providing large, unobstructed roof area, either south facing or flat, for future photovoltaic (PV) mounting.
  - Providing electrical conduit chases to possible future renewable sites.

Life-Cycle Cost Analysis

- Include initial cost, operating cost, replacement cost, and maintenance cost over the life of the building when cost justifying low-energy systems. Previously successful examples include the following:
  - Additional first costs of ground-coupled systems can partially be offset by reduced maintenance costs of well fields, as compared to traditional cooling towers or heat-rejection condensers.
  - Additional first cost of light-emitting diode (LED) fixtures can partially be offset by reduced re-lamping and maintenance costs, as compared to traditional exterior lighting fixtures.

Cost Trade-Offs

- Include installation and labor costs with material costs when evaluating total system costs. Previously successful examples include the following:
  - Insulated concrete form (ICF) walls may be more expensive from a material standpoint, but the additional expense can be partially offset by reduced installation time and the fact that the electrical contractor does not have to be on site during wall framing.
- Focus on modular, pre-built systems to reduce installation costs and construction time.
- Re-invest first-costs savings from removing unnecessary amenities (overly glazed facades, excessive finishes, water fountains, etc.) for efficiency upgrades.

- U.S. Environmental Protection Agency and U.S. Department of Energy ENERGY STAR™ Portfolio Manager rating
- Commercial Buildings Energy Consumption Survey (CBECS) for new, average buildings
- California End Use Survey (CEUS)

It is possible to benchmark the proposed design against the BAU and its pre-existing peers to demonstrate that substantial steps have been taken toward energy use reduction. Designers often successfully compare their designs to the "typical" equivalent building in the pre-existing stock, or to the number of houses that could be powered on the energy savings, to make it easier for lay people to understand the magnitude of energy savings.

Historic data, however, is not the inspiration for future good design. This is where more aspirational benchmarking can benefit the project team. The most frequently used benchmarks are as follows:

- Energy savings as designated by percentage annual costs savings as compared to ASHRAE/IES Standard 90.1 Appendix G (typically used by codes and policies, also used by USGBC LEED rating systems)

Value Added

- Create additional value beyond energy savings by considering efficiency strategies that have multiple benefits. Examples include the following:
  - Use PV systems or wind turbines as both renewable generation and curriculum.
  - Use M&V data to hold energy savings competitions among classrooms, grades, wings, etc.
  - Use M&V data as part of a science or math curriculum analyzing performance data.
  - Provide an enhanced learning environment though daylighting.
  - Use PV systems that can be integrated into an uninterruptable power supply.
  - Use computer carts in place of computer labs to save unnecessary square footage costs while also providing more efficient computing.
  - Passive survivability concepts.
  - High mass structure for disaster resistance.
  - Utilize daylighting to provide light during extended power outages.
  - Utilize natural ventilation to provide some outdoor air during extended power outages.

Hiring an Experienced Design Team

- Select a design and construction team with experience successfully and cost-effectively implementing efficiency strategies in schools. Benefits include the following:
  - Better understanding of actual costs and cost trade-offs that are available.
  - Understanding how to leverage the benefits of integrated design to ensure that all of the efficiency strategies work together.
  - Reduced subcontractor contingency costs associated with traditionally untrusted and risky systems and strategies.
  - Avoiding unnecessary and costly equipment oversizing due to system performance uncertainties by leveraging lessons learned from past projects. Applications include the following:
    - Ground heat exchanger well sizing based on seasonal loads and actual ground characteristics.
    - Ventilation system sizing based on actual occupancy patterns.

Alternative Financing

- Leverage all possible rebates from nonprofits, utilities, state energy offices, etc. for efficiency upgrades and renewable energy systems (NREL 2011).
- Team up with third-party financing to eliminate first costs for systems that exceed capital budget limitations and to leverage for-profit tax incentives not available to typical school districts.

- Absolute EUI definitions (occasionally used by campuses, regularly used by the General Services Administration, easiest to measure and verify after construction)
- Net zero energy definitions

As noted above, it is important for the design team to agree to move away from the design practices that led to older, poor-performing buildings and move toward a quantifiable target that is consistent with the available job funding.

Budget Sharing

One often heard but fundamentally unnecessary question is "Whose budget pays for improved energy efficiency?" The answer is always, "The owner's budget!" When a team commits itself to delivering low energy, holistic solutions, it is virtually impossible to separate by trade or discipline the cost of energy efficiency measures "purchased" during the course of the project through its respective design decisions. A classic example is the cost of shading: there are increased structural and façade costs, but these may be offset by reduced capital costs for window glazing and air conditioning. These trade-offs are absolutely necessary to explore in consideration of the particular goals and context of the building. As long as the overall building

Key Design Strategies for Controlling Capital Costs

The following strategies and best practices detail key design strategies for controlling costs in high performance K-12 school projects.

Site Design

- Properly orient the school on your site—good orientation allows for significant energy savings without additional costs
- Utilize existing trees for shading
- Retain site features that can later serve as teaching tools
- If a prototype design is used, make sure the prototype is flexible enough to allow for optimal placement on the site
- Locate ground heat exchanger wells under parking lots or athletic fields to share site preparation costs

Daylight and Windows

- Use clear, double-glazing in the glass areas that are integral to your daylighting strategy to maximizing visible light transmission. High visible transmittance daylighting glass maximizes daylight transmission while minimizing daylighting aperture cost.
- Don't use any more glass in your daylighting strategy than is necessary to achieve your lighting level objective during peak cooling times. Excess glass costs more and results in higher heating and cooling energy use.
- Eliminate east and west facing glass and only utilize view glass where there is a purpose – not just to aesthetically balance the design elevation.
- Where east and west facing windows are required, select tinted glazing to help reduce peak cooling loads and, in turn, reduce installed cooling equipment.
- Understand that daylighting always contributes light to the space and because of different lighting requirements between day and night less light fixtures can be installed initially while still maintaining daytime illuminance requirements.
- Use architectural features to shade classroom projection areas, not operable window shades.

Building Shell

- Use white, single-ply roofing material to maximize daylight reflectance and minimize cooling.
- Paint interior walls light colors, select highly reflective ceiling materials, and don't pick extremely dark floor finishes. Darker surfaces can require more installed lighting power to meet illuminance levels resulting in higher costs and less effective daylighting.
- Develop the design based upon even modules for materials. It will reduce material waste and save time, in turn savings cost.
- Maximize the use of modular construction techniques and focus on simple forms that minimize complex wall detailing and curved surfaces.

Electrical Systems

- Select the more energy-efficient computers, vending machines, televisions, appliances, and kitchen equipment. Best in class efficiency plug load efficiency can be achieved with minimal additional cost.
- Consider PV lighting for remote locations where conduit and trenching costs can exceed the cost of the PV system.
- Limit exterior lighting to critical areas only.
- Don't over light hallways.
- Use multiple lamp fluorescent fixtures that can be switched and/or dimmed to provide multiple light levels in daylighted gymnasiums. They can cost less and provide an additional advantage by being able to be dimmed.

Mechanical Systems

- Analyze your seasonal and hourly loads carefully to determine full-load conditions.
- Make sure you accurately account for the benefits of daylighting in terms of cooling load reduction.
- Lay out the chilled- and hot-water piping, and ductwork, to minimize turns and reduce pressure losses.
- Optimize the mechanical system as a complete entity to allow for the interaction of various building system components.
- When sizing your mechanical equipment, investigate the unit sizes—it may make more sense to improve the energy efficiency of other design elements to help reduce the overall cooling load downward to the next unit size
- Correctly account for the impact of an energy recovery device(s) on the outdoor air cooling and heating system capacities.

construction budget remains consistent with the OPR and the building performs as designed, it doesn't matter where the money is spent.

What this tells us, however, is that discipline-based construction budget allocations might be inappropriate for the integrated design paradigm and should be reviewed early in the project. Similarly, traditional fee percentages may also unintentionally prevent the disciplines most capable of proposing and proving energy reduction techniques from applying their analytical technologies and abilities to solutions.

Lastly, the EUI "budget" itself also must be equitably shared. The building envelope does not consume energy but significantly affects the energy use of mechanical and lighting systems. Therefore, it is important for design teams to carefully review the relative proportion of energy use by discretionary design choice and collectively tackle those systems/features that represent the greediest energy users. A classic example of an energy-wasting feature is the use of all-glass facades with the expectation that highly efficient HVAC systems will somehow compensate for the extravagant and inefficient design; thankfully, the energy codes are now biased to avoid this practice. Another, more subtle example is the issue of plug loads in highly efficient buildings. As lighting and mechanical energy use is intentionally reduced, the relative proportion of plug load energy use grows toward 50% of the total. This immediately highlights the need to address plug loads, either with automatic shutdown controls or with substantial reduction in required, desired, or assumed load on the part of the owner and design team. If the team knows that it shares the responsibility for end energy use burden, it sets the tone for sharing the energy savings burden as well.

Investment Financial Analysis

Many of the examples so far have discussed trade-offs made by the design team to reduce total building energy use. In order to confirm that each decision contributes to affordable energy savings, energy modeling can be coupled with a series of financial analyses to show which ECM pays off best. The three most typical tools include the following:

- *Life-cycle cost analysis* is a calculation method that adds first costs to 20–25 years of annual energy and maintenance costs, inclusive of equipment replacement costs and an estimate on inflation. The option with the lowest life-cycle cost is usually chosen if the budget allows. LCCA is the financial tool most often used by institutional owners planning to hold and operate a building through a few generations of equipment technology.

    For school projects, the industry standard assumes a system life span of about 30 years, and that figure is generally used for long-range planning. However, schools could remain in service (if properly maintained and renovated) for longer. Features such as the envelope, well fields, site development, and building orientation could last 100 years. While most school bonds are issued for a 20 year period, when considering the functional life of the building, it would be appropriate to use 30 years for life-cycle planning
- *Simple payback period* is a calculation method that divides first costs by the annual energy savings to determine how long it will take to break even on the investment. Simple payback is most often used by developers looking to recoup costs before divesting of a property, or by long-term building owners with limited funding for retrofits.
- *Return on investment* (ROI) is a calculation that takes the ratio of the energy savings over a predefined number of years minus the first costs divided by the first costs. It is somewhat comparable to the rate of return used in the financial markets. The ROI method is usually used by wealth-holding clients to compare relative opportunity costs when looking to invest in stable profit growth. In downturn economies burdened with the ever-rising cost of energy throughout the world, some financial institutions have begun to provide financing for energy-efficiency upgrades based on projected ROI through vehicles based on ROI calculations.

It is important for all of these financial comparisons that the project team agrees on appropriate inflation and depreciation rates to use. It is essential to take the volatility of certain rates (especially fossil fuel and electricity rates) into account as well. Prices can increase rapidly in a

Green Design on a Budget

There are Ways to Be Green without Spending the Green

Although many green building options have lower construction and operational costs than conventional approaches, the designers that pursue higher degrees of sustainability are challenged by initial costs. To achieve the highest level of sustainability within budget, begin the design by implementing strategies, systems, materials and products that have a lower initial cost.

Projects have many design trade-offs, which still will meet or exceed the owner's objectives without impacting quality. If designers begin the project with the belief that sustainability is an important component of the design, they will view potential trade-offs in different ways. The result likely will be the implementation of more sustainable concepts while staying within the overall project budget. By making smart trade-offs, firms can integrate sustainable design strategies and still keep projects an average of 5% under budget.

Start with basic objectives such as saving energy and water, helping the environment, improving indoor environment quality and using resources efficiently. Judge the solutions based on impact. Considering the budget, determine what strategy or groups of strategies will make the most positive impact.

Form Follows Function

A basic concept taught to every architectural student is that form follows function. When this concept is practiced, the result is almost always cost and resource savings. Unfortunately, designers often ignore this creed. Poor examples are everywhere. There are ramifications when functional benefits can only be rationalized after the architects created design elements based primarily on aesthetics.

Complementary Strategies

Think whole building, not individual measures. Typically, a single green approach, by itself, will be more expensive than conventional approaches. But, in combination with other green elements, the overall impact may be significant enough to lower first costs and improve sustainability."

Dual Function Approaches

Whether designing building or site components, the more functions that can be served by one design element, the more resourceful and cost efficient the design.

short amount of time, drastically changing payback calculations. Life-cycle costing is generally built around what is known at that time, but it should also consider first costs against future risks that are not known. The ability to identify and minimize risks (especially unknown ones) is critical to successful projects.

Building Configuration and Floor Area Minimization

For first cost reasons, there is a drive towards minimizing built square footage, and the entire project team should review the actual requested occupancies to determine if space can be shared as flexible space between uses otherwise listed separately. For instance, shared conference or lounge spaces can reduce redundancy while also encouraging interdepartmental synergy. Another area often under scrutiny for costs savings (both first costs and operating costs) is the transient gross square footage associated with circulation space and lobbies. Space planning exercises are recommended to determine if there are ways for these types of spaces to be reduced in size by merging with other functions or to be limited in scope and controllability for energy use under low-occupancy conditions.

The second major item for the project team to address is the architectural configuration of the building. Facade square footage represents a source of conductive heat loss or heat gain as outdoor air temperatures fluctuate; therefore, the larger the façade area, the greater the impact

Greatest Benefit to Initial Cost

A client may look at the investment in terms of what is the least costly way to provide the green benefit, the greatest benefit to initial cost. If the goal is to provide a healthy indoor environment, increase productivity or even provide the least costly way of ensuring low, long-term operational costs, the decision-making process in selecting the least costly avenue will certainly be different. For example, when education is the key driver, health and productivity often are a higher priority than operational savings associated with energy and water.

There is an extensive list of strategies implemented by designers that initially cost more but are good investments for the building owner. Strategies such as improved lighting and control options have paybacks within months; others like solar water heating and geothermal systems have longer returns. The options are many.

Sustainability Perspective

A client may choose to look at cost from a global sustainability perspective. For most clients, this viewpoint, while well appreciated by most, is beyond local financial capabilities to pursue. However, from a societal standpoint, this is precisely the perspective we must develop and somehow afford.

The Design Community's Challenge

Currently, skilled design teams can reduce energy consumption to 50% below current levels and still meet most reasonable construction budgets. Our immediate need from a sustainability standpoint is getting a greater part of the design community philosophically committed, increasing skill levels within the design community and better disseminating improved design tools.

Owners need to educate themselves about what can be accomplished with the budget and establish appropriate energy and water budgets. Architectural and engineering students should focus on more holistic system thinking and learning to analyze energy and water issues. Joint architectural and engineering classes will help make addressing engineering issues early in the design process the norm.

It is becoming more widely understood within our industry that buildings account for 48% of greenhouse gas emissions. The buildings we design today will be with us for 50 to 100 years. The cost to address environmental issues through better building design today is just a fraction of what it will cost society to deal with the ramifications of insufficient action.

Excerpted from "Green on a Budget" (Nicklas 2008)

of heat loss/gain. Additionally, most facades for K-12 schools buildings contain windows for the benefit of the occupants. Glazing is a poorer insulator than most opaque constructions and should be reviewed with regard to its placement and size. In general, daylighting and natural ventilation are possible within about 25 ft of a façade, a value that may govern the depth of building floorplate intended to include greater connectivity to the outdoors.

Beyond the impact on the interior floorplate, the shape of the building also informs where and how the building self-shades and begins to inform where glazing can be most effectively placed. In the northern hemisphere, glazing that points toward the north captures sky-reflected daylight with minimal solar heat content, making it the ideal source of "even" light. Eastern and western glazing is impacted by low-angle sun throughout the year, which can cause glare and thermal discomfort if not mitigated properly.

Lastly, in the northern hemisphere, southern facades with glazing benefit from overhangs that reduce solar load during the summer.

Safety Factors and Diversity Factors

It is important for all members of the design team to openly reveal their safety factors so that systems are not oversized. The judicious application of diversity factors, based on how normal buildings operate, is important to control "right-sizing" of equipment for optimum efficiency. A classic example is the plug-load allowance requested by the owner. The owner knows what the nameplates are—this can be up to four times higher than normal actual operating levels. The HVAC designer accepts that load, and then applies a factor of +20% to account for future expansion, and then, as per the code, is allowed to size equipment by an additional 20%–30% to accommodate morning warm-up and boost. Then fans are all sized by an additional 10% for air leakage, and the electrical engineer takes the mechanical loads and adds an extra 15% for unforeseen additional load or to effectively follow the National Electrical Code by taking everything at face value simultaneously. All told, one can find transformers sized over three times larger than the largest load ever likely to be experienced. The result of this drastic oversizing is that some equipment may be operating in inefficient ranges, distribution flows may become unstable at low turndown rates, and excessive material is installed compared to what was actually needed. It is strongly recommended that a map of all safety factors and diversity assumptions is clearly laid out in a transparent way so that the whole team can judge them together.

Diversity factors differ greatly from safety factors. The latter deal with unknown uncertainties in future operations, while the former deal with known uncertainties or fluctuations based on professional judgment and industry practice. For instance, in HVAC and electrical design, it is common to find the following diversity factors applied:

- Solar diversity embedded in most computer modeling software for calculating energy use and total peak load
- Diversity assumptions about occupant attendance
- Diversity assumptions about computer use with links to occupancy diversity
- Diversity assumptions with regards to likely simultaneity of peak airflows or peak water flows occurring on a single system—often used to downsize system capacity

It is important to note that diversity factors are independent of schedules and, as such, must be reviewed with the schedules to ensure that the appropriate level of fluctuation is accounted for only once (especially when the schedule is a percent of load type of schedule). It is crucial that the entire project team agree on the diversity factors, as using them to downsize equipment for energy efficiency may run the risk of reduced capacity on peak days. It is necessary to project the extreme internal conditions arising with these peak conditions.

Schedule of Occupancy, Use, Utility Rates

It is essential that the project team understand the schedules related to utility rates, especially any embedded demand charges and on/off/high/low/seasonal peak period definitions local to the site and its service utility. This is because the prevailing benchmarks for energy savings in ASHRAE/IES Standard 90.1 and most energy codes are based on annual cost not absolute energy savings. Most importantly, the owner pays for the demand and consumption charges. This means that discretionary decisions by the team to avoid onerous demand charges through load shifting may be appropriate when trying to reduce annual operating expenditures.

It is important that the project team map the anticipated schedules of use and occupancy for each area of the building. This information is crucial to energy modeling and can greatly affect the outcomes with regard to estimated energy savings over a known benchmark or LCCA. It is important to note that most energy models run the same schedule week after week, so schedules should be configured to cover not only typical weeks, but also changed to account for any known long periods of building closure.

The last item to bear in mind regarding scheduling is whether a standardized schedule will be imposed on the energy model through regulatory requirements. For compliance modeling in particular, some codes, such as the California Energy Code, require that prescribed schedules be used instead of a schedule grounded in a realistic review of assumptions. It is important for the entire team to be aware of such constraints ahead of time.

Redundant and Standby Capacity Sizing Protocols

It is recommended that a thorough discussion of redundancy be conducted with the owner early in the design process—in particular, how redundancy is achieved and if it is necessary. Redundancy is the creation of spare capacity so that a single piece of equipment can be down for maintenance and the rest of the system can continue to operate at some level. Redundancy is usually defined by percentage of capacity.

For instance, in a system in which two pumps are each sized at 60% of total load, the facility can lose one pump and still operate at 60% capacity. In a real life installation, it would be necessary to ensure that the selection of that pump had the optimum efficiency for the normal usage instead of an artificially high peak design flow.

If 100% capacity is desired at all times, some engineers prefer to use standby equipment— a whole spare unit capable of running when any of the normal "run" equipment is not functional. In this case, it might be appropriate to have three pumps, each sized for 50% capacity, available in the system—this would be a two run/one standby approach, and the pumps would generally be rotated in their operation in order to equalize run time.

Charettes and Design Reviews

Design teams working toward significant energy savings should early in the process conduct design charettes that involve all team members and follow up with periodic design reviews. This practice of team members holding one another accountable throughout the design process helps ensure that unintentional myopic thinking doesn't accidentally create vulnerabilities not caught until commissioning. The entire team must understand the multidisciplinary, multilateral agreements as noted herein, must acknowledge and support the achievement of stated energy-use goals, and must comb through the documents as they develop to ensure that the holistic system survives through detailing and value-engineering processes.

Typically kick-off charettes are convened by a named facilitator who sets the ground rules to encourage people to contribute and, most importantly, to listen. There should be agreed-upon time limits for both the length of the brainstorming session as well as the time each person is allowed to speak. All ideas are welcome and can be voiced without dialogue or judgment. It is often useful to start with a brainstorming period related to project and team goals, followed by a discernment session that allows the "brain-dump" list to be prioritized for time and cost investment. This can then be followed by a "blue-sky" brainstorming period related to energy-efficiency measures. During this session, it is necessary to refrain from actually starting to design or else the value of the limited-time creative output from all team members may be diminished. There will be months to include the ideas generated by the brainstorming into the design.

Design reviews can benefit from reviewers that are both internal and external to the team. Internal reviewers are intimately aware of all of the step-by-step decisions that led to the current state. External reviewers provide a level of objectivity and can offer advice from past experience of similar challenges. The CxA's job is to review the content for commissionability and minimized energy use. Again, a facilitator may be necessary to ensure that all reviewers have time to speak without their suggestions being immediately contested by those with an investment in the status quo or those who are biased for whatever reason. It is often beneficial to capture in writing all of the comments in an objective manner so they can be respectfully addressed in sequence, and a resolution on change of or continuance of design direction can be achieved and shared by the entire team.

Use of Energy Modeling as Design Guidance

Energy modeling is a powerful design tool for reviewing the relative energy savings of various ECMs. It can be further exploited when coupled with investment financial analysis to ensure that the investment in first costs will pay for itself in annual energy savings. The whole design team should understand that the current state of energy modeling software is insufficient to predict the actual energy use of a building but is adequate to compare options. It should be noted that there is no federal standard for verifying the absolute accuracy of the energy modeling engine as compared to real life in uncontrolled circumstances. Unlike many repeatable calculation techniques, error ranges are inconsistent based on systems used and user input, so there is no published percent accuracy associated with the algorithms. Additionally, the design team must acknowledge that the current software's algorithms are limited in many ways with regard to the manipulation of certain variables and control techniques and that energy modeling is as much an art as a science when it comes to working around the limitations of the current energy-modeling software. As a rule of thumb, results of at least a 5% relative energy savings arising from comparative energy models with ECMs applied to the same source file are probably a true indicator of measurable savings in real life. Anything less should be reviewed by the design team in a careful risk management process.

The energy modeling process involves a very large amount of data input, and in some software programs it is extremely difficult to change geometry after the fact without re-entering the entire model. As such, the design team should determine how it will spend its limited energy modeling fee from the start and ensure that each model run is absolutely necessary to confirm the design is moving in a direction consistent with project goals. Many tips in this Guide have proven energy reduction benefits and are now best practice and do not need to be analyzed individually for cost effectiveness. For instance, any non-technical person would acknowledge that reducing plug and lighting loads will reduce overall energy use, assuming usage of those loads remains constant. In order to achieve 50% reduction in building energy use as compared to ASHRAE/IESNA Standard 90.1-2004, energy modeling should confirm the relative size of a known benefit rather than support a bad position for resistant team members.

REFERENCES AND RESOURCES

AIA. 2007. *Integrated Project Delivery: A Guide*. Washington, DC: American Institute of Architects. www.aia.org/contractdocs/AIA077630.

ASHRAE. 2004. ANSI/ASHRAE/IESNA Standard 90.1-2004, Energy Standard for Buildings Except Low-Rise Residential Buildings. Atlanta: American Society of Heating, Refrigerating and Air-Conditioning Engineers.

ASHRAE. 2009. *Indoor Air Quality Guide: Best Practices for Design, Construction, and Commissioning*. Atlanta: American Society of Heating, Refrigerating and Air-Conditioning Engineers.

ASHRAE. 2010a. ANSI/ASHRAE/IES Standard 90.1-2010, Energy Standard for Buildings Except Low-Rise Residential Buildings. Atlanta: American Society of Heating, Refrigerating and Air-Conditioning Engineers.

ASHRAE. 2010b. ANSI/ASHRAE/USGBC/IES Standard 189.1-2009, *Standard for the Design of High-Performance Green Buildings*. Atlanta: American Society of Heating, Refrigerating and Air-Conditioning Engineers.

ASHRAE. 2010c. *Performance Measurement Protocols for Commercial Buildings*. Atlanta: American Society of Heating, Refrigerating and Air-Conditioning Engineers.

Bonnema, E., M. Leach, M., S. Pless. 2011. Technical support document: Development of the *Advanced Energy Design Guide for K-12 Schools—50% Energy Savings*. NREL/TP-5500-51437, National Renewable Energy Laboratory, Golden, CO. http://www.nrel.gov/docs/fy11osti/51437.pdf" www.nrel.gov/docs/fy11osti/51437.pdf

Colliver, D., R.S. Gates, T.F. Burks, and H. Zhang. 1997. Determination of the 0.4%, 1% and 2% annual occurrences of temperature and moisture and the 99% and 98% occurrences of temperature for 1400 national and international locations. Final Report, ASHRAE Research Project RP-890. Atlanta: American Society of Heating, Refrigerating and Air-Conditioning.

DOE. 2011a. Operating and maintaining energy smart schools training. U.S. Department of Energy, Washington, DC, and the Council of Educational Facility Planners International (CEFPI), Arlington, VA. http://doe.cefpi.org/.

DOE. 2011b. Weather data. EnergyPlus Energy Simulation Software, U.S. Department of Energy, Energy Efficiency and Renewable Energy, Washington, DC. http://apps1.eere.energy.gov/buildings/energyplus/cfm/weather_data.cfm.

Energy Information Administration, Residential Energy Consumption Survey. Table 5a. U.S. Residential Using Site Energy by Census Region and Type of Housing Unit, 1978- 2005. http://www.eia.doe.gov/emeu/efficiency/recs_5a_table.pdf, U.S. Total for 2005 was used.

Nicklas, M. 2008. Green on a budget. *High Performance Buildings* Fall:7–16.

NOAA. 2005. Climate maps of the United States. NOAA Satellite and Information Service. National Climatic Data Center. Washington, DC: National Oceanic and Atmospheric Administration. http://cdo.ncdc.noaa.gov/cgi-bin/climaps/climaps.pl.

NREL. 2005. Global Horizontal Solar Radiation—Annual. Golden, CO: National Renewable Energy Laboratory. Image "solar_glo" available at www.nrel.gov/gis/images.

NREL. 2011. Database of state incentives for renewables & efficiency. Subcontract XEU-0-99515-01, National Renewable Energy Laboratory, U.S. Department of Energy. http://www.dsireusa.org/.

Performance Targets and Case Studies

3

ENERGY TARGETS

Building energy-efficient schools takes careful planning. The goal of this Guide is a building that consumes at least 50% less energy than a computer-modeled baseline that follows the minimum requirements set forth in ASHRAE/IESNA Standard 90.1-2004. To better define this goal, an absolute whole-building energy use intensity (EUI) should be defined as a best practice. Designers and owners should strive to set their own whole-building EUI targets to provide focused and measurable 50% savings goals. These EUI targets can be used to select design teams as part of a procurement strategy, to set early design goals, to track design development progress, and to verify performance during operations. EUI targets can be generated from multiple data sources, including the following:

- ENERGYSTAR™ Target Finder (DOE 2011)
- Other local schools in your district or in neighboring districts
- Case studies of high-performance schools with similar programs and climate zones (see case studies in this chapter)
- The energy target tables in this chapter. The recommended EUIs in Tables 3-1 and 3-2 are based on a typical set configuration for schools. It is a good target goal, but may not apply if your school has specific high-use energy loads or other special circumstances.

In general, the energy targets in this guide are applicable to most K-12 schools with typical programs and use profiles. For the purposes of using these targets, we define a K-12 school as having the following common space types:

- Administrative and office areas
- Classrooms, hallways, and restrooms
- Gymnasiums with locker rooms and showers
- Assembly spaces with either flat or tiered seating
- Food preparation spaces
- Libraries

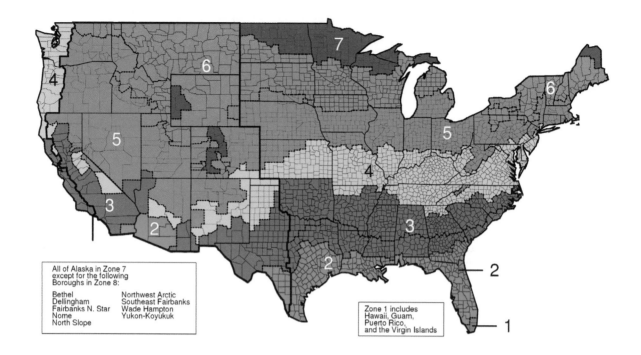

Figure 3-1   United States Climate Zone Map

However, these energy targets do not include atypical spaces, such as indoor pools, wet labs with fume hoods (e.g., chemistry), "dirty" dry labs (e.g., woodworking and auto shops), or other unique spaces with extraordinary heat or pollution generation. They assume a typical weather year for a typical climate zone. They also contain specific plug load and control assumptions and assume properly operating, well-maintained equipment. Caution should be used when applying these energy targets, especially if your school has atypical spaces, high-use energy loads, etc. The targets for K-12 schools in this guide apply to all sizes and classifications (primary and secondary schools) of new-construction K-12 school buildings. Targets are based on two different prototype designs: a 74,000 ft^2 elementary school and a 211,000 ft^2 high school. The models assume some year-round use in the gym and common space areas, and nine months of use for classrooms and the rest of the school. The whole-building models are designed to meet minimum ventilation requirements and maintain ASHRAE comfort standards year round. Ventilation and other internal load requirements are to be reduced during times of reduced occupancy. It has been shown through whole-building annual energy modeling that following the prescriptive recommendations of Chapter 4 will result in meeting or exceeding the energy targets for all three recommended HVAC system types. For additional details, see the technical support document for this Guide (Bonnema et al. 2011).

These energy targets can be used to give designers flexibility while still reaching the goal of at least 50% energy savings. The numbers given in the tables below are annual whole-building and subsystem energy consumption targets. Following the recommendations in Chapter 4 has been shown through precomputed energy modeling to result in at least 50% energy savings. However, if there is a specific recommendation that is not feasible for a specific project, this guide can still be used to achieve at least 50% energy savings. For instance, if the project team decides not to daylight the school, then the annual energy consumption of the recommended lighting system must achieve the lighting target value. Similarly, if one of the three recommended HVAC system types is not feasible, than the recommended system type must meet the HVAC target in Tables 3-1 for primary schools or Table 3-2 for secondary schools to reach the goal of at least 50% energy savings. Ultimate flexibility is provided to a

Table 3-1 Primary School Energy Use Targets for 50% Energy Savings

Climate Zone	Plug/Process Loads, kBtu/ft^2·yr	Lighting, kBtu/ft^2·yr	HVAC, kBtu/ft^2·yr	Total, kBtu/ft^2·yr
1A			20	37
2A			20	37
2B			20	37
3A			15	32
3B:CA			8	25
3B			14	31
3C			10	27
4A			19	36
4B	11	6	15	32
4C			15	32
5A			22	39
5B			17	34
6A			27	44
6B			22	39
7			30	47
8			45	62

Table 3-2 Secondary School Energy Use Targets for 50% Energy Savings

Climate Zone	Plug/Process Loads, kBtu/ft^2·yr	Lighting, kBtu/ft^2·yr	HVAC, kBtu/ft^2·yr	Total, kBtu/ft^2·yr
1A			21	36
2A			21	36
2B			21	36
3A			18	33
3B:CA			10	25
3B			17	32
3C			13	28
4A			22	37
4B	8	7	18	33
4C			19	34
5A			25	40
5B			21	36
6A			31	46
6B			26	41
7			34	49
8			48	63

project team by allowing a project to meet the whole building targets without consideration to subsystem or prescriptive recommendations.

Tables 3-1 and 3-2 represent energy targets based on end use (lighting, HVAC, plug/process loads). There are two tables, one for the primary school and one for the secondary school. All tables provide energy targets by the 16 defined climate zones as shown in Figure 3-1. For more information on setting EUI targets in your building, please see *Setting Absolute Energy Use Targets for High Performance Buildings* (Leach et al. 2011).

REFERENCES AND RESOURCES

DOE. 2011. ENERGYSTAR Target Finder. U.S. Department of Energy, Washington, DC. www.energystar.gov/index.cfm?c=new_bldg_design.bus_target_finder.

Bonnema, E., M. Leach, and S. Pless. 2011. Technical support document: Development of the *Advanced Energy Design Guide for K-12 Schools—50% Energy Savings*. NREL/TP-5500-51437, National Renewable Energy Laboratory, Golden, CO. www.nrel.gov/docs/fy11osti/51437.pdf.

Leach, M., E. Bonnema, and S. Pless. 2011. Setting absolute energy use targets for high performance buildings. NREL/TP-5500-52590, National Renewable Energy Laboratory, Golden, CO. www.nrel.gov/docs/fy11osti/52590.pdf.

CASE STUDIES

GLORIA MARSHALL ELEMENTARY SCHOOL

Gloria Marshall Elementary School in the Spring Independent School District is a 105,000 ft^2 two-story school that accommodates 800 students. The school achieved the goal of creating a fun, well lighted, high comfort, low energy consumption, high-performance elementary school that emphasizes math and science curriculum using the building as a teaching tool for sustainability. Completed in 2010, Gloria Marshall was the first school of its kind in the Houston, TX, area to use geothermal heating and cooling, sophisticated lighting controls with daylight harvesting, roof-mounted photovoltaic (PV) electrical generation, a wind generator, and rainwater collection for toilet flushing.

Gloria Marshall Elementary School Exterior
Source: SHW Group

Building Orientation/Design/Envelope

The building orientation was set to true north to take full benefit of daylight harvesting. The majority of classrooms were located on the first and second floors of the south exposure, with the remaining classrooms located on the second floor of the north exposure. Texas elementary schools are traditionally single story; in this case, the facility was changed to a rectangular two-story structure with courtyard. This resulted in a smaller footprint and roof for energy efficiency and more windows for daylighting the classrooms. The roof is a cold liquid applied membrane, reflective white with low heat gain, that structurally supports the Velcro® applied flexible PV located on the roof. The walls are structural steel with metal stud construction and dense glass sheeting with a full adhesive water-proofing membrane over the sheeting to

Daylighted Classroom
Source: SHW Group

Exterior Shading
Source: CMTA Engineers

greatly reduce air infiltration. Three types of windows were used on the project: (1) clear insulated windows with no low-e coating for the north exposure and daylighting panes at the top of classrooms, (2) clear insulated windows with low-e coating for visual windows with a south exposure, and (3) green insulated low-e coating for east and west exposures and the main entry into the auditorium.

HVAC

The HVAC systems were designed around a geothermal or water-source heat pump (WSHP) system. System efficiencies were increased by using two-speed compressors in the WSHP units. This was due to past experience, which indicated that 80% of run hours would be at part load. School heating and cooling zones were broken into two classrooms per zone, with averaging thermostats for heating and cooling. The well fields for this geothermal system were located in the parking lot and green areas of the school grounds where there were approximately 180 closed-loop wells all piped into a distribution vault, with mains piped into the building. Each WSHP is paired with a single circulating water pump sized specifically to the unit, which eliminates the need to balance based on gallon-per-minute flows specified for each pump. Fresh air is introduced into each occupied space by a variable-air-volume (VAV) box supplied by a dedicated outdoor air system (DOAS). The DOAS unit includes a total energy recovery wheel and variable-frequency drives (VFDs) to vary the outdoor air delivered to each classroom, independent of the WSHP system. The VAV boxes are controlled by a central CO_2 testing system that determines how much if any outdoor air is required.

Lighting Controls and Daylighting

The lighting system was designed to 0.75 W/ft^2 and a minimum of 40 fc. Daylight harvesting was accomplished by using daylight windows with exterior and interior light shelves. Each second-floor classroom was fitted with two tubular daylighting devices for a southern exposure and four tubular daylighting devices in classrooms with a northern exposure. Classrooms were designed with two zones, one closest to exterior windows and the other furthest from the windows. Photo sensors determine lighting levels and ramp up dimmable florescent fixtures to reach minimum foot candles in each zone. Teachers were given three control buttons—ON, OFF, and a "Media" button—to control classroom lighting. The ON button only enables the controls to turn on lights if lighting levels are too low. The ON button also allows the use of lights after hours for a timed two hours, at which time the occupant is notified by a flash of the light fixtures that the lights will turn off. The Media button reduces florescence lighting and closes tubular daylighting device dampers to a classroom light level of 10 fc. Occupancy sensors were converted to vacancy sensors to turn off lights when no one is present. The lighting system was designed to totally shut off all lights on campus at specified times to create a completely dark

Table 3-3   Building Data for Gloria Marshall Elementary School

Building Data	
Cold applied liquid membrane roof	Overall U-factor = 0.065 Reflectivity = 95
Metal stud exterior walls	Overall U-factor = 0.075
Windows (view)	U-factor – 0.505 SHGC – 0.25
Windows (daylighting)	U-factor – 0.98 SHGC – 0.4
Simulated energy use intensity (EUI)	33.4kBtu/ft^2
Total construction cost	$15.6 million
Cost per square foot	$149/ft^2

campus. This condition was coordinated and supported by the local police department to make it easier for them to identify when someone is in the building. The interior lighting package was completed with three lamp types: 32 W super T8, 54 W T5 high output, and 42 W compact fluorescent. The exterior lighting package was completed with two lamp types: metal halide for most common areas, and LED fixtures where night custodial crews would park. This allows for the majority of the metal halides to be turned off and for the LEDs to be left on until the night crews leave.

Rainwater Collection

A rainwater system was designed to collect 30,000 gal of rainwater from 50% of the roof to be used to flush toilets. A clear 6 in. polyvinyl chloride stormwater line was run through the science lab for students to witness the amount of water running off the roof. Low-volume urinals and water closets were installed with dual flush valves to reduce the amount of water needed. Landscaping was designed with all native plantings to eliminate the need for irrigation.

Power Generation/Monitoring

A 10 kW PV system was installed on the roof, and a small PV display and 3.7 kW wind turbine were installed on the playground as teaching aids integrated into the EcoScreen® dashboard. The EcoScreen dashboard is an interactive real-time interface that displays a snapshot and trending of energy systems. The electrical design included submetering for all systems to allow the school district to gather data on Gloria Marshall's performance and to provide data for future school designs.

MARIN COUNTY DAY SCHOOL

Marin County Day School, founded in 1955, includes both grades K-4 and 5-8 schools and provides an atmosphere that encourages both creativity and personal involvement, while educating students and teachers on resource conservation. Located on 35 acres in Corte Madera, CA, the campus includes 40 classrooms, music and art rooms, a gymnasium, an auditorium, and a learning resource center. Since the school includes environmental sustainability in their programs and teaching practices, it was very important that the new buildings fit the school's vision.

Marin County Day School Exterior
Source: Michael David Rose

Marin County Day School Surrounding Natural Campus
Source: Josh Partee

Improvements initiated in 2007 followed a multiphase master plan for six new buildings and renovations to existing structures. The goal was to preserve the feel of the natural campus with sustainable building measures, maintain the existing campus footprint, and minimize disruption to on-going programs.

There was a total of 33,000 ft^2 of new construction, and the updates were completed in winter of 2009. Phase one, completed in 2008, was LEED® Gold-certified by the U.S. Green Building Council. The east-side campus built in phase two reached LEED Platinum certification and net zero energy with a 40% energy savings over California's Title 24.

Daylighting

Daylighting brings more light into the classrooms and provides a positive effect on student performance. New buildings are connected to outdoor learning spaces and are intentionally thin to allow daylight on two sides as well as easy cross ventilation. In the new learning resource center, an open-air hallway connects the second floor, the library, and the renovated classrooms.

Glazed facades, deep louvers, and low-emissivity glass reduce solar energy heat gain, while still allowing for natural light and views of the surrounding campus grounds. More daylighting is provided by a solar chimney lined with light shelves, which also provides stack-effect cooling.

HVAC

Covered walkways, shade trees, and light-colored paving/roofing materials help reduce the heat from hot days. Heating is provided via water circulating through tubes in the concrete slab floor. A 15,000 gal rainwater cistern is buried below grade to hold water chilled from a night-time-operated cooling tower. This greywater is pumped into the building for radiant cooling on hot days and for toilet flushing. By not using forced air for heating and cooling, air quality is improved and the system uses about one-tenth the energy of a compressor. Carbon dioxide sensors indicate when fresh air is needed.In order to help students participate in the energy management process, an energy-monitoring system was installed as a teaching tool. Students can test actual energy use versus the net zero energy goal, see if they are generating more energy than they are consuming, and make adjustments as needed.

(Right) Exterior Shading and (Left) Louvers on Classroom Windows
Source: EHDD Architecture

Additional Sustainable Features

- An on-site PV array (95 kW) provides all of the new structures' energy needs and, in conjunction with the efficiency strategies used, allows the achievement of net zero energy use. Monitoring systems are in place both for verification and for use in the school curriculum, integrating design with education. The cost of the PV was approximately 1.5% of the total construction cost.
- The 15,000 gal cistern used for radiant cooling in the summer is also used for toilet flushing, and the washrooms use water-efficient fixtures for minimal use of resources.
- The surrounding watershed was rehabilitated and new site lines were opened to the surrounding mountains. Bioswales were used to filter water runoff and provide areas for students to enjoy nature, and they return overflow to a stream near the edge of the campus. The creek that crosses the campus was widened, and pools were added to prevent erosion. The seventh-grade science classes monitor both water quality and creek levels.
- The landscaping uses drought-tolerant plants that best thrive in the climate. A green roof was added to the administrative building to help regulate interior building temperature.
- Forest Stewardship Council certified wood was used for rough framing, exterior guardrails, and for siding, which also helps to maintain a continuity and similar feel to the older buildings already present.

MANASSAS PARK ELEMENTARY SCHOOL AND PREKINDERGARTEN

Located in Manassas Park, VA, Manassas Park Elementary school serves 840 students and educators and includes 59 classrooms, gymnasium, cafeteria, media center, offices, and breakout spaces for informal learning, plus a dedicated pre-kindergarten building housed in 140,463 ft^2 (gross) of building. The LEED Gold certified school was designed not only for energy efficiency but also as an educational tool for students.

(Right) Educational House Exterior and (Left) Section View
Source: VMDO Architects

Utilizing lessons learned from schools previously constructed in the district, the design team strove to build a green, sustainable facility that would provide educational opportunities incorporated into the building itself. The result is a building so efficient that the 2010 summer school program for the entire school system was conducted there, which allowed the other school buildings to be programmed into unoccupied mode for the summer.

Thermal Envelope

The building footprint was constrained by the narrow area on the site available for building. The final design created an E-shaped footprint with three 3-story educational houses for the classrooms, which face north or south. The east side of the building houses spaces that don't require many windows (gymnasium, loading dock, mechanical rooms) to minimize solar heat gain.

The cubic shape of the buildings minimizes building envelope exposure. The walls have an overall R-value of 20.8 and are constructed of cold formed metal studs, sheathing, two inches of closed-cell spray foam insulation, and either brick or metal siding. A cool roof of white thermoplastic polyolefin membrane provides an overall R-value 24.2.

Daylighting/Lighting

Courtyards between the educational houses are 70 ft wide so that daylight reaches the full southern elevation of each house. Over 78% of the regularly occupied spaces benefit from daylighting:

- The pre-kindergarten building utilizes north facing monitors.
- Tubular skylights provide daylighting without glare in the gymnasium.
- The classrooms have continuous glazing from 3 ft above finished floor to the 11 ft high ceilings.
- Exterior sunshades block direct sunlight from south-facing classrooms.
- Parabolic light louvers in clerestory windows redirect sunlight to the ceiling.
- Ambient light is further reflected by sloped ceilings in the classrooms.

Electric lighting in classrooms is supplied by three rows of pendant fluorescent fixtures that automatically dim as needed. Motion sensors with auto-off, manual-on further control lighting, based on occupancy.

(Right) Daylighted Classroom and (Left) Gymnasium
Source: VMDO Architects

(Right) Green-Light Ventilation System and (Left) Building Systems Cut Away and Signs
Source: VMDO Architects

HVAC

The school employs a ground-source heat pump (GSHP) mechanical system with 221 vertical bores at 350 ft. There is a dedicated GSHP for each of the classrooms, with setpoints determined by the building automation system (BAS); the temperature can be manually adjusted by 2° in either direction. The pumps are located away from the classrooms to minimize noise but to also provide easy access for maintenance. Natural ventilation is employed during favorable outdoor conditions (60°F–75°F and less a than 40% chance of rain). A fan-assisted stack effect moves the fresh air through the room. Additional energy-efficiency measures include variable-speed pumps; high-volume, low-speed fans in the gymnasium; and mini-tank water heaters positioned at point of use locations in the classrooms and restrooms.

Water Conservation

Rainwater from the site is filtered and collected in a cistern and moved to a bioretention area and, finally, into a stormwater management pond. A portion of the water is treated and used to flush toilets; the rest is used for irrigation. Low-consumption fixtures and kitchen equipment reduce the potable water amount requirements.

Table 3-4   Building Data for Manassas Park Elementary School and Prekindergarten

Building Data	
Energy use intensity (site)	37.28 kBtu/ft^2
Annual energy cost index (ECI)	$1.14/ft^2
Total construction cost	$24,698,200 $28,026,925 (with site work)
Cost per square foot	$175.83 $199.53 (total hard costs)

Educational Features

Each building at the school has seasonal- and forest-related themes in the classrooms and corridors. Signs and building cutaways illustrate and explain the building systems—pipes are painted red and blue analogous to human veins and arteries. A green-light system tied to the BAS signals when classroom windows can be opened to provide natural ventilation and allows students to become directly involved in energy conservation. Signs adjacent to the system describe attributes and benefits of both daylighting and natural ventilation.

The principal water retention area can be used as an outdoor classroom or performance stage. Other exterior learning spaces allow students to explore the surrounding landscape. Maps on the grounds illustrate how rainwater flows through nearby rivers. A mural on the side of the cistern shows the rainwater system and explains the water cycle.

Additional information on the Manassas Park Elementary School and the how the building provides educational opportunities can be found in the Fall 2010 issue of *High Performance Buildings* (Knox and Davis 2010).

RICHARDSVILLE ELEMENTARY SCHOOL

Richardsville Elementary School, a 74,000 ft^2, two-story school that accommodates 500 students, is the culmination of 10 years of energy successes for Warren County Public Schools in Bowling Green, KY. Envisioned as a net zero energy building, the school design focused on achieving an energy consumption goal of 17 kBtu/ft^2/yr.

An integrated design process was used that involved participants including school district officials, building users, the architectural/engineering design team, the state department of education, and the local power generation company. In order to design and operate a net zero energy school within a public school budget, all of these entities had to understand the vision and be willing to implement strategies to make energy reduction feasible and make a solar power generation system affordable.

A leader in reducing energy consumption, the Warren County School District's first step was to hire a district energy manager whose task was to educate and empower the staff on building operation. Successive construction projects over an eight-year period showed a continuous improvement in energy consumption. With a focus on better thermal envelopes, improved geothermal system designs, and efficient building operation, the district employed new construction techniques to improve building energy efficiency.

Thermal Envelope

Insulated concrete form (ICF) was used for the wall assemblies because of its improved thermal performance, reduced air infiltration, and high speed of construction. Richardsville further improved the thermal envelope by making the building a two-story rectangular shape to reduce exterior wall and roof area.

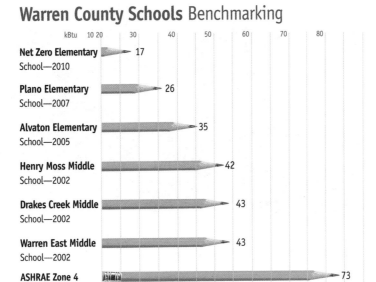

Figure 3-2 Energy Use Reduction in Projects over an 8 Year Period

Daylighting

Richardsville was the district's first attempt at daylight harvesting. The two-story rectangular design made it simpler to align the building on an east/west axis. The daylight glazing is 20 in. high and has an interior light shelf. The second floor classrooms are provided with tubular daylighting devices to supplement the natural light in the rear of the classrooms. All classrooms have a digital, addressable daylight control system. The school's electric lighting systems were designed to minimize energy intensity, averaging 0.68 W/ft². The daylighting design is a good example of collaboration with the Kentucky Department of Education (KDE). KDE standards require electric lighting to provide 50 fc in classrooms. On this project, they reduced their standards to 40 fc to save on project costs. This reduction was allowed because with the natural light supplement, the illumination would be greater than 50 fc for 95% of class teaching hours.

HVAC

Geothermal was used in the project and reduced energy consumption through the use of dual compressor heat-pump units and a distributive pumping system. The dual compressor units were chosen because of the impressive part-load performance. Measured data for another school in the district indicated that 80% of run hours were at part load. The distributive water pumping allows for a simpler variable flow system. One water pump is mounted adjacent to each unit. System pump head is reduced by designing to lower water velocities, which reduces installed pump horsepower.

The geothermal heat-pump units are coupled with a constant-volume DOAS. The DOAS unit includes a total energy recovery wheel and delivers outside air directly to the classroom, independent of the heat-pump system. To further reduce energy consumption, demand-control ventilation was integrated into the DOAS. CO_2 is monitored throughout all rooms, and the quantity of outside air introduced is varied based on measured indoor and outdoor CO_2. Each classroom is provided with an outdoor air VAV box, and the DOAS supply/exhaust fans have variable-frequency drives to vary airflow. A central CO_2 testing system was provided so that reliable, consistent measurements can be used as the basis of control. The VAV boxes can mea-

Richardsville Elementary School
Source: Sherman-Carter-Barnhart Architects

(Right) Daylighted Classroom and (Left) Rooftop Thin Film and Crystalline PV Panels
Source: Rachel Paul Photography (for CMTA Engineers)

sure OA flow to each classroom, which allows for trending of airflow for measurement and verification.

Technology/Plug Loads

Laptop computers were selected in lieu of desktop machines, and a wireless system was provided throughout the school. Multiple mobile computer carts are made available so that any classroom can operate as a computer room. Eliminating the classroom computer stations and separate computer classroom reduced the building size by 1200 ft^2 and proved to be an unexpected strategy to reduce energy consumption and costs. The fully wireless school was the first in Kentucky and another example of collaboration with state agencies.

Kitchen

Measured data from a previously built school indicated that the all-electric kitchen was consuming 22% of power used annually. Meeting Richardsville's energy goal required that kitchen power consumption be reduced, but lunch quality needed to be maintained. The kitchen staff was involved throughout the process and tested various new types of equipment. Combination steamer/ovens and tilt kettles were selected, thus eliminating high-heat-producing cooking equipment. An additional benefit was the use of type II range hoods that significantly reduced the exhaust air quantity.

Table 3-5 Richardsville Elementary School Power Consumption by Month

Month	Power Consumed
October 2010	37,200 Kwh
November 2010	35,200 Kwh
December 2010	32,000 Kwh
January 2011	28,400 Kwh
February 2011	33,800 Kwh
Monthly Average	33,800 Kwh

Table 3-6 Building Data for Richardsville Elementary School

Building Data	
Single-ply membrane with rigid insulation on metal decking	Overall R-value = R-30 Reflectivity = 95
ICF exterior walls	Overall R-value = R-28.6
View windows (center of glass)	U-factor – 0.29 SHGC – 0.40
Daylighting windows (center of glass)	U-factor – 0.47 SHGC – 0.78
Energy use intensity	17 kBtu/ft^2
Total construction cost	$14.2 million
Cost per square foot	$197/ft^2

Measurement & Verification

Many of the new strategies developed for this project required post-occupancy power measurements, so Richardsville was designed with a power monitoring system. Individual systems that can be trended for energy consumption include HVAC, DOAS, exterior and interior lighting, kitchen, IT rooms, and plug loads. Consumption can be measured hourly, daily, monthly, or annually and compared to the energy model results. The first unexpected trend identified was the unoccupied hours' power consumption. The effect that the 24/7 operation of the kitchen refrigeration equipment, IT servers and other parasitic loads, has on annual power usage are significant.

The building's power consumption has been on target with projected usage. The first two months were higher while the school was being commissioned and time schedules set correctly. The average usage to date is 1.55 kBtu/month. The building is generally unoccupied in the summer, so the targeted 17 kBtu/ft^2·yr appears to be tracking well.

Power Generation

The power generation design was delayed until the energy consumption goal was met. The final energy model indicated that the annual consumption would be 421,300 kWh. Solar power is generated via thin film and crystalline panels: 208 kW of thin film was placed on the building's flat roof, and 140 kW of crystalline panels were installed on an adjacent shade structure. The total cost of the system was $2,650,000. Warren County received a $1,400,000 stimulus grant to help support the system's cost. In support of the net zero energy design, the local power utility (Tennessee Valley Authority) agreed to purchase all power generated at a price $0.12/kW greater than the cost they sell power. This agreement improved the financial model of the project.

GREENSBURG K-12 SCHOOL

Greensburg K-12, a 120,000 ft^2, two-story facility located in Greensburg, KS, accommodates 375 students from pre-kindergarten through high school. The campus includes a library, a cafeteria, a kitchen, science labs, two gymnasiums, an art/music wing, courtyards, playgrounds, and a football stadium. After 95% of the town was destroyed by an EF5 tornado in May of 2007, the school was rebuilt as part of Greensburg's plan for a model "eco-community." Ground was broken on the facility in October of 2008, and the school's grand opening was held in August of 2010.

Designed to achieve the U.S. Green Building Council's LEED for Schools Platinum designation, Greensburg K-12 anticipates a 60% energy-use cost savings. Energy analysis modeling of this school versus an ASHRAE/IESNA Standard 90.1-compliant building of the same size and shape indicates a reduction of more than 50% before adding savings gained from the 50 kW on-site wind turbine, which could provide an additional 10% in annual electricity savings.

As part of Greensburg's overall plan of efficiency and sustainability, Greensburg K-12 was designed from the ground up to be an environmentally responsible model school. Many techniques were used to make the most efficient use of materials and energy.

Thermal Envelope

The walls and parts of the roof are insulated with R-30 to R-40 rated structural insulated panels in order to eliminate heat/cold migration through the exterior building envelope that can occur with more traditional metal stud framing. Overhangs on the south-facing windows reduce summer solar gains and allow winter passive solar tempering for more energy efficiency.

Lighting

The school was built facing east-west to make use of abundant daylight from north and south for both lighting and winter heating. Daylighting is used in all regularly occupied spaces:

- The classrooms and hallways are naturally lit to diminish the need for electric lighting and to improve student performance.
- Electronic timer light switches, indoor occupancy switches, and photoelectric switches are used to manage lighting levels and power usage.

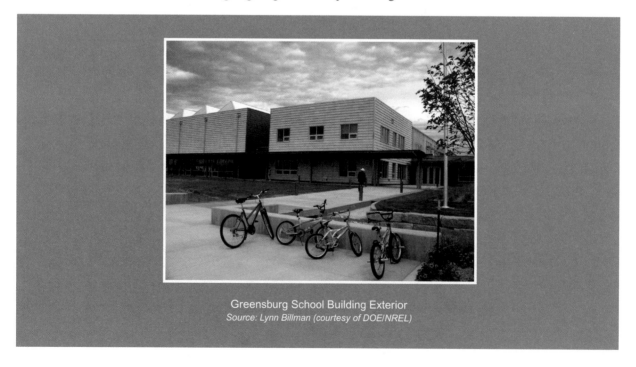

Greensburg School Building Exterior
Source: Lynn Billman (courtesy of DOE/NREL)

- Skylights are used to reduce the use of electricity during daylight hours and to provide plenty of light to corridors and other common areas.

HVAC

Heating and cooling are supplied by a hybrid closed-loop GSHP system, combined with a fluid cooler, through almost one hundred 410 ft deep vertical wells. A sensor-controlled outdoor air system lets in outdoor air as needed. The heating and hot-water system are electric to best utilize both the on-site wind turbine as well as the abundant energy produced by the Greensburg wind farm. Carbon dioxide sensors control a dedicated outdoor air system with energy recovery ventilators to provide outdoor air ventilation as needed. All classrooms and most of the offices have operable windows in order to allow natural ventilation.

Other Sustainable Features

- Operable windows provide natural ventilation in classrooms, offices, and other spaces.
- An on-site wind generator provides 50 kW of power that supplements the 12.5 MW generated from the community wind farm.
- Rainwater is captured and stored, and bioswales are used to filter parking lot runoff. Waterless urinals and low-flow fixtures, faucets, and toilets minimize water usage.

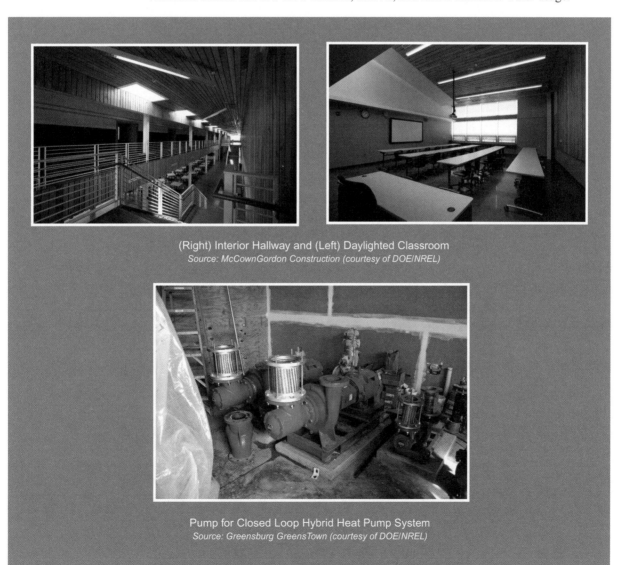

(Right) Interior Hallway and (Left) Daylighted Classroom
Source: McCownGordon Construction (courtesy of DOE/NREL)

Pump for Closed Loop Hybrid Heat Pump System
Source: Greensburg GreensTown (courtesy of DOE/NREL)

- Recycled and reclaimed materials were used where possible, including reclaimed Douglas fir board paneling for use in the ceilings and wood salvaged from Hurricane Katrina for use on the building exterior.

Additional information on the Greensburg K-12 project is available from the U.S. Department of Energy, Energy Efficiency and Renewable Energy Web site (DOE 2011a, 2011b).

KINARD JUNIOR HIGH SCHOOL

Poudre School District, located in Fort Collins, CO, includes 50 schools serving 24,000 students and is the ninth largest school district in Colorado. The 113,000 ft^2 Kinard Junior High School is the most energy-efficient school in the Poudre School District—it was qualified as "Designed to Earn the ENERGY STAR" before it completed construction. The building's annual energy use is 25 kBtu/ft^2·yr, which exceeds ASHRAE/IESNA Standard 90.1 requirements by 50% and saves $40,000 per year in energy costs as compared to the most recently constructed district junior high school in the Poudre School District.

Thermal Envelope

Building materials included high-mass R-20 walls with brick, foam insulation, block, and drywall. The roof is rated R-30. Compared to other schools in the area, Kinard has an excellent record for comfort, with few heating or cooling complaints. The windows incorporate colored glass panels that add interest and hide views of the roof.

Lighting

Kinard Junior High School is built on a long east-west axis to make best use of daylighting features that include tubular daylighting devices for interior spaces. Daylighting is used in all regularly occupied areas, providing students and staff with a connection to the outdoors from all occupied spaces. Many of the classrooms and other common areas use no electric light during daylight hours. A building energy management system and individual classroom controls provide precise lighting level controls when electric light is needed.

Kinard Junior High School Building Exterior
Source: Time Frame Images (courtesy of RB+B Architects)

HVAC

A geoexchange borefield consisting of one hundred 350 ft deep boreholes is used to provide or reject heat through a series of piping loops manifolded together and piped to the mechanical room. This rejects heat from the building for cooling in the summer and is a source of heat for in the winter. In addition, the following apply:

- Each classroom uses geoexchange heat pumps with electronically commutated fan motors (ECMs) and fresh air ventilation through a heat recovery ventilation system.
- The cafeteria employs a variable-speed air-handling system served by geoexchange water-to-water heat pumps and backed up by a natural-gas-fired condensing boiler heating plant.
- The kitchen has a dedicated variable-speed air-handling unit (AHU) integrated with the exhaust hoods and utilizes the condensing boiler plant for heating along with direct evaporative cooling.

(Right) Daylighted Classroom and (Left) Windows with Colored Glass Panels Overlooking Cafeteria
Source: Time Frame Images (courtesy of RB+B Architects)

Geoexchange Heat Pumps
Source: RB+B Architects

- The gymnasiums employ a variable-speed air-handling system with economizer control and demand controlled ventilation, while locker-room ventilation and exhaust make up are provided by geoexchange heat pumps through a heat recovery systems that is backed by the condensing boiler plant heating water system.
- A direct digital control and energy management system makes sure the energy savings and operating cost reductions are maintained throughout the scheduled occupied periods as well as during morning warm up and evening cool down.

Water Usage

Parking lots drain through bioswales and into a retention pond. Through the use of automated water controls and an on-site weather station exterior, water usage has been reduced by 50%. Recycled content artificial turf was used for the school's football field, and native turf in other areas was designed to require no irrigation after five years.

TWO HARBORS HIGH SCHOOL

The 190,000 ft^2 Two Harbors High School, located near Duluth, MN, was built to replace a 1935 vintage existing building. The project offered the opportunity to design and construct an energy-efficient facility with low maintenance, low operating costs, and multi-use spaces available for use by both the school and the community. An integrated design approach improved the performance of the daylighting controls and the ventilation systems.

Completed in 2005, the school has received a number of awards, including a CEFPI Design Concept award (2005), an ASHRAE technology award (2009), and the Minnesota Governors' Partnership Award (2008).

Two Harbors High School
Source: John Gregor, Coldsnap Photography

Daylighting/Lighting

Abundant daylighting is available due to the architectural design of the building. The choice of mechanical systems reduced overhead ductwork, allowing for greater ceiling and window heights, which improved daylighting penetration into perimeter spaces. High clerestory windows provide daylighting for interior spaces. The lighting systems are integrated with the building management system and utilize occupancy schedules and both daylighting and occupancy sensors. These controls also operate as part of the security system. One lesson learned from the project was that while the south-facing orientation of the clerestory windows helps with natural ventilation, glare would be reduced by the use of north-facing clerestories.

HVAC

The school utilizes a DOAS that delivers air via thermal displacement ventilation (TDV) diffusers and high ΔT low-temperature hot-water distribution. These systems combined with demand-controlled ventilation in the classrooms and the use of a CO_2 override for high occupancy situations help reduce energy transport loads and heating energy. Outdoor air is preconditioned with energy recovery ventilators and conventional air-handling units. By locating the DOAS air handlers near to the areas being serviced, the size of the handlers and the length of the ductwork were reduced.

Air conditioning is accomplished via a TDV diffuser from the AHU. Chilled water is provided to chilled-water coils by air-cooled water-chiller units with integral pumps and chilled-water buffer tanks. The closer tolerance control of the air discharge temperature afforded by this system was a consideration in the system choice.

Radiant floor heating was used in the classrooms in order to maximize space for cabinets and storage. Modeling and analysis suggested that radiant heating would work well with thermal displacement ventilation as long as the floor temperature remained below 80°F.

The original design concept, as determined by a manufacturer's design program, was to have two TDV diffusers per classroom. This was recommended in order to minimize the likelihood of

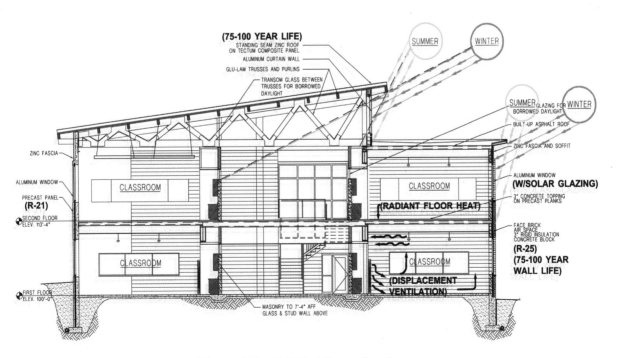

Figure 3-3 Building Cross Section
Source: LHB

Daylighted Classroom and Windows with Colored Glass Panels Overlooking Cafeteria
Source: John Gregor, Coldsnap Photography

TYPICAL CLASSROOM AIRFLOW SCHEMATIC.

**DEDICATED OUTDOOR AIR SYSTEM WITH
AIR TO AIR ENERGY RECOVERY UNITS
THERMAL DISPLACEMENT DIFFUSERS,
RADIANT FLOOR SKIN HEATING SYSTEM
OCCUPANCY/CO2 CONTROL AT THE ROOM LEVEL.**

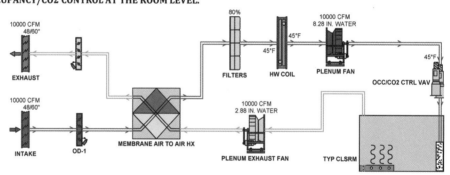

Figure 3-4   Classroom Ventilation System Schematic
Source: LHB

uncomfortable drafts in the spaces. However, by employing high-performance insulation and windows, and through adjustments in the layout, the final design included just one diffuser at the front of each classroom, thus allowing for the desired performance at a lower cost.

Additional systems employed include the following:

- Conventional return air central units for the media center and administrative areas
- Thermal displacement ventilation cooling system in the media lab
- Ceiling cassette mini-split units for computer instructions areas
- Hydronic heating system that provides hot water at 140°F and returns it to the boilers at 100°F

The HVAC equipment worked together to not only save energy but also provide thermal comfort that exceeds the industry standard of 80% satisfied. This is mainly due to the radiant

Table 3-7   Building Data for Two Harbors High School

Building Data	
Energy use intensity (site)	56 kBtu/ft^2
Construction budget	$25,000,000
Actual construction cost	$24,500,000
Cost per square foot	$127 (vs. the $161/ft^2 average in MN in 2005)

floor, efficient glazing system, and low-velocity air-distribution system. Not only did the HVAC system provide exceptional thermal comfort, it also cost less than a conventional AHU-based VAV system because of less ductwork, fewer diffusers, and smaller pipes.

Additional Sustainable Features

Energy efficiency measures in other/specialty spaces include the following:

- An engineered pool recovery unit provides ventilation in the championship pool area.
- An automated dust collector valve system reduces the needed size of the system by serving only equipment that is in operation.
- Point-of-use electric water heaters supply water to the classrooms and a semi-instantaneous system supplies water to restrooms, locker rooms, and the kitchen.

High performance features incorporated into the site design include the following:

- Walkways and bicycle paths connect to the town and recreational areas.
- Most stormwater from the site is retained in a number of small ponds.
- Native plantings and limited lawn spaces limit irrigation requirements.

Additional information on the Two Harbors High School and the lessons learned from the project can be found in the Spring 2009 issue of *High Performance Buildings* (Williams 2009).

REFERENCES AND RESOURCES

Knox, W., and S. Davis. 2010. Nature as the teacher. *High Performance Buildings* Fall:37–45.

Williams, D.T. 2009. Lake Superior's remedy. *High Performance Buildings* Spring:7–17.

DOE. 2011a. EERE Information Center. Energy Efficiency and Renewable Energy, U.S. Department of Energy, Washington, DC. www.eere.energy.gov/informationcenter.

DOE. 2011b. Rebuilding green in Greensburg, Kansas. Energy Efficiency and Renewable Energy, U.S. Department of Energy, Washington, DC. www.buildings.energy.gov/greensburg/.

Design Strategies and Recommendations by Climate Zone 4

INTRODUCTION

Users should determine the recommendations for their design and construction project by first locating the correct climate zone. The U.S. Department of Energy (DOE) has identified eight climate zones for the United States. Each is defined by county borders, as shown in Figure 4-1. This Guide uses these DOE climate zones in defining energy recommendations that vary by climate. The definitions for the climate zones are provided in Appendix B, so that the information can be applied outside the United States.

This chapter contains a unique set of energy-efficient recommendations for each climate zone. The recommendation tables represent *a* way, but not *the only* way, for reaching the 50% energy savings target over ASHRAE/IESNA Standard 90.1-2004. Other approaches may also save energy, and Chapter 3 provides energy target and benchmarking information to guide teams pursuing other options. Confirmation of energy savings for those uniquely designed systems is left to the design team. The user should note that the recommendation tables do not include all of the components listed in ASHRAE/IESNA Standard 90.1 since the Guide focuses only on the primary energy systems within a building.

When "Comply with Standard 90.1" is indicated, the user must meet the more stringent of either the applicable version of ASHRAE/IES Standard 90.1 or the local code requirements.

Each of the climate zone recommendation tables includes a set of common items arranged by building subsystem: envelope, daylighting/lighting, plug loads, service water heating (SWH), and HVAC. Recommendations are included for each item or subsystem by component within that subsystem. For some subsystems, recommendations depend on the construction type. For example, insulation values are given for mass and steel-framed and wood-framed wall types. For other subsystems, recommendations are given for each subsystem attribute. For example, vertical fenestration recommendations are given for thermal transmittance, solar heat gain coefficient (SHGC), and exterior sun control.

There are three possible HVAC system types included in the recommendation tables: ground-source heat pumps with a dedicated outdoor air system (DOAS), four-pipe fan coils with a DOAS, and central variable-air-volume (VAV) air-handling units combined with a DOAS (see HV1–3 in Chapter 5 for detailed descriptions). Unique recommendations are included for each HVAC system type, based on practicality of implementation and the 50% energy reduction goal.

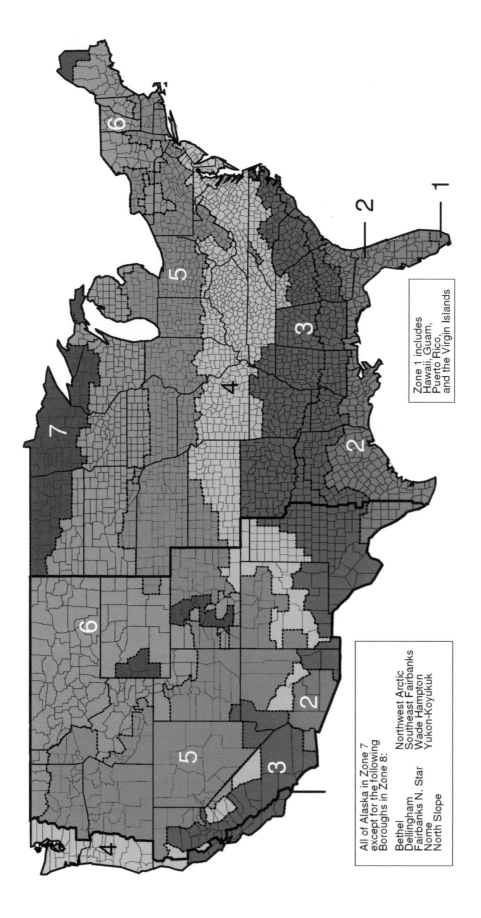

Figure 4-1 Climate Zone Map

The fourth column in each table lists references to how-to tips for implementing the recommended criteria. The tips are found in Chapter 5 under separate sections coded for envelope (EN), daylighting (DL), electric lighting (EL), plug loads (PL), service water heating systems and equipment (WH), HVAC systems and equipment (HV), and quality assurance (QA). In addition to how-to advice that represents good practice for design and maintenance suggestions, these tips include cautions for what to avoid. Important QA considerations and recommendations are also given for the building design, construction, and post-occupancy phases. Note that each tip is tied to the applicable climate zone in Chapter 4. The final column is provided as a simple checklist to identify the recommendations being used for a specific building design and construction.

CLIMATE ZONE RECOMMENDATIONS

The recommendations presented in the following tables are minimum, maximum, or specific values (which are both the minimum and maximum values).

Minimum values include the following:

- R-values
- Solar Reflectance Index (SRI)
- Whole window visible transmittance (VT)
- Projection factor (PF)
- Interior surface average reflectance
- Mean lumens per watt
- Gas water heater or boiler efficiency
- Thermal efficiency (E_t)
- Energy factor (EF)
- Energy efficiency ratio (EER)
- Integrated part-load value (IPLV)
- Coefficient of performance (COP)
- Energy recovery enthalpy (or dry bulb temperature) reduction
- Motor efficiency
- Duct or pipe insulation thickness

Maximum values include the following:

- Fenestration and door U-factors
- Fenestration solar heat gain coefficient (SHGC)
- Fenestration-to-floor ratio (FFR)
- Lighting power density (LPD)
- Fan input power per cfm of supply airflow (W/cfm)

BONUS SAVINGS

Chapter 5 provides additional recommendations and strategies for savings for toplighting, natural ventilation, and renewable energy that are over and above the 50% savings recommendations contained in the following eight climate regions.

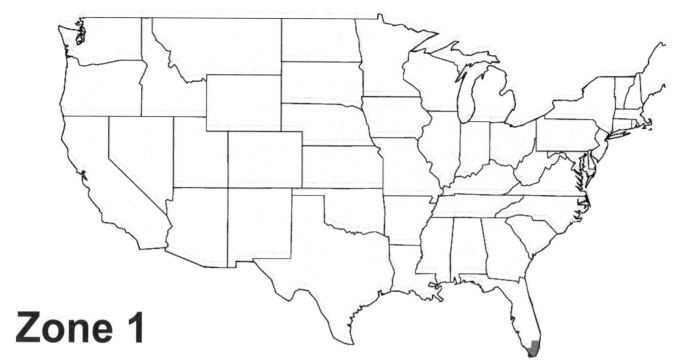

Zone 1

Florida
Broward
Miami-Dade
Monroe

Guam

Hawaii

Puerto Rico

U.S. Virgin Islands

Climate Zone 1 Recommendation Table for K-12 School Buildings

	Item	Component	Recommendation	How-To Tips	✓
Envelope	Roofs	Insulation entirely above deck	R-20.0 c.i.	EN1,2,17,19,21,22	
		Attic and other	R-38.0	EN1,3,17,19,20,21	
		Metal building	R-10.0 + R-19.0 FC	EN1,4,17,19,21,22	
		Solar Reflectance Index (SRI)	78	EN1	
	Walls	Mass (HC > 7 Btu/ft^2)	R-5.7 c.i.	EN5,17,19, 21	
		Steel framed	R-13.0 + R-7.5 c.i.	EN6,17,19, 21	
		Wood framed and other	R-13.0	EN7,17,19, 21	
		Metal building	R-0.0 + R-9.8 c.i.	EN8,17,19, 21	
		Below grade walls	Comply with Standard 90.1*	EN17,19, 21	
	Floors	Mass	R-4.2 c.i.	EN10,17,19, 21	
		Steel framed	R-19.0	EN11,17,19, 21	
		Wood framed and other	R-19.0	EN11,17,19, 21	
	Slabs	Unheated	Comply with Standard 90.1*	EN17,19, 21	
		Heated	R-7.5 c.i.	EN13,14,17,19, 21,22	
	Doors	Swinging	U-0.70	EN15,17	
		Nonswinging	U-1.45	EN16,17	
	Vestibules	At building entrance	Comply with Standard 90.1*	EN17	
	Vertical Fenestration	Thermal transmittance	Nonmetal framing = U-0.56 Metal framing = U-0.65	EN24	
		Fenestration-to-floor-area ratio (FFR)	E or W orientation = 5% maximum N or S orientation = 7% maximum	EN24–25	
		Solar heat gain coefficient (SHGC)	E or W orientation = 0.25 N orientation = 0.62 S orientation = 0.25	EN24,28–29	
		Exterior sun control	S orientation only = PF-0.5	EN26	
Daylighting/Lighting	Daylighting	Visible transmittance (VT)	See Table 5-5 for appropriate VT value	DL1,5–6,23	
		Interior/exterior sun control (S orientation only)	S orientation = no glare during school hours	DL1,9,12,13,31	
		Classroom, resource rooms, cafeteria, gym, and multipurpose rooms	Daylight 100% of floor area for 2/3 of school hours	DL1–5,7–21, 24–30,32–41	
		Administration areas	Daylight perimeter floor area (15 ft) for 2/3 of school hours	DL1–5,8–12	
	Interior Finishes	Interior surface average reflectance for daylighted rooms	Ceilings = 80% Wall surfaces = 70%	DL14	
	Interior Lighting	Lighting power density (LPD)	Whole building = 0.70 W/ft^2 Gyms, multipurpose rooms = 1.0 W/ft^2 Classrooms, art rooms, kitchens, libraries, media centers = 0.8 W/ft^2 Cafeterias, lobbies = 0.7 W/ft^2 Offices = 0.60 W/ft^2 Auditoriums, restrooms = 0.5 W/ft^2 Corridors, mechanical rooms = 0.4 W/ft^2	EL12–19	
		Light source lamp efficacy (mean lumens per watt)	T8 & T5 > 2 ft = 92, T8 & T5 ≤ 2 ft = 85, All other > 50	EL4–6	
		T8 ballasts	Non-dimming = NEMA Premium Instant Start Dimming= NEMA Premium Program Start	EL4–6	
		T5/T5HO ballasts	Electronic program start		
		CFL and HID ballasts	Electronic		
		Dimming controls daylight harvesting	Dim all fixtures in daylight zones	EL8,9,11–19	
		Lighting controls	Manual ON, auto/timed OFF in all areas as possible	EL8,9,11–20	
	Exterior Lighting	Façade and landscape lighting	LPD = 0.075 W/ft^2 in LZ-3 & LZ-4 LPD = 0.05 W/ft^2 in LZ-2 Controls = auto OFF between 12am and 6am	EL23	
		Parking lots and drives	LPD = 0.1 W/ft^2 in LZ-3 & LZ-4 LPD = 0.06 W/ft^2 in LZ-2 Controls = auto reduce to 25% (12am to 6am)	EL21	
		Walkways, plaza, and special feature areas	LPD = 0.16 W/ft^2 in LZ-3 & LZ-4 LPD = 0.14 W/ft^2 in LZ-2 Controls = auto reduce to 25% (12am to 6am)	EL22	
		All other exterior lighting	LPD = Comply with Standard 90.1* Controls = auto reduce to 25% (12am to 6am)	EL25	
Plug Loads	Equipment Choices	Laptop computers	Minimum 2/3 of total computers	PL2,3	
		ENERGY STAR equipment	All computers, equipment, and appliances	PL3,5	
		Vending machines	De-lamp and specify best in class efficiency	PL3,5	
	Controls/ Programs	Computer power control	Network control with power saving modes and control OFF during unoccupied hours	PL2,3	
		Power outlet control	Controllable power outlets with auto OFF during unoccupied hours for classrooms, office, library/media spaces All plug-in equipment not requiring continuous operation to use controllable outlets		
		Policies	Implement at least one: • District/school policy on allowed equipment • School energy teams	PL3,4	

*Note: Where the table says "Comply with Standard 90.1," the user must meet the more stringent of either the applicable version of ASHRAE/IES Standard 90.1 or the local code requirements.

Climate Zone 1 Recommendation Table for K-12 School Buildings *(Continued)*

	Item	Component	Recommendation	How-To Tips	✓
Kitchen	Kitchen Equipment	Cooking equipment	ENERGY STAR or California rebate-qualified equipment	KE1,2	
		Walk-in refrigeration equipment	6 in. insulation on low-temp walk-in equipment, Insulated floor, LED lighting, floating-head pressure controls, liquid pressure amplifier, subcooled liquid refrigerant, evaporative condenser	KE2,5	
		Exhaust hoods	Side panels, larger overhangs, rear seal at appliances, proximity hoods, VAV demand-based exhaust	KE3,6	
SWH	Service Water Heating	Gas water heater (condensing)	95% efficiency	WH1–5	
		Electric storage EF (≤12 kW, ≥20 gal)	EF>0.99 – 0.0012 × Volume	WH1–5	
		Point-of-use heater selection	0.81 EF or 81% E_t	WH1–5	
		Electric heat-pump water heater efficiency	COP 3.0 (interior heat source)	WH1–5	
		Solar hot-water heating	30% solar hot-water fraction when LCC effective	WH7	
		Pipe insulation (d < 1.5 in./d ≥ 1.5 in.)	1/1.5 in.	WH6	
HVAC	Ground Source Heat-Pump (GSHP) System with DOAS	GSHP cooling efficiency	17.1 EER	HV1,11	
		GSHP heating efficiency	3.6 COP	HV1,11	
		GSHP compressor capacity control	Two stage or variable speed	HV1,11	
		Water-circulation pumps	VFD and NEMA Premium Efficiency	HV8	
		Cooling tower/fluid cooler	VFD on fans	HV1,8,11	
		Boiler efficiency	90% E_c	HV1,7,11	
		Maximum fan power	0.4 W/cfm	HV12	
		Exhaust air energy recovery in DOAS	A (humid) zones = 60% enthalpy reduction B (dry) zones = 60% dry-bulb temperature reduction	HV4,5	
		DOAS ventilation control	DCV with VFD	HV4,10,15	
	Fan-Coil System with DOAS	Water-cooled chiller efficiency	Comply with Standard 90.1*	HV2,6,11	
		Water circulation pumps	VFD and NEMA Premium Efficiency	HV6,7	
		Boiler efficiency	90% E_c	HV2,7,11	
		Maximum fan power	0.4 W/cfm	HV12	
		FCU fans	Multiple speed	HV2,12	
		Economizer	Comply with Standard 90.1*	HV2,14	
		Exhaust air energy recovery in DOAS	A (humid) zones = 60% enthalpy reduction B (dry) zones = 60% dry-bulb temperature reduction	HV4,5	
		DOAS ventilation control	DCV with VFD	HV4,10,15	
	VAV Air-Handling System with DOAS	Air-cooled chiller efficiency	10 EER; 12.75 IPLV	HV3,6,11	
		Water-cooled chiller efficiency	Comply with Standard 90.1*	HV3,6,11	
		Water circulation pumps	VFD and NEMA Premium Efficiency	HV6,7	
		Boiler efficiency	90% E_c	HV3,7,11	
		Maximum fan power	0.8 W/cfm	HV12	
		Economizer	Comply with Standard 90.1*	HV3,14	
		Exhaust air energy recovery in DOAS	A (humid) zones = 60% enthalpy reduction B (dry) zones = 60% dry-bulb temperature reduction	HV4,5	
		DOAS ventilation control	DCV with VFD	HV4,10,15	
	Ducts and Dampers	Outdoor air damper	Motorized damper	HV10	
		Duct seal class	Seal Class A	HV20	
		Insulation level	R-6	HV19	
M&V	M&V/ Benchmarking	Electrical submetering	Separately meter lighting, HVAC, general 120V, renewables, and whole building	QA14–17	
		Benchmarking	Begin submetering early to address issues during warranty period Benchmark monthly energy use Provide training on benchmarking	QA14–17	

*Note: Where the table says "Comply with Standard 90.1," the user must meet the more stringent of either the applicable version of ASHRAE/IES Standard 90.1 or the local code requirements.

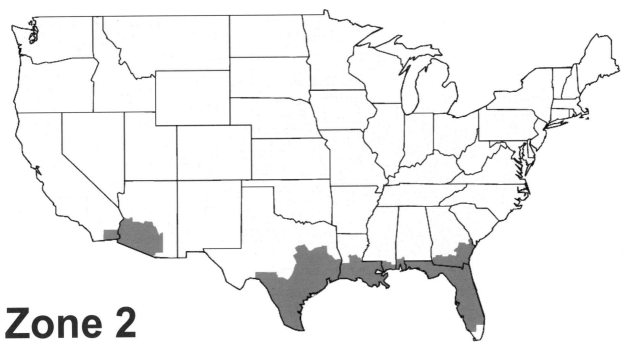

Zone 2

Alabama

Baldwin
Mobile

Arizona

La Paz
Maricopa
Pima
Pinal
Yuma

California

Imperial

Florida

Alachua
Baker
Bay
Bradford
Brevard
Calhoun
Charlotte
Citrus
Clay
Collier
Columbia
DeSoto
Dixie
Duval
Escambia
Flagler
Franklin
Gadsden
Gilchrist
Glades
Gulf

Hamilton
Hardee
Hendry
Hernando
Highlands
Hillsborough
Holmes
Indian River
Jackson
Jefferson
Lafayette
Lake
Lee
Leon
Levy
Liberty
Madison
Manatee
Marion
Martin
Nassau
Okaloosa
Okeechobee
Orange
Osceola
Palm Beach
Pasco
Pinellas
Polk
Putnam
Santa Rosa
Sarasota
Seminole
St. Johns
St. Lucie
Sumter
Suwannee
Taylor

Union
Volusia
Wakulla
Walton
Washington

Georgia

Appling
Atkinson
Bacon
Baker
Berrien
Brantley
Brooks
Bryan
Camden
Charlton
Chatham
Clinch
Colquitt
Cook
Decatur
Echols
Effingham
Evans
Glynn
Grady
Jeff Davis
Lanier
Liberty
Long
Lowndes
McIntosh
Miller
Mitchell
Pierce
Seminole
Tattnall

Thomas
Toombs
Ware
Wayne

Louisiana

Acadia
Allen
Ascension
Assumption
Avoyelles
Beauregard
Calcasieu
Cameron
East Baton
  Rouge
East Feliciana
Evangeline
Iberia
Iberville
Jefferson
Jefferson Davis
Lafayette
Lafourche
Livingston
Orleans
Plaquemines
Pointe Coupee
Rapides
St. Bernard
St. Charles
St. Helena
St. James
St. John the
  Baptist
St. Landry
St. Martin
St. Mary

St. Tammany
Tangipahoa
Terrebonne
Vermilion
Washington
West Baton
  Rouge
West Feliciana

Mississippi

Hancock
Harrison
Jackson
Pearl River
Stone

Texas

Anderson
Angelina
Aransas
Atascosa
Austin
Bandera
Bastrop
Bee
Bell
Bexar
Bosque
Brazoria
Brazos
Brooks
Burleson
Caldwell
Calhoun
Cameron
Chambers
Cherokee

Colorado
Comal
Coryell
DeWitt
Dimmit
Duval
Edwards
Falls
Fayette
Fort Bend
Freestone
Frio
Galveston
Goliad
Gonzales
Grimes
Guadalupe
Hardin
Harris
Hays
Hidalgo
Hill
Houston
Jackson
Jasper
Jefferson
Jim Hogg
Jim Wells
Karnes
Kenedy
Kinney
Kleberg
La Salle
Lavaca
Lee
Leon
Liberty
Limestone

Live Oak
Madison
Matagorda
Maverick
McLennan
McMullen
Medina
Milam
Montgomery
Newton
Nueces
Orange
Polk
Real
Refugio
Robertson
San Jacinto
San Patricio
Starr
Travis
Trinity
Tyler
Uvalde
Val Verde
Victoria
Walker
Waller
Washington
Webb
Wharton
Willacy
Williamson
Wilson
Zapata
Zavala

Climate Zone 2 Recommendation Table for K-12 School Buildings

	Item	Component	Recommendation	How-To Tips	✓
Envelope	Roofs	Insulation entirely above deck	R-25.0 c.i.	EN1,2,17,19,21,22	
		Attic and other	R-38.0	EN1,3,17,19,20,21	
		Metal building	R-10.0 + R-19.0 FC	EN1,4,17,19,21,22	
		Solar Reflectance Index (SRI)	78	EN1	
	Walls	Mass (HC > 7 Btu/ft^2)	R-7.6 c.i.	EN5,17,19, 21	
		Steel framed	R-13.0 + R-7.5 c.i.	EN6,17,19, 21	
		Wood framed and other	R-13.0 + R-3.8 c.i.	EN7,17,19, 21	
		Metal building	R-0.0 + R-9.8 c.i.	EN8,17,19, 21	
		Below grade walls	Comply with Standard 90.1*	EN17,19, 21	
	Floors	Mass	R-10.4 c.i.	EN10,17,19, 21	
		Steel framed	R-19.0	EN11,17,19, 21	
		Wood framed and other	R-19.0	EN11,17,19, 21	
	Slabs	Unheated	Comply with Standard 90.1*	EN17,19, 21	
		Heated	R-10 for 24 in.	EN13,14,17,19,21, 22	
	Doors	Swinging	U-0.70	EN15,17	
		Nonswinging	U-0.50	EN16,17	
	Vestibules	At building entrance	Comply with Standard 90.1*	EN17	
	View Fenestration	Thermal transmittance	Nonmetal framing = U-0.45 Metal framing = U-0.64	EN24	
		Fenestration-to-floor-area ratio (FFR)	E or W orientation = 5% maximum N or S orientation = 7% maximum	EN24–25	
		Solar heat gain coefficient (SHGC)	E or W orientation = 0.25 N orientation = 0.62 S orientation = 0.50	EN24,28–29	
		Exterior sun control	S orientation only = PF-0.5	EN26	
	Daylight Fenestration	Visible transmittance (VT)	See Table 5-5 for appropriate VT value	DL1,5–6,23	
		Interior/exterior sun control (S orientation only)	S orientation = no glare during school hours	DL1,9,12,13,31	
Daylighting/Lighting	Daylighting	Classroom, resource rooms, cafeteria, gym, and multipurpose rooms	Daylight 100% of floor area for 2/3 of school hours	DL1–5,7–21, 24–30,32–41	
		Administration areas	Daylight perimeter floor area (15 ft) for 2/3 of school hours	DL1–5,8–12	
	Interior Finishes	Interior surface average reflectance for daylighted rooms	Ceilings = 80% Wall surfaces = 70%	DL14	
	Interior Lighting	Lighting power density (LPD)	Whole building = 0.70 W/ft^2 Gyms, multipurpose rooms = 1.0 W/ft^2 Classrooms, art rooms, kitchens, libraries, media centers= 0.8 W/ft^2 Cafeterias, lobbies = 0.7 W/ft^2 Offices = 0.60 W/ft^2 Auditoriums, restrooms = 0.5 W/ft^2 Corridors, mechanical rooms = 0.4 W/ft^2	EL12–19	
		Light source lamp efficacy mean lumens per watt)	T8 & T5 > 2 ft = 92, T8 & T5 ≤ 2 ft = 85, All other > 50	EL4–6	
		T8 ballasts	Non-dimming = NEMA Premium Instant Start Dimming= NEMA Premium Program Start	EL4–6	
		T5/T5HO ballasts	Electronic program start		
		CFL and HID ballasts	Electronic		
		Dimming controls daylight harvesting	Dim all fixtures in daylight zones	EL8,9,11–19	
		Lighting controls	Manual ON, auto/timed OFF in all areas as possible	EL8,9,11–20	
	Exterior Lighting	Façade and landscape lighting	LPD = 0.075 W/ft^2 in LZ-3 & LZ-4 LPD = 0.05 W/ft^2 in LZ-2 Controls = auto OFF between 12am and 6am	EL23	
		Parking lots and drives	LPD = 0.1 W/ft^2 in LZ-3 & LZ-4 LPD = 0.06 W/ft^2 in LZ-2 Controls = auto reduce to 25% (12am to 6am)	EL21	
		Walkways, plaza, and special feature areas	LPD = 0.16 W/ft^2 in LZ-3 & LZ-4 LPD = 0.14 W/ft^2 in LZ-2 Controls = auto reduce to 25% (12am to 6am)	EL22	
		All other exterior lighting	LPD = Comply with Standard 90.1* Controls = auto reduce to 25% (12am to 6am)	EL25	
Plug Loads	Equipment Choices	Laptop computers	Minimum 2/3 of total computers	PL2,3	
		ENERGY STAR equipment	All computers, equipment, and appliances	PL3,5	
		Vending machines	De-lamp and specify best in class efficiency	PL3,5	
	Controls/ Programs	Computer power control	Network control with power saving modes and control off during unoccupied hours	PL2,3	
		Power outlet control	Controllable power outlets with auto OFF during unoccupied hours for classrooms, office, library/ media spaces All plug-in equipment not requiring continuous operation to use controllable outlets	PL3,4	
		Policies	Implement at least one: • District/school policy on allowed equipment • School energy teams	PL3,4	

*Note: Where the table says "Comply with Standard 90.1," the user must meet the more stringent of either the applicable version of ASHRAE/IES Standard 90.1 or the local code requirements.

Climate Zone 2 Recommendation Table for K-12 School Buildings *(Continued)*

	Item	Component	Recommendation	How-To Tips	✓
Kitchen	Kitchen Equipment	Cooking equipment	ENERGY STAR or California rebate-qualified equipment	KE1,2	
		Walk-in refrigeration equipment	6 in. insulation on low-temp walk-in equipment, Insulated floor, LED lighting, floating-head pressure controls, liquid pressure amplifier, subcooled liquid refrigerant, evaporative condenser	KE2,5	
		Exhaust hoods	Side panels, larger overhangs, rear seal at appliances, proximity hoods, VAV demand-based exhaust	KE3,6	
SWH	Service Water Heating	Gas water heater (condensing)	95% efficiency	WH1–5	
		Electric storage EF (≤12 kW, ≥20 gal)	$EF > 0.99 - 0.0012 \times$ Volume	WH1–5	
		Point-of-use heater selection	0.81 EF or 81% E_t	WH1–5	
		Electric heat-pump water heater efficiency	COP 3.0 (interior heat source)	WH1–5	
		Solar hot-water heating	30% solar hot-water fraction when LCC effective	WH7	
		Pipe insulation ($d < 1.5$ in./$d ≥ 1.5$ in.)	1/1.5 in.	WH6	
HVAC	Ground Source Heat-Pump (GSHP) System with DOAS	GSHP cooling efficiency	17.1 EER	HV1,11	
		GSHP heating efficiency	3.6 COP	HV1,11	
		GSHP compressor capacity control	Two stage or variable speed	HV1,11	
		Water-circulation pumps	VFD and NEMA Premium Efficiency	HV8	
		Cooling tower/fluid cooler	VFD on fans	HV1,8,11	
		Boiler efficiency	90% E_c	HV1,7,11	
		Maximum fan power	0.4 W/cfm	HV12	
		Exhaust air energy recovery in DOAS	A (humid) zones = 60% enthalpy reduction B (dry) zones = 60% dry-bulb temperature reduction	HV4,5	
		DOAS ventilation control	DCV with VFD	HV4,10,15	
	Fan-Coil System with DOAS	Water-cooled chiller efficiency	Comply with Standard 90.1*	HV2,6,11	
		Water circulation pumps	VFD and NEMA Premium Efficiency	HV6,7	
		Boiler efficiency	90% E_c	HV2,7,11	
		Maximum fan power	0.4 W/cfm	HV12	
		FCU fans	Multiple speed	HV2,12	
		Economizer	Comply with Standard 90.1*	HV2,14	
		Exhaust air energy recovery in DOAS	A (humid) zones = 60% enthalpy reduction B (dry) zones = 60% dry-bulb temperature reduction	HV4, 5	
		DOAS ventilation control	DCV with VFD	HV4,10,15	
	VAV Air-Handling System with DOAS	Air-cooled chiller efficiency	10 EER; 12.75 IPLV	HV3,6,11	
		Water-cooled chiller efficiency	Comply with Standard 90.1*	HV3,6,11	
		Water circulation pumps	VFD and NEMA Premium Efficiency	HV6,7	
		Boiler efficiency	90% E_c	HV3,7,11	
		Maximum fan power	0.8 W/cfm	HV12	
		Economizer	Comply with Standard 90.1*	HV3,14	
		Exhaust air energy recovery in DOAS	A (humid) zones = 60% enthalpy reduction B (dry) zones = 60% dry-bulb temperature reduction	HV4,5	
		DOAS ventilation control	DCV with VFD	HV4,10,15	
	Ducts and Dampers	Outdoor air damper	Motorized damper	HV10	
		Duct seal class	Seal Class A	HV20	
		Insulation level	R-6	HV19	
M&V	M&V/ Benchmarking	Electrical submeters	Disaggregate submeters for lighting, HVAC, general 120V, renewables, and whole building	QA14–17	
		Benchmarking	Begin submetering early to address issues during warranty period Benchmark monthly energy use Provide training on benchmarking	QA14–17	

*Note: Where the table says "Comply with Standard 90.1," the user must meet the more stringent of either the applicable version of ASHRAE/IES Standard 90.1 or the local code requirements.

Zone 3

Alabama

All counties except:
Baldwin
Mobile

Arizona

Cochise
Graham
Greenlee
Mohave
Santa Cruz

Arkansas

All counties except:
Baxter
Benton
Boone
Carroll
Fulton
Izard
Madison
Marion
Newton
Searcy
Stone
Washington

California

All counties except:
Alpine
Amador
Calaveras
Del Norte
El Dorado
Humboldt
Imperial
Inyo
Lake
Lassen
Mariposa
Modoc
Mono
Nevada
Plumas
Sierra
Siskiyou
Trinity
Tuolumne

Georgia

All counties except:
Appling
Atkinson
Bacon
Baker
Banks
Berrien
Brantley
Brooks
Bryan
Catoosa
Camden
Charlton
Chatham
Chattooga
Clinch
Colquitt
Cook
Dade
Dawson
Decatur
Echols
Effingham
Evans
Fannin
Floyd
Franklin
Gilmer
Glynn
Gordon
Grady
Habersham
Hall
Jeff Davis
Lanier
Liberty
Long
Lowndes
Lumpkin
McIntosh
Miller
Mitchell
Murray
Pickens
Pierce
Rabun
Seminole
Stephens
Tattnall
Thomas
Toombs
Towns
Union

Walker
Ware
Wayne
White
Whitfield

Louisiana

Bienville
Bossier
Caddo
Caldwell
Catahoula
Claiborne
Concordia
De Soto
East Carroll
Franklin
Grant
Jackson
La Salle
Lincoln
Madison
Morehouse
Natchitoches
Ouachita
Red River
Richland
Sabine
Tensas
Union
Vernon
Webster
West Carroll
Winn

Mississippi

All counties except:
Hancock
Harrison
Jackson
Pearl River
Stone

New Mexico

Chaves
Dona Ana
Eddy
Hidalgo
Lea
Luna
Otero

Nevada

Clark

Texas

Andrews
Archer
Baylor
Blanco
Borden
Bowie
Brewster
Brown
Burnet
Callahan
Camp
Cass
Childress
Clay
Coke
Coleman
Collingsworth
Collin
Comanche
Concho
Cottle
Cooke
Crane
Crockett
Crosby
Culberson
Dallas
Dawson
Delta
Denton
Dickens
Eastland
Ector
El Paso
Ellis
Erath
Fannin
Fisher
Foard
Franklin
Gaines
Garza
Gillespie
Glasscock
Grayson
Gregg
Hall
Hamilton
Hardeman

Harrison
Haskell
Hemphill
Henderson
Hood
Hopkins
Howard
Hudspeth
Hunt
Irion
Jack
Jeff Davis
Johnson
Jones
Kaufman
Kendall
Kent
Kerr
Kimble
King
Knox
Lamar
Lampasas
Llano
Loving
Lubbock
Lynn
Marion
Martin
Mason
McCulloch
Menard
Midland
Mills
Mitchell
Montague
Morris
Motley
Nacogdoches
Navarro
Nolan
Palo Pinto
Panola
Parker
Pecos
Presidio
Rains
Reagan
Reeves
Red River
Rockwall
Runnels
Rusk
Sabine
San Augustine

San Saba
Schleicher
Scurry
Shackelford
Shelby
Smith
Somervell
Stephens
Sterling
Stonewall
Sutton
Tarrant
Taylor
Terrell
Terry
Throckmorton
Titus
Tom Green
Upshur
Upton
Van Zandt
Ward
Wheeler
Wichita
Wilbarger
Winkler
Wise
Wood
Young

Utah

Washington

North Carolina

Anson
Beaufort
Bladen
Brunswick
Cabarrus
Camden
Carteret
Chowan
Columbus
Craven
Cumberland
Currituck
Dare
Davidson
Duplin
Edgecombe
Gaston
Greene
Hoke
Hyde

Johnston
Jones
Lenoir
Martin
Mecklenburg
Montgomery
Moore
New Hanover
Onslow
Pamlico
Pasquotank
Pender
Perquimans
Pitt
Randolph
Richmond
Robeson
Rowan
Sampson
Scotland
Stanly
Tyrrell
Union
Washington
Wayne
Wilson

Oklahoma

All counties except:
Beaver
Cimarron
Texas

South Carolina

All counties

Tennessee

Chester
Crockett
Dyer
Fayette
Hardeman
Hardin
Haywood
Henderson
Lake
Lauderdale
Madison
McNairy
Shelby
Tipton

Climate Zone 3 Recommendation Table for K-12 School Buildings

	Item	Component	Recommendation	How-To Tips	✓
Envelope	Roofs	Insulation entirely above deck	R-25.0 c.i.	EN1,2,17,19,21,22	
		Attic and other	R-38.0	EN1,3,17,19,20,21	
		Metal building	R-10.0 + R-19.0 FC	EN1,4,17,19,21,22	
		Solar Reflectance Index (SRI)	78	EN1	
	Walls	Mass (HC > 7 Btu/ft^2)	R-11.4 c.i.	EN5,17,19, 21	
		Steel framed	R-13.0 + R-7.5 c.i.	EN6,17,19, 21	
		Wood framed and other	R-13.0 + R-3.8 c.i.	EN7,17,19, 21	
		Metal building	R-0.0 + R-13.0 c.i.	EN8,17,19, 21	
		Below grade walls	R-7.5 c.i. (Comply with Std 90.1* in CZ 3A)	EN9,17,19, 21,22	
	Floors	Mass	R-12.5 c.i.	EN10,17,19, 21	
		Steel framed	R-30.0	EN11,17,19, 21	
		Wood framed and other	R-30.0	EN11,17,19, 21	
	Slabs	Unheated	Comply with Standard 90.1*	EN17,19, 21	
		Heated	R-15 for 24 in.	EN13,14,17,19, 21,22	
	Doors	Swinging	U-0.70	EN15,17	
		Nonswinging	U-0.50	EN16,17	
	Vestibules	At building entrance	Yes for buildings > 10,000 SF only	EN17,18	
	View Fenestration	Thermal transmittance	Nonmetal framing = U-0.41 Metal framing = U-0.60	EN24	
		Fenestration-to-floor-area ratio (FFR)	E or W orientation = 5% maximum N or S orientation = 7% maximum	EN24–25	
		Solar heat gain coefficient (SHGC)	E or W orientation = 0.25 N orientation = 0.62 S orientation = 0.75	EN24,28–29	
		Exterior sun control	S orientation only = PF-0.5	EN26	
	Daylight Fenestration	Visible transmittance (VT)	See Table 5-5 for appropriate VT value	DL1,5–6,23	
		Interior/exterior sun control (S orientation only)	S orientation = no glare during school hours	DL1,9,12,13,31	
Daylighting/Lighting	Daylighting	Classroom, resource rooms, cafeteria, gym and multipurpose rooms	Daylight 100% of floor area for 2/3 of school hours	DL1–5,7–21, 24–30,32–41	
		Administration areas	Daylight perimeter floor area (15 ft) for 2/3 of school hours	DL1–5,8–12	
	Interior Finishes	Interior surface average reflectance for daylighted rooms	Ceilings = 80% Wall surfaces = 70%	DL14	
	Interior Lighting	Lighting power density (LPD)	Whole building = 0.70 W/ft^2 Gyms, multipurpose rooms = 1.0 W/ft^2 Classrooms, art rooms, kitchens, libraries, media centers= 0.8 W/ft^2 Cafeterias, lobbies = 0.7 W/ft^2 Offices = 0.60 W/ft^2 Auditoriums, restrooms = 0.5 W/ft^2 Corridors, mechanical rooms = 0.4 W/ft^2	EL12–19	
		Light source lamp efficacy (mean lumens per watt)	T8 & T5 > 2 ft = 92, T8 & T5 ≤ 2 ft = 85, All other > 50	EL4–6	
		T8 ballasts	Non-dimming = NEMA Premium Instant Start Dimming= NEMA Premium Program Start	EL4–6	
		T5/T5HO ballasts	Electronic program start		
		CFL and HID ballasts	Electronic		
		Dimming controls daylight harvesting	Dim all fixtures in daylight zones	EL8,9,11–19	
		Lighting controls	Manual ON, auto/timed OFF in all areas as possible	EL8,9,11–20	
	Exterior Lighting	Façade and landscape lighting	LPD = 0.075 W/ft^2 in LZ-3 & LZ-4 LPD = 0.05 W/ft^2 in LZ-2 Controls = auto OFF between 12am and 6am	EL23	
		Parking lots and drives	LPD = 0.1 W/ft^2 in LZ-3 & LZ-4 LPD = 0.06 W/ft^2 in LZ-2 Controls = auto reduce to 25% (12am to 6am)	EL21	
		Walkways, plaza, and special feature areas	LPD = 0.16 W/ft^2 in LZ-3 & LZ-4 LPD = 0.14 W/ft^2 in LZ-2 Controls = auto reduce to 25% (12am to 6am)	EL22	
		All other exterior lighting	LPD = Comply with Standard 90.1* Controls = auto reduce to 25% (12am to 6am)	EL25	
Plug Loads	Equipment Choices	Laptop computers	Minimum 2/3 of total computers	PL2,3	
		ENERGY STAR equipment	All computers, equipment, and appliances	PL3,5	
		Vending machines	De-lamp and specify best in class efficiency	PL3,5	
	Controls/ Programs	Computer power control	Network control with power saving modes and control off during unoccupied hours	PL2,3	
		Power outlet control	Controllable power outlets with auto OFF during unoccupied hours for classrooms, office, library/media spaces All plug-in equipment not requiring continuous operation to use controllable outlets	PL3,4	
		Policies	Implement at least one: • District/school policy on allowed equipment • School energy teams	PL3,4	

*Note: Where the table says "Comply with Standard 90.1," the user must meet the more stringent of either the applicable version of ASHRAE/IES Standard 90.1 or the local code requirements.

Climate Zone 3 Recommendation Table for K-12 School Buildings *(Continued)*

	Item	Component	Recommendation	How-To Tips	✓
Kitchen	Kitchen Equipment	Cooking equipment	ENERGY STAR or California rebate-qualified equipment	KE1,2	
		Walk-in refrigeration equipment	6 in. insulation on low-temp walk-in equipment, Insulated floor, LED lighting, floating-head pressure controls, liquid pressure amplifier, subcooled liquid refrigerant, evaporative condenser	KE2,5	
		Exhaust hoods	Side panels, larger overhangs, rear seal at appliances, proximity hoods, VAV demand-based exhaust	KE3,6	
SWH	Service Water Heating	Gas water heater (condensing)	95% efficiency	WH1–5	
		Electric storage EF (≤12 kW, ≥20 gal)	EF > 0.99 − 0.0012 × Volume	WH1–5	
		Point-of-use heater selection	0.81 EF or 81% E_t	WH1–5	
		Electric heat-pump water heater efficiency	COP 3.0 (interior heat source)	WH1–5	
		Solar hot-water heating	30% solar hot-water fraction when LCC effective	WH7	
		Pipe insulation (d < 1.5 in./d ≥ 1.5 in.)	1/1.5 in.	WH6	
HVAC	Ground Source Heat-Pump (GSHP) System with DOAS	GSHP cooling efficiency	17.1 EER	HV1,11	
		GSHP heating efficiency	3.6 COP	HV1,11	
		GSHP compressor capacity control	Two stage or variable speed	HV1,11	
		Water-circulation pumps	VFD and NEMA Premium Efficiency	HV8	
		Cooling tower/fluid cooler	VFD on fans	HV1,8,11	
		Boiler efficiency	90% E_c	HV1,7,11	
		Maximum fan power	0.4 W/cfm	HV12	
		Exhaust air energy recovery in DOAS	A (humid) zones = 60% enthalpy reduction B (dry) zones = 60% dry-bulb temp reduction C (marine) zones = 60% enthalpy reduction	HV4,5	
		DOAS ventilation control	DCV with VFD	HV4,10,15	
	Fan-Coil System with DOAS	Water-cooled chiller efficiency	Comply with Standard 90.1*	HV2,6,11	
		Water circulation pumps	VFD and NEMA Premium Efficiency	HV6,7	
		Boiler efficiency	90% E_c	HV2,7,11	
		Maximum fan power	0.4 W/cfm	HV12	
		FCU fans	Multiple speed	HV2,12	
		Economizer	Comply with Standard 90.1*	HV2,14	
		Exhaust air energy recovery in DOAS	A (humid) zones = 60% enthalpy reduction B (dry) zones = 60% dry-bulb temp reduction C (marine) zones = 60% enthalpy reduction	HV4,5	
		DOAS ventilation control	DCV with VFD	HV4,10,15	
	VAV Air-Handling System with DOAS	Air-cooled chiller efficiency	10 EER; 12.75 IPLV	HV3,6,11	
		Water-cooled chiller efficiency	Comply with Standard 90.1*	HV3,6,11	
		Water circulation pumps	VFD and NEMA Premium Efficiency	HV6,7	
		Boiler efficiency	90% E_c	HV3,7,11	
		Maximum fan power	0.8 W/cfm	HV12	
		Economizer	Comply with Standard 90.1*	HV3,14	
		Exhaust air energy recovery in DOAS	A (humid) zones = 60% enthalpy reduction B (dry) zones = 60% dry-bulb temp reduction C (marine) zones = 60% enthalpy reduction	HV4,5	
		DOAS ventilation control	DCV with VFD	HV4,10,15	
	Ducts and Dampers	Outdoor air damper	Motorized damper	HV10	
		Duct seal class	Seal Class A	HV20	
		Insulation level	R-6	HV19	
M&V	M&V/ Benchmarking	Electrical submeters	Disaggregate submeters for lighting, HVAC, general 120V, renewables, and whole building	QA14–17	
		Benchmarking	Begin submetering early to address issues during warranty period Benchmark monthly energy use Provide training on benchmarking	QA14–17	

*Note: Where the table says "Comply with Standard 90.1," the user must meet the more stringent of either the applicable version of ASHRAE/IES Standard 90.1 or the local code requirements.

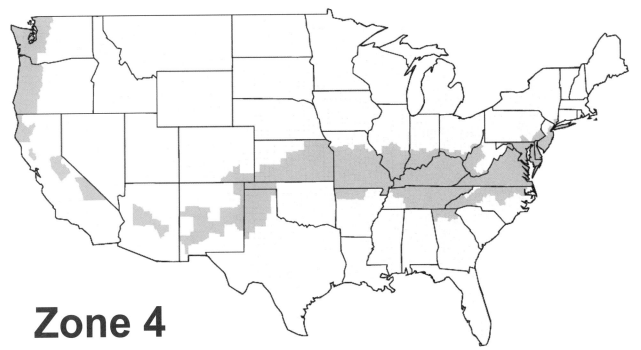

Zone 4

Arizona
Gila
Yavapai

Arkansas
Baxter
Benton
Boone
Carroll
Fulton
Izard
Madison
Marion
Newton
Searcy
Stone
Washington

California
Amador
Calaveras
Del Norte
El Dorado
Humboldt
Inyo
Lake
Mariposa
Trinity
Tuolumne

Colorado
Baca
Las Animas
Otero

Delaware
All counties

**District of
Columbia**

Georgia
Banks
Catoosa
Chattooga
Dade
Dawson
Fannin
Floyd
Franklin
Gilmer
Gordon
Habersham
Hall
Lumpkin
Murray
Pickens
Rabun
Stephens
Towns
Union

Walker
White
Whitfield

Illinois
Alexander
Bond
Brown
Christian
Clay
Clinton
Crawford
Edwards
Effingham
Fayette
Franklin
Gallatin
Hamilton
Hardin
Jackson
Jasper
Jefferson
Johnson
Lawrence
Macoupin
Madison
Marion
Massac
Monroe
Montgomery
Perry
Pope
Pulaski
Randolph
Richland
Saline
Shelby
St. Clair
Union
Wabash
Washington
Wayne
White
Williamson

Indiana
Clark
Crawford
Daviess
Dearborn
Dubois
Floyd
Gibson
Greene
Harrison
Jackson
Jefferson
Jennings
Knox
Lawrence
Martin
Monroe
Ohio

Orange
Perry
Pike
Posey
Ripley
Scott
Spencer
Sullivan
Switzerland
Vanderburgh
Warrick
Washington

Kansas
All counties except:
Cheyenne
Cloud
Decatur
Ellis
Gove
Graham
Greeley
Hamilton
Jewell
Lane
Logan
Mitchell
Ness
Norton
Osborne
Phillips
Rawlins
Republic
Rooks
Scott
Sheridan
Sherman
Smith
Thomas
Trego
Wallace
Wichita

Kentucky
All counties

Maryland
All counties except:
Garrett

Missouri
All counties except:
Adair
Andrew
Atchison
Buchanan
Caldwell
Chariton
Clark
Clinton
Daviess
DeKalb
Gentry

Grundy
Harrison
Holt
Knox
Lewis
Linn
Livingston
Macon
Marion
Mercer
Nodaway
Pike
Putnam
Ralls
Schuyler
Scotland
Shelby
Sullivan
Worth

New Jersey
All counties except:
Bergen
Hunterdon
Mercer
Morris
Passaic
Somerset
Sussex
Warren

New Mexico
Bernalillo
Cibola
Curry
DeBaca
Grant
Guadalupe
Lincoln
Quay
Roosevelt
Sierra
Socorro
Union
Valencia

New York
Bronx
Kings
Nassau
New York
Queens
Richmond
Suffolk
Westchester

North Carolina
Alamance
Alexander
Bertie
Buncombe
Burke

Caldwell
Caswell
Catawba
Chatham
Cherokee
Clay
Cleveland
Davie
Durham
Forsyth
Franklin
Gates
Graham
Granville
Guilford
Halifax
Harnett
Haywood
Henderson
Hertford
Iredell
Jackson
Lee
Lincoln
Macon
Madison
McDowell
Nash
Northampton
Orange
Person
Polk
Rockingham
Rutherford
Stokes
Surry
Swain
Transylvania
Vance
Wake
Warren
Wilkes
Yadkin

Ohio
Adams
Brown
Clermont
Gallia
Hamilton
Lawrence
Pike
Scioto
Washington

Oklahoma
Beaver
Cimarron
Texas

Oregon
Benton

Clackamas
Clatsop
Columbia
Coos
Curry
Douglas
Jackson
Josephine
Lane
Lincoln
Linn
Marion
Multnomah
Polk
Tillamook
Washington
Yamhill

Pennsylvania
Bucks
Chester
Delaware
Montgomery
Philadelphia
York

Tennessee
All counties except:
Chester
Crockett
Dyer
Fayette
Hardeman
Hardin
Haywood
Henderson
Lake
Lauderdale
Madison
McNairy
Shelby
Tipton

Texas
Armstrong
Bailey
Briscoe
Carson
Castro
Cochran
Dallam
Deaf Smith
Donley
Floyd
Gray
Hale
Hansford
Hartley
Hockley
Hutchinson
Lamb
Lipscomb
Moore
Ochiltree

Oldham
Parmer
Potter
Randall
Roberts
Sherman
Swisher
Yoakum

Virginia
All counties

Washington
Clallam
Clark
Cowlitz
Grays Harbor
Island
Jefferson
King
Kitsap
Lewis
Mason
Pacific
Pierce
San Juan
Skagit
Snohomish
Thurston
Wahkiakum
Whatcom

West Virginia
Berkeley
Boone
Braxton
Cabell
Calhoun
Clay
Gilmer
Jackson
Jefferson
Kanawha
Lincoln
Logan
Mason
McDowell
Mercer
Mingo
Monroe
Morgan
Pleasants
Putnam
Ritchie
Roane
Tyler
Wayne
Wirt
Wood
Wyoming

Climate Zone 4 Recommendation Table for K-12 School Buildings

	Item	Component	Recommendation	How-To Tips	✓
Envelope	Roofs	Insulation entirely above deck	R-30.0 c.i.	EN2,17,19,21,22	
		Attic and other	R-49.0	EN3,17,19,20,21	
		Metal building	R-19.0 + R-11 L_s	EN4,17,19,21,22	
		Solar Reflectance Index (SRI)	Comply with Standard 90.1*		
	Walls	Mass (HC > 7 Btu/ft^2)	R-13.3 c.i.	EN5,17,19, 21	
		Steel framed	R-13.0 + R-7.5 c.i.	EN6,17,19, 21	
		Wood framed and other	R-13.0 + R-7.5 c.i.	EN7,17,19, 21	
		Metal building	R-0.0 + R-19.0 c.i.	EN8,17,19, 21	
		Below grade walls	R-7.5 c.i.	EN9,17,19, 21,22	
	Floors	Mass	R-14.6 c.i.	EN10,17,19, 21	
		Steel framed	R-38.0	EN11,17,19, 21	
		Wood framed and other	R-38.0	EN11,17,19, 21	
	Slabs	Unheated	Comply with Standard 90.1*	EN17,19, 21	
		Heated	R-20 for 24 in.	EN13,14,17,19, 21,22	
	Doors	Swinging	U-0.50	EN15,17	
		Nonswinging	U-0.50	EN16,17	
	Vestibules	At building entrance	Yes	EN17,18	
	View Fenestration	Thermal transmittance	Nonmetal framing = U-0.38 Metal framing = U-0.44	EN24	
		Fenestration-to-floor-area ratio (FFR)	E or W orientation = 5% maximum N or S orientation = 7% maximum	EN24–25	
		Solar heat gain coefficient (SHGC)	E or W orientation = 0.40 N orientation = 0.62 S orientation = 0.75	EN24,28–29	
		Exterior sun control	S orientation only = PF-0.5	EN26	
	Daylight Fenestration	Visible transmittance (VT)	See Table 5-5 for appropriate VT value	DL1,5–6,23	
		Interior/exterior sun control (S orientation only)	S orientation = no glare during school hours	DL1,9,12,13,31	
Daylighting/Lighting	Daylighting	Classroom, resource rooms, cafeteria, gym, and multipurpose rooms	Daylight 100% of floor area for 2/3 of school hours	DL1–5,7–21, 24–30,32–41	
		Administration areas	Daylight perimeter floor area (15 ft) for 2/3 of school hours	DL1–5,8–12	
	Interior Finishes	Interior surface average reflectance for daylighted rooms	Ceilings = 80% Wall surfaces = 70%	DL14	
	Interior Lighting	Lighting power density (LPD)	Whole building = 0.70 W/ft^2 Gyms, multipurpose rooms = 1.0 W/ft^2 Classrooms, art rooms, kitchens, libraries, media centers= 0.8 W/ft^2 Cafeterias, lobbies = 0.7 W/ft^2 Offices = 0.60 W/ft^2 Auditoriums, restrooms = 0.5 W/ft^2 Corridors, mechanical rooms = 0.4 W/ft^2	EL12–19	
		Light source lamp efficacy (mean lumens per watt)	T8 & T5 > 2 ft = 92, T8 & T5 ≤ 2 ft = 85, All other > 50	EL4–6	
		T8 ballasts	Non-dimming = NEMA Premium Instant Start Dimming= NEMA Premium Program Start	EL4–6	
		T5/T5HO ballasts	Electronic program start		
		CFL and HID ballasts	Electronic		
		Dimming controls daylight harvesting	Dim all fixtures in daylight zones	EL8,9,11–19	
		Lighting controls	Manual ON, auto/timed OFF in all areas as possible	EL8,9,11–20	
	Exterior Lighting	Façade and landscape lighting	LPD = 0.075 W/ft^2 in LZ-3 & LZ-4 LPD = 0.05 W/ft^2 in LZ-2 Controls = auto OFF between 12am and 6am	EL23	
		Parking lots and drives	LPD = 0.1 W/ft^2 in LZ-3 & LZ-4 LPD = 0.06 W/ft^2 in LZ-2 Controls = auto reduce to 25% (12am to 6am)	EL21	
		Walkways, plaza, and special feature areas	LPD = 0.16 W/ft^2 in LZ-3 & LZ-4 LPD = 0.14 W/ft^2 in LZ-2 Controls = auto reduce to 25% (12am to 6am)	EL22	
		All other exterior lighting	LPD = Comply with Standard 90.1* Controls = auto reduce to 25% (12am to 6am)	EL25	
Plug Loads	Equipment Choices	Laptop computers	Minimum 2/3 of total computers	PL2,3	
		ENERGY STAR equipment	All computers, equipment, and appliances	PL3,5	
		Vending machines	De-lamp and specify best in class efficiency	PL3,5	
	Controls/ Programs	Computer power control	Network control with power saving modes and control off during unoccupied hours	PL2,3	
		Power outlet control	Controllable power outlets with auto OFF during unoccupied hours for classrooms, office, library/media spaces All plug-in equipment not requiring continuous operation to use controllable outlets	PL3,4	
		Policies	Implement at least one: • District/school policy on allowed equipment • School energy teams	PL3,4	

*Note: Where the table says "Comply with Standard 90.1," the user must meet the more stringent of either the applicable version of ASHRAE/IES Standard 90.1 or the local code requirements.

Climate Zone 4 Recommendation Table for K-12 School Buildings *(Continued)*

	Item	Component	Recommendation	How-To Tips	✓
Kitchen	Kitchen Equipment	Cooking equipment	ENERGY STAR or California rebate-qualified equipment	KE1,2	
		Walk-in refrigeration equipment	6 in. insulation on low-temp walk-in equipment, Insulated floor, LED lighting, floating-head pressure controls, liquid pressure amplifier, subcooled liquid refrigerant, evaporative condenser	KE2,5	
		Exhaust hoods	Side panels, larger overhangs, rear seal at appliances, proximity hoods, VAV demand-based exhaust	KE3,6	
SWH	Service Water Heating	Gas water heater (condensing)	95% efficiency	WH1–5	
		Electric storage EF (≤12 kW, ≥20 gal)	EF > 0.99 − 0.0012 × Volume	WH1–5	
		Point-of-use heater selection	0.81 EF or 81% E_t	WH1–5	
		Electric heat-pump water heater efficiency	COP 3.0 (interior heat source)	WH1–5	
		Solar hot-water heating	30% solar hot-water fraction when LCC effective	WH7	
		Pipe insulation (d < 1.5 in./d ≥ 1.5 in.)	1/1.5 in.	WH6	
HVAC	Ground Source Heat-Pump (GSHP) System with DOAS	GSHP cooling efficiency	17.1 EER	HV1,11	
		GSHP heating efficiency	3.6 COP	HV1,11	
		GSHP compressor capacity control	Two stage or variable speed	HV1,11	
		Water-circulation pumps	VFD and NEMA Premium Efficiency	HV8	
		Cooling tower/fluid cooler	VFD on fans	HV1,8,11	
		Boiler efficiency	90% E_c	HV1,7,11	
		Maximum fan power	0.4 W/cfm	HV12	
		Exhaust air energy recovery in DOAS	A (humid) zones = 60% enthalpy reduction B (dry) zones = 60% dry-bulb temp reduction C (marine) zones = 60% enthalpy reduction	HV4,5	
		DOAS ventilation control	DCV with VFD	HV4,10,15	
	Fan-Coil System with DOAS	Water-cooled chiller efficiency	Comply with Standard 90.1*	HV2,6,11	
		Water circulation pumps	VFD and NEMA Premium Efficiency	HV6,7	
		Boiler efficiency	90% E_c	HV2,7,11	
		Maximum fan power	0.4 W/cfm	HV12	
		FCU fans	Multiple speed	HV2,12	
		Economizer	Comply with Standard 90.1*	HV2,14	
		Exhaust air energy recovery in DOAS	A (humid) zones = 60% enthalpy reduction B (dry) zones = 60% dry-bulb temp reduction C (marine) zones = 60% enthalpy reduction	HV4,5	
		DOAS ventilation control	DCV with VFD	HV4,10,15	
	VAV Air-Handling System with DOAS	Air-cooled chiller efficiency	10 EER; 12.75 IPLV	HV3,6,11	
		Water-cooled chiller efficiency	Comply with Standard 90.1*	HV3,6,11	
		Water circulation pumps	VFD and NEMA Premium Efficiency	HV6,7	
		Boiler efficiency	90% E_c	HV3,7,11	
		Maximum fan power	0.8 W/cfm	HV12	
		Economizer	Comply with Standard 90.1*	HV3,14	
		Exhaust air energy recovery in DOAS	A (humid) zones = 60% enthalpy reduction B (dry) zones = 60% dry-bulb temp reduction C (marine) zones = 60% enthalpy reduction	HV4,5	
		DOAS ventilation control	DCV with VFD	HV4,10,15	
	Ducts and Dampers	Outdoor air damper	Motorized damper	HV10	
		Duct seal class	Seal Class A	HV20	
		Insulation level	R-6	HV19	
M&V	M&V/ Benchmarking	Electrical submeters	Disaggregate submeters for lighting, HVAC, general 120V, renewables, and whole building	QA14–17	
		Benchmarking	Begin submetering early to address issues during warranty period Benchmark monthly energy use Provide training on benchmarking	QA14–17	

*Note: Where the table says "Comply with Standard 90.1," the user must meet the more stringent of either the applicable version of ASHRAE/IES Standard 90.1 or the local code requirements.

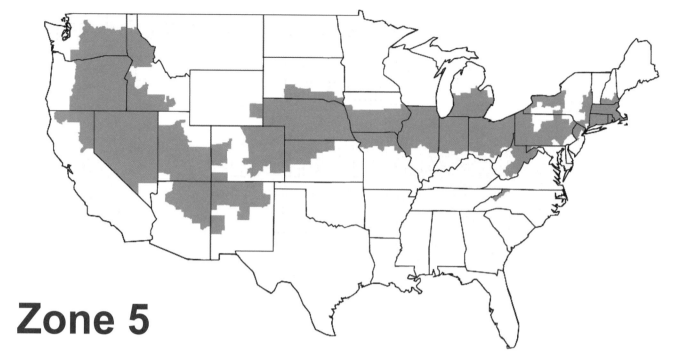

Zone 5

Arizona
Apache
Coconino
Navajo

California
Lassen
Modoc
Nevada
Plumas
Sierra
Siskiyou

Colorado
Adams
Arapahoe
Bent
Boulder
Cheyenne
Crowley
Delta
Denver
Douglas
Elbert
El Paso
Fremont
Garfield
Gilpin
Huerfano
Jefferson
Kiowa
Kit Carson
La Plata
Larimer
Lincoln
Logan
Mesa
Montezuma
Montrose
Morgan
Phillips
Prowers
Pueblo
Sedgwick
Teller
Washington
Weld
Yuma

Connecticut
All counties

Idaho
Ada
Benewah
Canyon
Cassia
Clearwater
Elmore
Gem
Gooding
Idaho
Jerome
Kootenai
Latah
Lewis
Lincoln
Minidoka
Nez Perce
Owyhee
Payette
Power

Shoshone
Twin Falls
Washington

Illinois
All counties except:
Alexander
Bond
Christian
Clay
Clinton
Crawford
Edwards
Effingham
Fayette
Franklin
Gallatin
Hamilton
Hardin
Jackson
Jasper
Jefferson
Johnson
Lawrence
Macoupin
Madison
Marion
Massac
Monroe
Montgomery
Perry
Pope
Pulaski
Randolph
Richland
Saline
Shelby
St. Clair
Union
Wabash
Washington
Wayne
White
Williamson
Brown

Indiana
All counties except:
Clark
Crawford
Daviess
Dearborn
Dubois
Floyd
Gibson
Greene
Harrison
Jackson
Jefferson
Jennings
Knox
Lawrence
Martin
Monroe
Ohio
Orange
Perry
Pike
Posey
Ripley
Scott
Spencer
Sullivan

Switzerland
Vanderburgh
Warrick
Washington

Iowa
All counties except:
Allamakee
Black Hawk
Bremer
Buchanan
Buena Vista
Butler
Calhoun
Cerro Gordo
Cherokee
Chickasaw
Clay
Clayton
Delaware
Dickinson
Emmet
Fayette
Floyd
Franklin
Grundy
Hamilton
Hancock
Hardin
Howard
Humboldt
Ida
Kossuth
Lyon
Mitchell
O'Brien
Osceola
Palo Alto
Plymouth
Pocahontas
Sac
Sioux
Webster
Winnebago
Winneshiek
Worth
Wright

Kansas
Cheyenne
Cloud
Decatur
Ellis
Gove
Graham
Greeley
Hamilton
Jewell
Lane
Logan
Mitchell
Ness
Norton
Osborne
Phillips
Rawlins
Republic
Rooks
Scott
Sheridan
Sherman
Smith
Thomas

Trego
Wallace
Wichita

Maryland
Garrett

Massachusetts
All counties

Michigan
Allegan
Barry
Bay
Berrien
Branch
Calhoun
Cass
Clinton
Eaton
Genesee
Gratiot
Hillsdale
Ingham
Ionia
Jackson
Kalamazoo
Kent
Lapeer
Lenawee
Livingston
Macomb
Midland
Monroe
Montcalm
Muskegon
Oakland
Ottawa
Saginaw
Shiawassee
St. Clair
St. Joseph
Tuscola
Van Buren
Washtenaw
Wayne

Missouri
Adair
Andrew
Atchison
Buchanan
Caldwell
Chariton
Clark
Clinton
Daviess
DeKalb
Gentry
Grundy
Harrison
Holt
Knox
Lewis
Linn
Livingston
Macon
Marion
Mercer
Nodaway
Pike
Putnam
Ralls
Schuyler

Scotland
Shelby
Sullivan
Worth

Nebraska
All counties

Nevada
All counties except:
Clark

New Hampshire
Cheshire
Hillsborough
Rockingham
Strafford

New Jersey
Bergen
Hunterdon
Mercer
Morris
Passaic
Somerset
Sussex
Warren

New Mexico
Catron
Colfax
Harding
Los Alamos
McKinley
Mora
Rio Arriba
Sandoval
San Juan
San Miguel
Santa Fe
Taos
Torrance

New York
Albany
Cayuga
Chautauqua
Chemung
Columbia
Cortland
Dutchess
Erie
Genesee
Greene
Livingston
Monroe
Niagara
Onondaga
Ontario
Orange
Orleans
Oswego
Putnam
Rensselaer
Rockland
Saratoga
Schenectady
Seneca
Tioga
Washington
Wayne
Yates

North Carolina
Alleghany
Ashe
Avery
Mitchell
Watauga
Yancey

Ohio
All counties except:
Adams
Brown
Clermont
Gallia
Hamilton
Lawrence
Pike
Scioto
Washington

Oregon
Baker
Crook
Deschutes
Gilliam
Grant
Harney
Hood River
Jefferson
Klamath
Lake
Malheur
Morrow
Sherman
Umatilla
Union
Wallowa
Wasco
Wheeler

Pennsylvania
All counties except:
Bucks
Cameron
Chester
Clearfield
Delaware
Elk
McKean
Montgomery
Philadelphia
Potter
Susquehanna
Tioga
Wayne
York

Rhode Island
All counties

South Dakota
Bennett
Bon Homme
Charles Mix
Clay
Douglas
Gregory
Hutchinson
Jackson
Mellette

Todd
Tripp
Union
Yankton

Utah
All counties except:
Box Elder
Cache
Carbon
Daggett
Duchesne
Morgan
Rich
Summit
Uintah
Wasatch
Washington

Washington
Adams
Asotin
Benton
Chelan
Columbia
Douglas
Franklin
Garfield
Grant
Kittitas
Klickitat
Lincoln
Skamania
Spokane
Walla Walla
Whitman
Yakima

Wyoming
Goshen
Platte

West Virginia
Barbour
Brooke
Doddridge
Fayette
Grant
Greenbrier
Hampshire
Hancock
Hardy
Harrison
Lewis
Marion
Marshall
Mineral
Monongalia
Nicholas
Ohio
Pendleton
Pocahontas
Preston
Raleigh
Randolph
Summers
Taylor
Tucker
Upshur
Webster
Wetzel

Climate Zone 5 Recommendation Table for K-12 School Buildings

	Item	Component	Recommendation	How-to Tips	✓
Envelope	Roofs	Insulation entirely above deck	R-30.0 c.i.	EN2,17,19,21,22	
		Attic and other	R-49.0	EN3,17,19,20,21	
		Metal building	R-25.0 + R-11 L_s	EN4,17,19,21,22	
		Solar Reflectance Index (SRI)	Comply with Standard 90.1*		
	Walls	Mass (HC > 7 Btu/ft^2)	R-13.3 c.i.	EN5,17,19, 21	
		Steel framed	R-13.0 + R-15.6 c.i.	EN6,17,19, 21	
		Wood framed and other	R-13.0 + R-10.0 c.i.	EN7,17,19, 21	
		Metal building	R-0.0 + R-19.0 c.i.	EN8,17,19, 21	
		Below grade walls	R-7.5 c.i.	EN9,17,19, 21,22	
	Floors	Mass	R-14.6 c.i.	EN10,17,19, 21	
		Steel framed	R-38.0	EN11,17,19, 21	
		Wood framed and other	R-38.0	EN11,17,19, 21	
	Slabs	Unheated	Comply with Standard 90.1*	EN17,19, 21	
		Heated	R-20 for 24 in.	EN13,14,17,19, 21,22	
	Doors	Swinging	U-0.50	EN15,17	
		Nonswinging	U-0.50	EN16,17	
	Vestibules	At building entrance	Yes	EN17,18	
	View Fenestration	Thermal transmittance	Nonmetal framing = U-0.35 Metal framing = U-0.44	EN24	
		Fenestration-to-floor-area ratio (FFR)	E or W orientation = 5% maximum N or S orientation = 7% maximum	EN24–25	
		Solar heat gain coefficient (SHGC)	E or W orientation = 0.42 N orientation = 0.62 S orientation = 0.75	EN24,32–33	
	Daylight Fenestration	Exterior sun control	S orientation only = PF-0.5	EN26,33	
		Visible transmittance (VT)	See Table 5-5 for appropriate VT value	DL1,5–6,23	
		Interior/exterior sun control (S orientation only)	S orientation = no glare during school hours	DL1,9,12,13,31	
Daylighting/Lighting	Daylighting	Classroom, resource rooms, cafeteria, gym, and multipurpose rooms	Daylight 100% of floor area for 2/3 of school hours	DL1–5,7–21, 24–30,32–41	
		Administration areas	Daylight perimeter floor area (15 ft) for 2/3 of school hours	DL1–5,8–12	
	Interior Finishes	Interior surface average reflectance for daylighted rooms	Ceilings = 80% Wall surfaces = 70%	DL14	
	Interior Lighting	Lighting power density (LPD)	Whole building = 0.70 W/ft^2 Gyms, multipurpose rooms = 1.0 W/ft^2 Classrooms, art rooms, kitchens, libraries, media centers= 0.8 W/ft^2 Cafeterias, lobbies = 0.7 W/ft^2 Offices = 0.60 W/ft^2 Auditoriums, restrooms = 0.5 W/ft^2 Corridors, mechanical rooms = 0.4 W/ft^2	EL12–19	
		Light source lamp efficacy (mean lumens per watt)	T8 & T5 > 2 ft = 92, T8 & T5 ≤ 2 ft = 85, All other > 50	EL4–6	
		T8 ballasts	Non-dimming = NEMA Premium Instant Start Dimming= NEMA Premium Program Start	EL4–6	
		T5/T5HO ballasts	Electronic program start		
		CFL and HID ballasts	Electronic		
		Dimming controls daylight harvesting	Dim all fixtures in daylight zones	EL8,9,11–19	
		Lighting controls	Manual ON, auto/timed OFF in all areas as possible	EL8,9,11–20	
	Exterior Lighting	Façade and landscape lighting	LPD = 0.075 W/ft^2 in LZ-3 & LZ-4 LPD = 0.05 W/ft^2 in LZ-2 Controls = auto OFF between 12am and 6am	EL23	
		Parking lots and drives	LPD = 0.1 W/ft^2 in LZ-3 & LZ-4 LPD = 0.06 W/ft^2 in LZ-2 Controls = auto reduce to 25% (12am to 6am)	EL21	
		Walkways, plaza, and special feature areas	LPD = 0.16 W/ft^2 in LZ-3 & LZ-4 LPD = 0.14 W/ft^2 in LZ-2 Controls = auto reduce to 25% (12am to 6am)	EL22	
		All other exterior lighting	LPD = Comply with Standard 90.1* Controls = auto reduce to 25% (12am to 6am)	EL25	
Plug Loads	Equipment Choices	Laptop computers	Minimum 2/3 of total computers	PL2,3	
		ENERGY STAR equipment	All computers, equipment, and appliances	PL3,5	
		Vending machines	De-lamp and specify best in class efficiency	PL3,5	
	Controls/ Programs	Computer power control	Network control with power saving modes and control off during unoccupied hours	PL2,3	
		Power outlet control	Controllable power outlets with auto OFF during unoccupied hours for classrooms, office, library/ media spaces All plug-in equipment not requiring continuous operation to use controllable outlets	PL3,4	
		Policies	Implement at least one: • District/school policy on allowed equipment • School energy teams	PL3,4	

*Note: Where the table says "Comply with Standard 90.1," the user must meet the more stringent of either the applicable version of ASHRAE/IES Standard 90.1 or the local code requirements.

Climate Zone 5 Recommendation Table for K-12 School Buildings *(Continued)*

	Item	Component	Recommendation	How-to Tips	✓
Kitchen	Kitchen Equipment	Cooking equipment	ENERGY STAR or California rebate-qualified equipment	KE1,2	
		Walk-in refrigeration equipment	6 in. insulation on low-temp walk-in equipment, Insulated floor, LED lighting, floating-head pressure controls, liquid pressure amplifier, subcooled liquid refrigerant, evaporative condenser	KE2,5	
		Exhaust hoods	Side panels, larger overhangs, rear seal at appliances, proximity hoods, VAV demand-based exhaust	KE3,6	
SWH	Service Water Heating	Gas water heater (condensing)	95% efficiency	WH1–5	
		Electric storage EF (≤12 kW, ≥20 gal)	EF > 0.99 − 0.0012 x Volume	WH1–5	
		Point-of-use heater selection	0.81 EF or 81% E_t	WH1–5	
		Electric heat-pump water heater efficiency	COP 3.0 (interior heat source)	WH1–5	
		Solar hot-water heating	30% solar hot-water fraction when LCC effective	WH7	
		Pipe insulation (d < 1.5 in./d ≥ 1.5 in.)	1/1.5 in.	WH6	
HVAC	Ground Source Heat-Pump (GSHP) System with DOAS	GSHP cooling efficiency	17.1 EER	HV1,11	
		GSHP heating efficiency	3.6 COP	HV1,11	
		GSHP compressor capacity control	Two stage or variable speed	HV1,11	
		Water-circulation pumps	VFD and NEMA Premium Efficiency	HV8	
		Cooling tower/fluid cooler	VFD on fans	HV1,8,11	
		Boiler efficiency	90% E_c	HV1,7,11	
		Maximum fan power	0.4 W/cfm	HV12	
		Exhaust air energy recovery in DOAS	A (humid) zones = 60% enthalpy reduction B (dry) zones = 60% dry-bulb temp reduction C (marine) zones = 60% enthalpy reduction	HV4,5	
		DOAS ventilation control	DCV with VFD	HV4,10,15	
	Fan-Coil System with DOAS	Water-cooled chiller efficiency	Comply with Standard 90.1*	HV2,6,11	
		Water circulation pumps	VFD and NEMA Premium Efficiency	HV6,7	
		Boiler efficiency	90% E_c	HV2,7,11	
		Maximum fan power	0.4 W/cfm	HV12	
		FCU fans	Multiple speed	HV2,12	
		Economizer	Comply with Standard 90.1*	HV2,14	
		Exhaust air energy recovery in DOAS	A (humid) zones = 60% enthalpy reduction B (dry) zones = 60% dry-bulb temp reduction C (marine) zones = 60% enthalpy reduction	HV4,5	
		DOAS ventilation control	DCV with VFD	HV4,10,15	
	VAV Air-Handling System with DOAS	Air-cooled chiller efficiency	10 EER; 12.75 IPLV	HV3,6,11	
		Water-cooled chiller efficiency	Comply with Standard 90.1*	HV3,6,11	
		Water circulation pumps	VFD and NEMA Premium Efficiency	HV6,7	
		Boiler efficiency	90% E_c	HV3,7,11	
		Maximum fan power	0.8 W/cfm	HV12	
		Economizer	Comply with Standard 90.1*	HV3,14	
		Exhaust air energy recovery in DOAS	A (humid) zones = 60% enthalpy reduction B (dry) zones = 60% dry-bulb temp reduction C (marine) zones = 60% enthalpy reduction	HV4,5	
		DOAS ventilation control	DCV with VFD	HV4,10,15	
	Ducts and Dampers	Outdoor air damper	Motorized damper	HV10	
		Duct seal class	Seal Class A	HV20	
		Insulation level	R-6	HV19	
M&V	M&V/ Benchmarking	Electrical submeters	Disaggregate submeters for lighting, HVAC, general 120V, renewables, and whole building	QA14–17	
		Benchmarking	Begin submetering early to address issues during warranty period Benchmark monthly energy use Provide training on benchmarking	QA14–17	

*Note: Where the table says "Comply with Standard 90.1," the user must meet the more stringent of either the applicable version of ASHRAE/IES Standard 90.1 or the local code requirements.

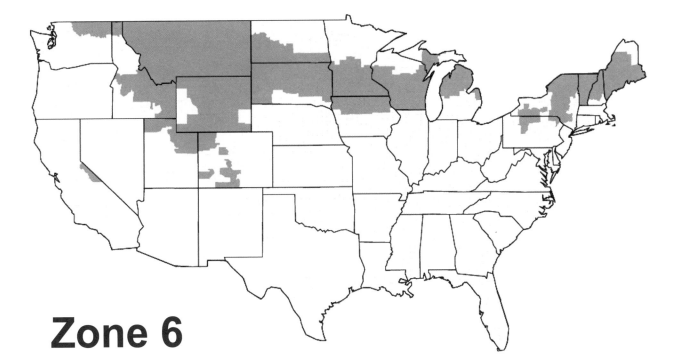

Zone 6

California

Alpine
Mono

Colorado

Alamosa
Archuleta
Chaffee
Conejos
Costilla
Custer
Dolores
Eagle
Moffat
Ouray
Rio Blanco
Saguache
San Miguel

Idaho

Adams
Bannock
Bear Lake
Bingham
Blaine
Boise
Bonner
Bonneville
Boundary
Butte
Camas
Caribou
Clark
Custer
Franklin
Fremont
Jefferson
Lemhi
Madison
Oneida
Teton
Valley

Iowa

Allamakee
Black Hawk
Bremer
Buchanan
Buena Vista
Butler
Calhoun
Cerro Gordo
Cherokee
Chickasaw
Clay
Clayton
Delaware
Dickinson
Emmet
Fayette
Floyd
Franklin
Grundy
Hamilton
Hancock
Hardin
Howard
Humboldt
Ida
Kossuth
Lyon
Mitchell
O'Brien
Osceola
Palo Alto
Plymouth
Pocahontas
Sac
Sioux
Webster
Winnebago
Winneshiek
Worth
Wright

Maine

All counties except:
Aroostook

Michigan

Alcona
Alger
Alpena
Antrim
Arenac
Benzie
Charlevoix
Cheboygan
Clare
Crawford
Delta
Dickinson
Emmet
Gladwin
Grand Traverse
Huron
Iosco
Isabella
Kalkaska
Lake
Leelanau
Manistee
Marquette
Mason
Mecosta
Menominee
Missaukee
Montmorency
Newaygo
Oceana
Ogemaw
Osceola
Oscoda
Otsego
Presque Isle
Roscommon
Sanilac
Wexford

Minnesota

Anoka
Benton
Big Stone
Blue Earth
Brown
Carver
Chippewa
Chisago
Cottonwood
Dakota
Dodge
Douglas
Faribault
Fillmore
Freeborn
Goodhue
Hennepin
Houston
Isanti
Jackson
Kandiyohi
Lac qui Parle
Le Sueur
Lincoln
Lyon
Martin
McLeod
Meeker
Morrison
Mower
Murray
Nicollet
Nobles
Olmsted
Pipestone
Pope
Ramsey
Redwood
Renville
Rice
Rock
Scott
Sherburne
Sibley
Stearns
Steele
Stevens
Swift
Todd
Traverse
Wabasha
Waseca
Washington
Watonwan
Winona
Wright
Yellow Medicine

Montana

All counties

New Hampshire

Belknap
Carroll
Coos
Grafton
Merrimack
Sullivan

New York

Allegany
Broome
Cattaraugus
Chenango
Clinton
Delaware
Essex
Franklin
Fulton
Hamilton
Herkimer
Jefferson
Lewis
Madison
Montgomery
Oneida
Otsego
Schoharie
Schuyler
Steuben
St. Lawrence
Sullivan
Tompkins
Ulster
Warren
Wyoming

North Dakota

Adams
Billings
Bowman
Burleigh
Dickey
Dunn
Emmons

Golden Valley
Grant
Hettinger
LaMoure
Logan
McIntosh
McKenzie
Mercer
Morton
Oliver
Ransom
Richland
Sargent
Sioux
Slope
Stark

Pennsylvania

Cameron
Clearfield
Elk
McKean
Potter
Susquehanna
Tioga
Wayne

South Dakota

All counties except:
Bennett
Bon Homme
Charles Mix
Clay
Douglas
Gregory
Hutchinson
Jackson
Mellette
Todd
Tripp
Union
Yankton

Utah

Box Elder
Cache
Carbon
Daggett
Duchesne
Morgan
Rich
Summit
Uintah
Wasatch

Vermont

All counties

Washington

Ferry
Okanogan
Pend Oreille
Stevens

Wisconsin

All counties except:
Ashland
Bayfield
Burnett
Douglas
Florence
Forest
Iron
Langlade
Lincoln
Oneida
Price
Sawyer
Taylor
Vilas
Washburn

Wyoming

All counties except:
Goshen
Platte
Lincoln
Sublette
Teton

Climate Zone 6 Recommendation Table for K-12 School Buildings

	Item	Component	Recommendation	How-To Tips	✓
Envelope	Roofs	Insulation entirely above deck	R-30.0 c.i.	EN2,17,19,21,22	
		Attic and other	R-49.0	EN3,17,19,20,21	
		Metal building	R-25.0 + R-11 L_s	EN4,17,19,21,22	
		Solar Reflectance Index (SRI)	Comply with Standard 90.1*		
	Walls	Mass (HC > 7 Btu/ft^2)	R-19.5 c.i.	EN5,17,19, 21	
		Steel framed	R13.0 + R-18.8 c.i.	EN6,17,19, 21	
		Wood framed and other	R-13.0 + R-12.5 c.i.	EN7,17,19, 21	
		Metal building	R-0.0 + R-19.0 c.i.	EN8,17,19, 21	
		Below grade walls	R-10.0 c.i.	EN9,17,19, 21,22	
	Floors	Mass	R-16.7 c.i.	EN10,17,19, 21	
		Steel framed	R-38.0	EN11,17,19, 21	
		Wood framed and other	R-38.0	EN11,17,19, 21	
	Slabs	Unheated	R-10 for 24 in.	EN12,14,17,19, 21, 22	
		Heated	R-20 for 48 in.	EN13,14,17,19, 21,22	
	Doors	Swinging	U-0.50	EN15,17	
		Nonswinging	U-0.50	EN16,17	
	Vestibules	At building entrance	Yes	EN17,18	
	View Fenestration	Thermal transmittance	Nonmetal framing = U-0.35 Metal framing = U-0.42	EN24	
		Fenestration-to-floor-area ratio (FFR)	E or W orientation = 5% maximum N or S orientation = 7% maximum	EN24–25	
		Solar heat gain coefficient (SHGC)	E or W orientation = 0.42 N orientation = 0.62 S orientation = 0.75	EN24,32–33	
		Exterior sun control	S orientation only = PF-0.5	EN26,33	
Daylighting/Lighting	Daylight Fenestration	Visible transmittance (VT)	See Table 5-5 for appropriate VT value	DL1,5–6,23	
		Interior/exterior sun control (S orientation only)	S orientation = no glare during school hours	DL1,9,12,13,31	
	Daylighting	Classroom, resource rooms, cafeteria, gym, and multipurpose rooms	Daylight 100% of floor area for 2/3 of school hours	DL1–5,7–21, 24–30,32–41	
		Administration areas	Daylight perimeter floor area (15 ft) for 2/3 of school hours	DL1–5,8–12	
	Interior Finishes	Interior surface average reflectance for daylighted rooms	Ceilings = 80% Wall surfaces = 70%	DL14	
	Interior Lighting	Lighting power density (LPD)	Whole building = 0.70 W/ft^2 Gyms, multipurpose rooms = 1.0 W/ft^2 Classrooms, art rooms, kitchens, libraries, media centers= 0.8 W/ft^2 Cafeterias, lobbies = 0.7 W/ft^2 Offices = 0.60 W/ft^2 Auditoriums, restrooms = 0.5 W/ft^2 Corridors, mechanical rooms = 0.4 W/ft^2	EL12–19	
		Light source lamp efficacy (mean lumens per watt)	T8 & T5 > 2 ft = 92, T8 & T5 ≤ 2 ft = 85, All other > 50	EL4–6	
		T8 ballasts	Non-dimming = NEMA Premium Instant Start Dimming= NEMA Premium Program Start	EL4–6	
		T5/T5HO ballasts	Electronic program start		
		CFL and HID ballasts	Electronic		
		Dimming controls daylight harvesting	Dim all fixtures in daylight zones	EL8,9,11–19	
		Lighting controls	Manual ON, auto/timed OFF in all areas as possible	EL8,9,11–20	
	Exterior Lighting	Façade and landscape lighting	LPD = 0.075 W/ft^2 in LZ-3 & LZ-4 LPD = 0.05 W/ft^2 in LZ-2 Controls = auto OFF between 12am and 6am	EL23	
		Parking lots and drives	LPD = 0.1 W/ft^2 in LZ-3 & LZ-4 LPD = 0.06 W/ft^2 in LZ-2 Controls = auto reduce to 25% (12am to 6am)	EL21	
		Walkways, plaza, and special feature areas	LPD = 0.16 W/ft^2 LZ-3 & LZ-4 LPD = 0.14 W/ft^2 in LZ-2 Controls = auto reduce to 25% (12am to 6am)	EL22	
		All other exterior lighting	LPD = Comply with Standard 90.1* Controls = auto reduce to 25% (12am to 6am)	EL25	
Plug Loads	Equipment Choices	Laptop computers	Minimum 2/3 of total computers	PL2,3	
		ENERGY STAR equipment	All computers, equipment, and appliances	PL3,5	
		Vending machines	De-lamp and specify best in class efficiency	PL3,5	
	Controls/ Programs	Computer power control	Network control with power saving modes and control off during unoccupied hours	PL2,3	
		Power outlet control	Controllable power outlets with auto OFF during unoccupied hours for classrooms, office, library/ media spaces All plug-in equipment not requiring continuous operation to use controllable outlets	PL3,4	
		Policies	Implement at least one: • District/school policy on allowed equipment • School energy teams	PL3,4	

*Note: Where the table says "Comply with Standard 90.1," the user must meet the more stringent of either the applicable version of ASHRAE/IES Standard 90.1 or the local code requirements.

Climate Zone 6 Recommendation Table for K-12 School Buildings *(Continued)*

	Item	Component	Recommendation	How-To Tips	✓
Kitchen	Kitchen Equipment	Cooking equipment	ENERGY STAR or California rebate-qualified equipment	KE1,2	
		Walk-in refrigeration equipment	6 in. insulation on low-temp walk-in equipment, Insulated floor, LED lighting, floating-head pressure controls, liquid pressure amplifier, subcooled liquid refrigerant, evaporative condenser	KE2,5	
		Exhaust hoods	Side panels, larger overhangs, rear seal at appliances, proximity hoods, VAV demand-based exhaust	KE3,6	
SWH	Service Water Heating	Gas water heater (condensing)	95% efficiency	WH1–5	
		Electric storage EF (≤12 kW, ≥20 gal)	$EF > 0.99 - 0.0012 \times Volume$	WH1–5	
		Point-of-use heater selection	0.81 EF or 81% E_t	WH1–5	
		Electric heat-pump water heater efficiency	COP 3.0 (interior heat source)	WH1–5	
		Solar hot-water heating	30% solar hot-water fraction when LCC effective	WH7	
		Pipe insulation ($d < 1.5$ in./$d \geq 1.5$ in.)	1/1.5 in.	WH6	
HVAC	Ground Source Heat-Pump (GSHP) System with DOAS	GSHP cooling efficiency	17.1 EER	HV1,11	
		GSHP heating efficiency	3.6 COP	HV1,11	
		GSHP compressor capacity control	Two stage or variable speed	HV1,11	
		Water-circulation pumps	VFD and NEMA Premium Efficiency	HV8	
		Cooling tower/fluid cooler	VFD on fans	HV1,8,11	
		Boiler efficiency	90% E_c	HV1,7,11	
		Maximum fan power	0.4 W/cfm	HV12	
		Exhaust air energy recovery in DOAS	A (humid) zones = 60% enthalpy reduction B (dry) zones = 60% dry-bulb temperature reduction	HV4,5	
		DOAS ventilation control	DCV with VFD	HV4,10,15	
	Fan-Coil System with DOAS	Water-cooled chiller efficiency	Comply with Standard 90.1*	HV2,6,11	
		Water circulation pumps	VFD and NEMA Premium Efficiency	HV6,7	
		Boiler efficiency	90% E_c	HV2,7,11	
		Maximum fan power	0.4 W/cfm	HV12	
		FCU fans	Multiple speed	HV2,12	
		Economizer	Comply with Standard 90.1*	HV2,14	
		Exhaust air energy recovery in DOAS	A (humid) zones = 60% enthalpy reduction B (dry) zones = 60% dry-bulb temperature reduction	HV4,5	
		DOAS ventilation control	DCV with VFD	HV4,10,15	
	VAV Air-Handling System with DOAS	Air-cooled chiller efficiency	10 EER; 12.75 IPLV	HV3,6,11	
		Water-cooled chiller efficiency	Comply with Standard 90.1*	HV3,6,11	
		Water circulation pumps	VFD and NEMA Premium Efficiency	HV6,7	
		Boiler efficiency	90% E_c	HV3,7,11	
		Maximum fan power	0.8 W/cfm	HV12	
		Economizer	Comply with Standard 90.1*	HV3,14	
		Exhaust air energy recovery in DOAS	A (humid) zones = 60% enthalpy reduction B (dry) zones = 60% dry-bulb temperature reduction	HV4,5	
		DOAS ventilation control	DCV with VFD	HV4,10,15	
	Ducts and Dampers	Outdoor air damper	Motorized damper	HV10	
		Duct seal class	Seal Class A	HV20	
		Insulation level	R-6	HV19	
M&V	M&V/ Benchmarking	Electrical submeters	Disaggregate submeters for lighting, HVAC, general 120V, renewables, and whole building	QA14–17	
		Benchmarking	Begin submetering early to address issues during warranty period Benchmark monthly energy use Provide training on benchmarking	QA14–17	

*Note: Where the table says "Comply with Standard 90.1," the user must meet the more stringent of either the applicable version of ASHRAE/IES Standard 90.1 or the local code requirements.

Zone 7

Alaska

Aleutians East
Aleutians West (CA)
Anchorage
Angoon (CA)
Bristol Bay
Denali
Haines
Juneau
Kenai Peninsula
Ketchikan (CA)
Ketchikan Gateway
Kodiak Island
Lake and Peninsula
Matanuska-Susitna
Prince of Wales-Outer
Sitka
Skagway-Hoonah-
Valdez-Cordova (CA)
Wrangell-Petersburg (CA)
Yakutat

Colorado

Clear Creek
Grand
Gunnison
Hinsdale
Jackson
Lake
Mineral
Park
Pitkin
Rio Grande
Routt
San Juan
Summit

Maine

Aroostook

Michigan

Baraga
Chippewa
Gogebic
Houghton

Iron
Keweenaw
Luce
Mackinac
Ontonagon
Schoolcraft

Minnesota

Aitkin
Becker
Beltrami
Carlton
Cass
Clay
Clearwater
Cook
Crow Wing
Grant
Hubbard
Itasca
Kanabec
Kittson
Koochiching
Lake
Lake of the Woods
Mahnomen
Marshall
Mille Lacs
Norman
Otter Tail
Pennington
Pine
Polk
Red Lake
Roseau
St. Louis
Wadena
Wilkin

North Dakota

Barnes
Benson
Bottineau
Burke
Cass
Cavalier

Divide
Eddy
Foster
Grand Forks
Griggs
Kidder
McHenry
McLean
Mountrail
Nelson
Pembina
Pierce
Ramsey
Renville
Rolette
Sheridan
Steele
Stutsman
Towner
Traill
Walsh
Ward
Wells
Williams

Wisconsin

Ashland
Bayfield
Burnett
Douglas
Florence
Forest
Iron
Langlade
Lincoln
Oneida
Price
Sawyer
Taylor
Vilas
Washburn

Wyoming

Lincoln
Sublette
Teton

Climate Zone 7 Recommendation Table for K-12 School Buildings

	Item	Component	Recommendation	How-To Tips	✓
Envelope	Roofs	Insulation entirely above deck	R-35.0 c.i.	EN2,17,19,21,22	
		Attic and other	R-60.0	EN3,17,19,20,21	
		Metal building	R-30.0 + R-11 L_s	EN4,17,19,21,22	
		Solar Reflectance Index (SRI)	Comply with Standard 90.1*		
	Walls	Mass (HC > 7 Btu/ft^2)	R-19.5 c.i.	EN5,17,19, 21	
		Steel framed	R13.0 + R-18.8 c.i.	EN6,17,19, 21	
		Wood framed and other	R-13.0 + R-15.0 c.i.	EN7,17,19, 21	
		Metal building	R-0.0 + R-22.1 c.i.	EN8,17,19, 21	
		Below grade walls	R-15.0 c.i.	EN9,17,19, 21,22	
	Floors	Mass	R-20.9 c.i.	EN10,17,19, 21	
		Steel framed	R-49.0	EN11,17,19, 21	
		Wood framed and other	R-49.0	EN11,17,19, 21	
	Slabs	Unheated	R-20 for 24 in.	EN12,14,17,19, 21, 22	
		Heated	R-25 for 48 in.	EN13,14,17,19, 21,22	
	Doors	Swinging	U-0.50	EN15,17	
		Nonswinging	U-0.50	EN16,17	
	Vestibules	At building entrance	Yes	EN17,18	
	View Fenestration	Thermal transmittance	Nonmetal framing = U-0.33 Metal framing = U-0.34	EN24	
		Fenestration-to-floor-area ratio (FFR)	E or W orientation = 5% maximum N or S orientation = 7% maximum	EN24–25	
		Solar heat gain coefficient (SHGC)	E or W orientation = 0.45 N orientation = 0.62 S orientation = 0.75	EN24,32–33	
		Exterior sun control	S orientation only = PF-0.5	EN26,33	
	Daylight Fenestration	Visible transmittance (VT)	See Table 5-5 for appropriate VT value	DL1,5–6,23	
		Interior/exterior sun control (S orientation only)	S orientation = no glare during school hours	DL1,9,12,13,31	
Daylighting/Lighting	Daylighting	Classroom, resource rooms, cafeteria, gym, and multipurpose rooms	Daylight 100% of floor area for 2/3 of school hours	DL1–5,7–21,24–30,32–41	
		Administration areas	Daylight perimeter floor area (15 ft) for 2/3 of school hours	DL1–5,8–12	
	Interior Finishes	Interior surface average reflectance for daylighted rooms	Ceilings = 80% Wall surfaces = 70%	DL14	
	Interior Lighting	Lighting power density (LPD)	Whole building = 0.70 W/ft^2 Gyms, multipurpose rooms = 1.0 W/ft^2 Classrooms, art rooms, kitchens, libraries, media centers= 0.8 W/ft^2 Cafeterias, lobbies = 0.7 W/ft^2 Offices = 0.60 W/ft^2 Auditoriums, restrooms = 0.5 W/ft^2 Corridors, mechanical rooms = 0.4 W/ft^2	EL12–19	
		Light source lamp efficacy (mean lumens per watt)	T8 & T5 > 2 ft = 92, T8 & T5 ≤ 2 ft = 85, All other > 50	EL4–6	
		T8 ballasts	Non-dimming = NEMA Premium Instant Start Dimming= NEMA Premium Program Start	EL4–6	
		T5/T5HO ballasts	Electronic program start		
		CFL and HID ballasts	Electronic		
		Dimming controls daylight harvesting	Dim all fixtures in daylight zones	EL8,9,11–19	
		Lighting controls	Manual ON, auto/timed OFF in all areas as possible	EL8,9,11–20	
	Exterior Lighting	Façade and landscape lighting	LPD = 0.075 W/ft^2 in LZ-3 & LZ-4 LPD = 0.05 W/ft^2 in LZ-2 Controls = auto OFF between 12am and 6am	EL23	
		Parking lots and drives	LPD = 0.1 W/ft^2 in LZ-3 & LZ-4 LPD = 0.06 W/ft^2 in LZ-2 Controls = auto reduce to 25% (12am to 6am)	EL21	
		Walkways, plaza, and special feature areas	LPD = 0.16 W/ft^2 in LZ-3 & LZ-4 LPD = 0.14 W/ft^2 in LZ-2 Controls = auto reduce to 25% (12am to 6am)	EL22	
		All other exterior lighting	LPD = Comply with Standard 90.1* Controls = auto reduce to 25% (12am to 6am)	EL25	
Plug Loads	Equipment Choices	Laptop computers	Minimum 2/3 of total computers	PL2,3	
		ENERGY STAR equipment	All computers, equipment, and appliances	PL3,5	
		Vending machines	De-lamp and specify best in class efficiency	PL3,5	
	Controls/ Programs	Computer power control	Network control with power saving modes and control off during unoccupied hours	PL2,3	
		Power outlet control	Controllable power outlets with auto OFF during unoccupied hours for classrooms, office, library/ media spaces All plug-in equipment not requiring continuous operation to use controllable outlets	PL3,4	
		Policies	Implement at least one: • District/school policy on allowed equipment • School energy teams	PL3,4	

*Note: Where the table says "Comply with Standard 90.1," the user must meet the more stringent of either the applicable version of ASHRAE/IES Standard 90.1 or the local code requirements.

Climate Zone 7 Recommendation Table for K-12 School Buildings

Item	Component	Recommendation	How-To Tips	✓
Kitchen / Kitchen Equipment	Cooking equipment	ENERGY STAR or California rebate-qualified equipment	KE1,2	
	Walk-in refrigeration equipment	6 in. insulation on low-temp walk-in equipment, Insulated floor, LED lighting, floating-head pressure controls, liquid pressure amplifier, subcooled liquid refrigerant, evaporative condenser	KE2,5	
	Exhaust hoods	Side panels, larger overhangs, rear seal at appliances, proximity hoods, VAV demand-based exhaust	KE3,6	
SWH / Service Water Heating	Gas water heater (condensing)	95% efficiency	WH1–5	
	Electric storage EF (≤12 kW, ≥20 gal)	EF > 0.99 – 0.0012 × Volume	WH1–5	
	Point-of-use heater selection	0.81 EF or 81% E_t	WH1–5	
	Electric heat-pump water heater efficiency	COP 3.0 (interior heat source)	WH1–5	
	Solar hot-water heating	30% solar hot-water fraction when LCC effective	WH7	
	Pipe insulation (d < 1.5 in./d ≥ 1.5 in.)	1/1.5 in.	WH6	
HVAC / Ground Source Heat-Pump (GSHP) System with DOAS	GSHP cooling efficiency	17.1 EER	HV1,11	
	GSHP heating efficiency	3.6 COP	HV1,11	
	GSHP compressor capacity control	Two stage or variable speed	HV1,11	
	Water-circulation pumps	VFD and NEMA Premium Efficiency	HV8	
	Cooling tower/fluid cooler	VFD on fans	HV1,8,11	
	Boiler efficiency	90% E_c	HV1,7,11	
	Maximum fan power	0.4 W/cfm	HV12	
	Exhaust air energy recovery in DOAS	A (humid) zones = 60% enthalpy reduction B (dry) zones = 60% dry-bulb temperature reduction	HV4,5	
	DOAS ventilation control	DCV with VFD	HV4,10,15	
Fan-Coil System with DOAS	Water-cooled chiller efficiency	Comply with Standard 90.1*	HV2,6,11	
	Water circulation pumps	VFD and NEMA Premium Efficiency	HV6,7	
	Boiler efficiency	90% E_c	HV2,7,11	
	Maximum fan power	0.4 W/cfm	HV12	
	FCU fans	Multiple speed	HV2,12	
	Economizer	Comply with Standard 90.1*	HV2,14	
	Exhaust air energy recovery in DOAS	A (humid) zones = 60% enthalpy reduction B (dry) zones = 60% dry-bulb temperature reduction	HV4,5	
	DOAS ventilation control	DCV with VFD	HV4,10,15	
VAV Air-Handling System with DOAS	Air-cooled chiller efficiency	10 EER; 12.75 IPLV	HV3,6,11	
	Water-cooled chiller efficiency	Comply with Standard 90.1*	HV3,6,11	
	Water circulation pumps	VFD and NEMA Premium Efficiency	HV6,7	
	Boiler efficiency	90% E_c	HV3,7,11	
	Maximum fan power	0.8 W/cfm	HV12	
	Economizer	Comply with Standard 90.1*	HV3,14	
	Exhaust air energy recovery in DOAS	A (humid) zones = 60% enthalpy reduction B (dry) zones = 60% dry-bulb temperature reduction	HV4,5	
	DOAS ventilation control	DCV with VFD	HV4,10,15	
Ducts and Dampers	Outdoor air damper	Motorized damper	HV10	
	Duct seal class	Seal Class A	HV20	
	Insulation level	R-6	HV19	
M&V / M&V/ Benchmarking	Electrical submeters	Disaggregate submeters for lighting, HVAC, general 120V, renewables, and whole building	QA14–17	
	Benchmarking	Begin submetering early to address issues during warranty period Benchmark monthly energy use Provide training on benchmarking	QA14–17	

*Note: Where the table says "Comply with Standard 90.1," the user must meet the more stringent of either the applicable version of ASHRAE/IES Standard 90.1 or the local code requirements.

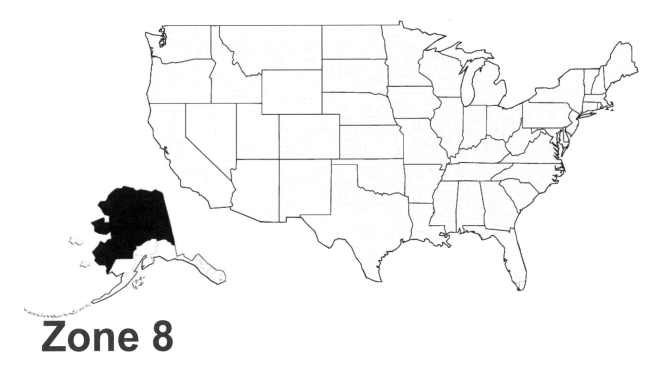

Zone 8

Alaska

Bethel (CA)
Dillingham (CA)
Fairbanks North Star
Nome (CA)
North Slope
Northwest Arctic
Southeast Fairbanks (CA)
Wade Hampton (CA)
Yukon-Koyukuk (CA)

Climate Zone 8 Recommendation Table for K-12 School Buildings

	Item	Component	Recommendation	How-To Tips	✓
Envelope	Roofs	Insulation entirely above deck	R-35.0 c.i.	EN2,17,19,21,22	
		Attic and other	R-60.0	EN3,17,19,20,21	
		Metal building	R-25.0 + R-11 + R-11 L_s	EN4,17,19,21,22	
		Solar Reflectance Index (SRI)	Comply with Standard 90.1*		
	Walls	Mass (HC > 7 Btu/ft^2)	R-19.5 c.i.	EN5,17,19, 21	
		Steel framed	R13.0 + R-18.8 c.i.	EN6,17,19, 21	
		Wood framed and other	R-13.0 + R-18.8 c.i.	EN7,17,19, 21	
		Metal building	R-0.0 + R-25.0 c.i.	EN8,17,19, 21	
		Below grade walls	R-15.0 c.i.	EN9,17,19, 21,22	
	Floors	Mass	R-23.0 c.i.	EN10,17,19, 21	
		Steel framed	R-60.0	EN11,17,19, 21	
		Wood framed and other	R-60.0	EN11,17,19, 21	
	Slabs	Unheated	R-20 for 24 in.	EN12,14,17,19, 21, 22	
		Heated	R-20 full slab.	EN13,14,17,19, 21,22	
	Doors	Swinging	U-0.50	EN15,17	
		Nonswinging	U-0.50	EN16,17	
	Vestibules	At building entrance	Yes	EN17,18	
	View Fenestration	Thermal transmittance	Nonmetal framing = U-0.25 Metal framing = U-0.34	EN24	
		Fenestration-to-floor-area ratio (FFR)	E or W orientation = 5% maximum N or S orientation = 7% maximum	EN24–25	
		Solar heat gain coefficient (SHGC)	E or W orientation = 0.45 N orientation = 0.62 S orientation = 0.75	EN24,32–33	
		Exterior sun control	S orientation only = PF-0.5	EN26,33	
	Daylight Fenestration	Visible transmittance (VT)	See Table 5-5 for appropriate VT value	DL1,5–6,23	
		Interior/exterior sun control (S orientation only)	S orientation = no glare during school hours	DL1,9,12,13,31	
Daylighting/Lighting	Daylighting	Classroom, resource rooms, cafeteria, gym, and multipurpose rooms	Daylight 100% of floor area for 2/3 of school hours	DL1–5,7–21, 24–30,32–41	
		Administration areas	Daylight perimeter floor area (15 ft) for 2/3 of school hours	DL1–5,8–12	
	Interior Finishes	Interior surface average reflectance for daylighted rooms	Ceilings = 80% Wall surfaces = 70%	DL14	
	Interior Lighting	Lighting power density (LPD)	Whole building = 0.70 W/ft^2 Gyms, multipurpose rooms = 1.0 W/ft^2 Classrooms, art rooms, kitchens, libraries, media centers= 0.8 W/ft^2 Cafeterias, lobbies = 0.7 W/ft^2 Offices = 0.60 W/ft^2 Auditoriums, restrooms = 0.5 W/ft^2 Corridors, mechanical rooms = 0.4 W/ft^2	EL12–19	
		Light source lamp efficacy (mean lumens per watt)	T8 & T5 > 2 ft = 92, T8 & T5 ≤ 2 ft = 85, All other > 50	EL4–6	
		T8 ballasts	Non-dimming = NEMA Premium Instant Start Dimming= NEMA Premium Program Start	EL4–6	
		T5/T5HO ballasts	Electronic program start		
		CFL and HID ballasts	Electronic		
		Dimming controls daylight harvesting	Dim all fixtures in daylight zones	EL8,9,11–19	
		Lighting controls	Manual ON, auto/timed OFF in all areas as possible	EL8,9,11–20	
	Exterior Lighting	Façade and landscape lighting	LPD = 0.075 W/ft^2 in LZ-3 & LZ-4 LPD = 0.05 W/ft^2 in LZ-2 Controls = auto OFF between 12am and 6am	EL23	
		Parking lots and drives	LPD = 0.1 W/ft2 in LZ-3 & LZ-4 LPD = 0.06 W/ft2 in LZ-2 Controls = auto reduce to 25% (12am to 6am)	EL21	
		Walkways, plaza, and special feature areas	LPD = 0.16 W/ft^2 in LZ-3 & LZ-4 LPD = 0.14 W/ft^2 in LZ-2 Controls = auto reduce to 25% (12am to 6am)	EL22	
		All other exterior lighting	LPD = Comply with Standard 90.1* Controls = auto reduce to 25% (12am to 6am)	EL25	
Plug Loads	Equipment Choices	Laptop computers	Minimum 2/3 of total computers	PL2,3	
		ENERGY STAR equipment	All computers, equipment, and appliances	PL3,5	
		Vending machines	De-lamp and specify best in class efficiency	PL3,5	
	Controls/ Programs	Computer power control	Network control with power saving modes and control off during unoccupied hours	PL2,3	
		Power outlet control	Controllable power outlets with auto OFF during unoccupied hours for classrooms, office, library/ media spaces All plug-in equipment not requiring continuous operation to use controllable outlets	PL3,4	
		Policies	Implement at least one: • District/school policy on allowed equipment • School energy teams	PL3,4	

*Note: Where the table says "Comply with Standard 90.1," the user must meet the more stringent of either the applicable version of ASHRAE/IES Standard 90.1 or the local code requirements.

Climate Zone 8 Recommendation Table for K-12 School Buildings

	Item	Component	Recommendation	How-To Tips	✓
Kitchen	Kitchen Equipment	Cooking equipment	ENERGY STAR or California rebate-qualified equipment	KE1,2	
		Walk-in refrigeration equipment	6 in. insulation on low-temp walk-in equipment, Insulated floor, LED lighting, floating-head pressure controls, liquid pressure amplifier, subcooled liquid refrigerant, evaporative condenser	KE2,5	
		Exhaust hoods	Side panels, larger overhangs, rear seal at appliances, proximity hoods, VAV demand-based exhaust	KE3,6	
SWH	Service Water Heating	Gas water heater (condensing)	95% efficiency	WH1–5	
		Electric storage EF (≤12 kW, ≥20 gal)	$EF > 0.99 - 0.0012 \times Volume$	WH1–5	
		Point-of-use heater selection	0.81 EF or 81% E_t	WH1–5	
		Electric heat-pump water heater efficiency	COP 3.0 (interior heat source)	WH1–5	
		Solar hot-water heating	30% solar hot-water fraction when LCC effective	WH7	
		Pipe insulation ($d < 1.5$ in./$d \geq 1.5$ in.)	1/1.5 in.	WH6	
HVAC	Ground Source Heat-Pump (GSHP) System with DOAS	GSHP cooling efficiency	17.1 EER	HV1,11	
		GSHP heating efficiency	3.6 COP	HV1,11	
		GSHP compressor capacity control	Two stage or variable speed	HV1,11	
		Water-circulation pumps	VFD and NEMA Premium Efficiency	HV8	
		Cooling tower/fluid cooler	VFD on fans	HV1,8,11	
		Boiler efficiency	90% Ec	HV1,7,11	
		Maximum fan power	0.4 W/cfm	HV12	
		Exhaust air energy recovery in DOAS	60% dry-bulb temperature reduction	HV4,5	
		DOAS ventilation control	DCV with VFD	HV4,10,15	
	Fan-Coil System with DOAS	Water-cooled chiller efficiency	Comply with Standard 90.1*	HV2,6,11	
		Water circulation pumps	VFD and NEMA Premium Efficiency	HV6,7	
		Boiler efficiency	90% E_c	HV2,7,11	
		Maximum fan power	0.4 W/cfm	HV12	
		FCU fans	Multiple speed	HV2,12	
		Economizer	Comply with Standard 90.1*	HV2,14	
		Exhaust air energy recovery in DOAS	60% dry-bulb temperature reduction	HV4,5	
		DOAS ventilation control	DCV with VFD	HV4,10,15	
	VAV Air-Handling System with DOAS	Air-cooled chiller efficiency	10 EER; 12.75 IPLV	HV3,6,11	
		Water-cooled chiller efficiency	Comply with Standard 90.1*	HV3,6,11	
		Water circulation pumps	VFD and NEMA Premium Efficiency	HV6,7	
		Boiler efficiency	90% E_c	HV3,7,11	
		Maximum fan power	0.8 W/cfm	HV12	
		Economizer	Comply with Standard 90.1*	HV3,14	
		Exhaust air energy recovery in DOAS	60% dry-bulb temperature reduction	HV4,5	
		DOAS ventilation control	DCV with VFD	HV4,10,15	
	Ducts and Dampers	Outdoor air damper	Motorized damper	HV10	
		Duct seal class	Seal Class A	HV20	
		Insulation level	R-6	HV19	
QA	Measurement &Verification	Electrical submeters	Disaggregate submeters for lighting, HVAC, general 120V, renewables, and whole building	QA14–17	
		Benchmarking	Begin submetering early to address issues during warranty period Benchmark monthly energy use Provide training on benchmarking	QA14–17	

*Note: Where the table says "Comply with Standard 90.1," the user must meet the more stringent of either the applicable version of ASHRAE/IES Standard 90.1 or the local code requirements.

How to Implement Recommendations

5

Recommendations are contained in the individual tables in Chapter 4, "Design Strategies and Recommendations by Climate Zone." The following how-to tips are intended to provide guidance on good practices for implementing the recommendations as well as cautions to avoid known problems in energy-efficient construction.

ENVELOPE

OPAQUE ENVELOPE COMPONENTS

Good Design Practice

EN1   *Cool Roofs* (Climate Zones: ❶ ❷ ❸)

To be considered a cool roof, a Solar Reflectance Index (SRI) of 78 or higher is recommended. A high reflectance keeps much of the sun's energy from being absorbed while a high thermal emissivity surface radiates away any solar energy that is absorbed, allowing the roof to cool more rapidly. Cool roofs are typically white and have a smooth surface. Commercial roof products that qualify as cool roofs fall into three categories: single-ply, liquid-applied, and metal panels. Examples are presented in Table 5-1.

Table 5-1   Examples of Cool Roofs

Category	Product	Reflectance	Emissivity	SRI
Single ply	White polyvinyl chloride (PVC)	0.86	0.86	107
	White chlorinated polyethylene (CPE)	0.86	0.88	108
	White chlorosulfonated polyethylene (CPSE)	0.85	0.87	106
	White thermoplastic polyolefin (TSO)	0.77	0.87	95
Liquid applied	White elastomeric, polyurethane, acrylic coating	0.71	0.86	86
	White paint (on metal or concrete)	0.71	0.85	86
Metal panels	Factory-coated white finish	0.90	0.87	113

The solar reflectance and thermal emissivity property values represent initial conditions as determined by a laboratory accredited by the Cool Roof Rating Council (CRRC). An SRI can be determined by the following equations:

$$SRI = 123.97 - 141.35(\chi) + 9.655(\chi^2)$$

where

$$\chi = \frac{20.797 \times \alpha - 0.603 \times \varepsilon}{9.5205 \times \varepsilon + 12.0}$$

and

α = solar absorptance = 1 – solar reflectance
ε = thermal emissivity

These equations were derived from ASTM E1980 assuming a medium wind speed. Note that cool roofs are not a substitute for the appropriate amount of insulation.

EN2 Roofs—Insulation Entirely above Deck (Climate Zones: all)

The insulation entirely above deck should be continuous insulation (c.i.) rigid boards. Continuous insulation is important because no framing members are present that would introduce thermal bridges or short circuits to bypass the insulation. When two layers of c.i. are used in this construction, the board edges should be staggered to reduce the potential for convection losses or thermal bridging. If an inverted or protected membrane roof system is used, at least one layer of insulation is placed above the membrane and a maximum of one layer is placed beneath the membrane.

EN3 Roofs—Attics, and Other Roofs (Climate Zones: all)

Attics and other roofs include roofs with insulation entirely below (inside of) the roof structure (i.e., attics and cathedral ceilings) and roofs with insulation both above and below the roof structure. Ventilated attic spaces need to have the insulation installed at the ceiling line. Unventilated attic spaces may have the insulation installed at the roof line. When suspended ceilings with removable ceiling tiles are used, the insulation performance is best when installed at the roof line. For buildings with attic spaces, ventilation should be provided equal to 1 ft^2 of open area per 100 ft^2 of attic space. This will provide adequate ventilation as long as the openings are split between the bottom and top of the attic space. Additional ventilation can further improve the performance of the building.

For single-rafter roofs, the roof above and ceiling below are both attached to the same wood rafter, and the cavity insulation is located between the wood rafters. Continuous insulation, when recommended, is installed at the bottom of the rafters and above the ceiling material. Single rafters can be constructed with solid wood or truss-type framing members. The cavity insulation should be installed between the wood rafters and in intimate contact with the ceiling to avoid the potential thermal short circuiting associated with open or exposed air spaces.

EN4 Roofs—Metal Buildings (Climate Zones: all)

Metal buildings pose particular challenges in the pursuit of designing and constructing advanced buildings. The metal skin and purlin/girt connection, even with compressed fiberglass between them, is highly conductive, which limits the effectiveness of the insulation. A purlin is a horizontal structural member that supports the roof covering. In metal building construction, this is typically a z-shaped cold-formed steel member; but a steel bar or open web joists can be used for longer spans.

The thermal performance of metal building roofs with fiberglass batts is improved by treating the thermal bridging associated with fasteners. Use of foam blocks is a proven technique to reduce the thermal bridging. Thermal blocks, with minimum dimensions of 1 × 3 in., should be R-5 rigid insulation installed parallel to the purlins. (See Figure 5-1.)

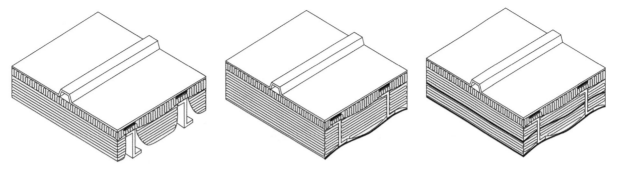

**Figure 5-1 (EN4) Prefabricated Metal Roofs Showing Thermal Blocking of Purlins—
(a) Filled Cavity; (b) Liner System, One Layer; and (c) Liner System, Two Layers**

Thermal blocks can be used successfully with standing seam roofs that utilize concealed clips of varying heights to accommodate the block. However, a thermal block cannot be used with a through-fastened roof that is screwed directly to the purlins because it diminishes the structural load carrying capacity by "softening" the connection and restraint provided to the purlin by the roof.

In climate zones 1 through 3, the recommended construction is a filled cavity that has the first layer of insulation, R-10, perpendicular to and over the top of the purlins, and the second layer of insulation, R-19, parallel to and between the purlins (see Figure 5-1a).

In climate zones 4 through 7, the recommended construction is a liner system that has the first layer of insulation parallel to and between the purlins, and the second layer of insulation perpendicular to and over the top of the purlins (see Figure 5-1b).

In climate zone 8, the recommended construction is a liner system with the first and second layers of insulation parallel to and between the purlins, and the third layer of insulation perpendicular to and over the top of the purlins (see Figure 5-1c).

Continuous rigid insulation can be added to provide additional insulation if required to meet the U-factors listed in Appendix A. In any case, rigid c.i. or other high-performance insulation systems may be used provided the total roof assembly has a U-factor that is less than or equal to the appropriate climate zone construction listed in Appendix A.

EN5 *Walls—Mass* **(Climate Zones: all)**

Mass walls are defined as those with a heat capacity exceeding 7 Btu/ft^2·°F. Insulation may be placed either on the inside or the outside of the mass wall. When insulation is placed on the exterior, rigid c.i. is recommended. When insulation is placed on the interior, a furring or framing system may be used, provided the total wall assembly has a U-factor that is less than or equal to the appropriate climate zone construction listed in Appendix A.

The greatest advantages of mass can be obtained when insulation is placed on its exterior. In this case, the mass absorbs heat from the interior spaces that is later released in the evenings when the buildings are not occupied. The thermal mass of a building (typically contained in the building envelope) absorbs heat during the day and reduces the magnitude of indoor air temperature swings, reduces peak cooling loads, and transfers some of the absorbed heat into the night hours. The cooling load can then be covered by passive cooling techniques (natural ventilation) when the outdoor conditions are more favorable. An unoccupied building can also be precooled during the night by natural or mechanical ventilation to reduce the cooling energy use. This same effect reduces heating load as well.

Thermal mass also has a positive effect on thermal comfort. High-mass buildings attenuate interior air and wall temperature variations and sustain a stable overall thermal environment. This increases thermal comfort, particularly during mild seasons (spring and fall), during large air temperature changes (high solar gain), and in areas with large day-night temperature swings.

Insulated Concrete Form Exterior Wall Assembly

Construction of an Insulated Concrete Form Wall

Alvaton Elementary school, a 70,000 ft^2 facility in Bowling Green, Kentucky, was the first school in the state to utilize an insulated concrete form (ICF) exterior wall assembly in lieu of the more traditional block/brick wall assembly. Since this school was completed in 2005, ICF has become a common exterior wall construction technique used in approximately 50 other education facilities in the state.

ICF exterior wall construction was originally chosen by the district to improve the thermal performance of the envelope. After one year of successful operation, the energy use intensity (EUI) was the lowest known for any school in Kentucky at that time.

While the ICF wall assembly bid was more expensive than that of traditional exterior wall systems, several surprises became apparent once construction began. First, construction was significantly faster which allowed the contractor to improve the project schedule. Second, while a traditional block wall system required an electrical contractor to work alongside the block contractor to install conduit in the wall, the electrical contractor was not required to be on site for the ICF walls construction, which resulted in savings on contractor labor. The construction costs for subsequent ICF projects became so competitive with brick and block projects that the ICF system is now being used for interior walls on many projects.

Designers should keep in mind that the occupants will be the final determinants of a building system's usability, including the effects of thermal mass. Changing the use of internal spaces and surfaces can drastically reduce the effectiveness of thermal storage. The final use of the space must be considered when making the heating and cooling load calculations and incorporating possible energy savings from thermal mass effects.

EN6   Walls—Steel Framed (Climate Zones: all)

Cold-formed steel framing members are thermal bridges to the cavity insulation. Adding exterior foam sheathing as c.i. is the preferred method to upgrade the wall thermal performance because it is not degraded by the thermal bridges.

Alternative combinations of cavity insulation and sheathing in thicker steel-framed walls can be used, provided that the proposed total wall assembly has a U-factor that is less than or equal to the U-factor for the appropriate climate zone construction listed in Appendix A. Batt insulation installed in cold-formed steel-framed wall assemblies is to be ordered as "full width batts" and installation is normally by friction fit. Batt insulation should fill the entire cavity and not be cut short.

EN7   *Walls—Wood Frame and Other* (Climate Zones: all)

Cavity insulation is used within the wood-frame wall, while rigid c.i. is placed on the exterior side of the framing. Care must be taken to have a vapor retarder on the warm side of the wall and to utilize a vapor-retarder-faced batt insulation product to avoid insulation sagging away from the vapor retarder.

Alternative combinations of cavity insulations and sheathings in thicker walls can be used, provided the total wall assembly has a U-factor that is less than or equal to the appropriate climate zone construction listed in Appendix A. Batt insulation should fill the entire cavity and not be cut short.

EN8   *Walls—Metal Building* (Climate Zones: all)

In all climate zones, rigid c.i. on the exterior of the girts is the recommendation. Alternate constructions are allowed provided the total wall assembly has a U-factor that is less than or equal to the appropriate climate zone construction listed in Appendix A.

If a single layer of faced fiberglass batt insulation is proposed, the insulation is installed continuously perpendicular to the exterior of the girts and is compressed as the metal panel is attached to the girts. If a layer of faced fiberglass batt insulation and a layer of rigid board insulation are proposed, the layer of faced fiberglass is installed continuously perpendicular to the exterior of the girts and is compressed as the rigid board insulation is installed continuously and perpendicular, then attached to the girts from the exterior (on top of the fiberglass). The metal panels are then attached over the rigid board insulation using screws that penetrate through the insulation assembly into the girts.

EN9   *Below-Grade Walls* (Climate Zones: ❸ ❹ ❺ ❻ ❼ ❽)

Insulation, when recommended, may be placed either on the inside or the outside of the below-grade wall. If placed on the exterior of the wall, rigid c.i. is recommended. If placed on the interior of the wall, a furring or framing system is recommended, provided the total wall assembly has a C-factor that is less than or equal to the appropriate climate zone construction listed in Appendix A.

When heated slabs are placed below grade, below-grade walls should meet the insulation recommendations for perimeter insulation according to the heated slab-on-grade construction.

EN10   *Floors—Mass* (Climate Zones: all)

Insulation should be continuous and either integral to or above the slab. This can be achieved by placing high-density extruded polystyrene above the slab, with either plywood or a thin layer of concrete on top. Placing insulation below the deck is not recommended due to losses through any concrete support columns or through the slab perimeter.

Exception: Buildings or zones within buildings that have durable floors for heavy machinery or equipment could place insulation below the deck.

EN11   *Floors—Metal Joist or Wood Joist/Wood Frame* (Climate Zones: all)

Insulation should be installed parallel to the framing members and in intimate contact with the flooring system supported by the framing member in order to avoid the potential thermal short circuiting associated with open or exposed air spaces. Non-rigid insulation should be supported from below, no less frequently than 24 in. on center.

EN12 *Slab-on-Grade Floors—Unheated* (Climate Zones: ⑥ ❼ ❽)

Rigid c.i. should be used around the perimeter of the slab and should reach the depth listed in the recommendation or to the bottom of the footing, whichever is less.

EN13 *Slab-on-Grade Floors—Heated* (Climate Zones: all)

Continuous rigid insulation should be used around the perimeter of the slab and should reach to the depth listed or to the frost line, whichever is deeper. Additionally, in climate zone 8, continuous insulation should be placed below the slab as well.

Note: In areas where termites are a concern and rigid insulation is not recommended for use under the slab, a different heating system should be used.

EN14 *Slab Edge Insulation* (Climate Zones: all)

Use of slab edge insulation improves thermal performance, but problems can occur in regions that have termites.

EN15 *Doors—Opaque, Swinging* (Climate Zones: all)

A U-factor of 0.5 corresponds to an insulated double-panel metal door. A U-factor of 0.7 corresponds to a double-panel metal door. If at all possible, single swinging doors should be used. Double swinging doors are difficult to seal at the center of the doors unless there is a center post. Double swinging doors without a center post should be minimized and limited to areas where width is important. Vestibules or revolving doors can be added to further improve the energy efficiency. See Figure 5-2.

EN16 *Doors—Opaque, Roll-Up, or Sliding* (Climate Zones: all)

Roll-up or sliding doors are recommended to have R-4.75 rigid insulation or meet the recommended U-factor. When meeting the recommended U-factor, the thermal bridging at the door and section edges is to be included in the analysis. Roll-up doors that have solar exposure should be painted with a reflective paint (or should be high emissivity) and should be shaded. Metal doors are a problem in that they typically have poor emissivity and collect heat, which is transmitted through even the best insulated door and causes cooling loads and thermal comfort issues.

If at all possible, use insulated panel doors over roll-up doors, as the insulation values can approach R-10 and provide a tighter seal to minimize infiltration.

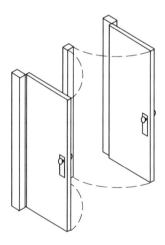

Figure 5-2   (EN15) Double Doors with a Center Post
Opaque doors with hinges on one side.

EN17 *Air Infiltration Control* (Climate Zones: all)

The building envelope should be designed and constructed with a continuous air barrier system to control air leakage into or out of the conditioned space and should extend over all surfaces of the building envelope (at the lowest floor, exterior walls, and ceiling or roof). An air barrier system should also be provided for interior separations between conditioned spaces and semi-conditioned spaces. Semi-conditioned spaces maintain temperature or humidity levels that vary significantly from those in conditioned space. The variance must be more than 50% of the difference between the conditioned space and design ambient conditions. If possible, a blower door should be used to depressurize the building to find leaks in the infiltration barrier. At a minimum, the air barrier system should have the following characteristics.

- It should be continuous, with all joints made airtight.
- Air barrier materials used in frame walls should have an air permeability not to exceed 0.004 cfm/ft^2 under a pressure differential of 0.3 in. H$_2$O (1.57 lb/ft^2) when tested in accordance with ASTM E 2178.
- The system should be able to withstand positive and negative combined design wind, fan, and stack pressures on the envelope without damage or displacement and should transfer the load to the structure. It should not displace adjacent materials under full load.
- It should be durable or maintainable.
- The air barrier material of an envelope assembly should be joined in an airtight and flexible manner to the air barrier material of adjacent assemblies, allowing for the relative movement of these assemblies and components due to thermal and moisture variations, creep, and structural deflection.
- Connections should be made between the following:
  a. Foundation and walls
  b. Walls and windows or doors
  c. Different wall systems
  d. Wall and roof
  e. Wall and roof over unconditioned space
  f. Walls, floors, and roof across construction, control, and expansion joints
  g. Walls, floors, and roof to utility, pipe, and duct penetrations
- All penetrations of the air barrier system and paths of air infiltration/exfiltration should be made airtight.

EN18 *Vestibules* (Climate Zones: ❸ ❹ ❺ ❻ ❼ ❽)

Vestibules are recommended for building entrances routinely used by occupants, not for emergency exits, maintenance doors, loading docks, or any other specialty entrances. Occupant entrances that separate conditioned space from the exterior shall be protected with an enclosed vestibule, with all doors opening into and out of the vestibule equipped with self-closing devices. Vestibules shall be designed so that in passing through the vestibule it is not necessary for the interior and exterior doors to open at the same time. Interior and exterior doors shall have a minimum distance between them of not less than 16 ft when in the closed position. Vestibules shall be designed only as areas to traverse between the exterior and the interior. The exterior envelope of conditioned vestibules shall comply with the requirements for a conditioned space. Either the interior or exterior envelope of unconditioned vestibules shall comply with the requirements for a conditioned space.

Options

EN19 *Alternative Constructions* (Climate Zones: all)

The climate zone recommendations provide only one solution for upgrading the thermal performance of the envelope. Other constructions can be equally effective, but they are not shown in this document. Any alternative construction that is less than or equal to the U-factor, C-factor, or F-factor presented in Appendix A for the appropriate climate zone construction is equally acceptable. U-factors, C-factors, and F-factors that correspond to all the recommendations are presented in Appendix A.

Procedures to calculate U-factors and C-factors are presented in *ASHRAE Handbook—Fundamentals* (ASHRAE 2009), and expanded U-factor, C-factor, and F-factor tables are presented in Appendix A of ASHRAE/IES Standard 90.1 (ASHRAE 2010a).

Cautions

The design of building envelopes for durability, indoor environmental quality, and energy conservation should not create conditions of accelerated deterioration or reduced thermal performance or problems associated with moisture, air infiltration, or termites.

The following cautions should be incorporated into the design and construction of the building.

EN20 *Truss Heel Heights* (Climate Zones: all)

When insulation levels are increased in attic spaces, the truss heel height should be raised to avoid or at least minimize the eave compression. Roof insulation should extend to the exterior of the walls to minimize edge effects.

EN21 *Moisture Control* (Climate Zones: all)

Building envelope assemblies (see Figures 5-3a and 5-3b) should be designed to prevent wetting, high moisture content, liquid water intrusion, and condensation caused by diffusion of water vapor. See Chapter 24 of *ASHRAE Handbook—Fundamentals* (ASHRAE 2009) for additional information.

EN22 *Thermal Bridging—Opaque Components* (Climate Zones: all)

Thermal bridging in opaque components occurs when continuous conductive elements connect internal and external surfaces. The adverse effects of thermal bridging are most notable in cold climates where frost can develop on internal surfaces and lead to water droplets when the indoor temperature increases. The solution to thermal bridging is to provide thermal breaks or continuous insulation. Common problem areas are parapets, foundations and penetrations of insulation.

The thermal bridge at parapets is shown in Figure 5-4a. The problem is that a portion of the wall construction is extended to create a parapet that extends above the roof to ensure worker safety per local code requirements. Since the wall insulation is on the outer face of the structure, it does not naturally connect to the insulation at the roof structure. The solution is to wrap the parapet with continuous insulation in the appropriate locations, as shown in Figure 5-4b; a structural solution is to have an independent parapet structure that periodically penetrates the roof insulation line to limit the thermal bridging effects.

Thermal bridges in foundations are shown in Figure 5-5a. This detail usually occurs because of construction sequences for the installation of below-grade works early in the design process. It is often an oversight to complete the connection between the below-grade and above-grade thermal protection because the installations of these elements are separate both in discipline and in time period on site. Design and construction teams must make it clear that action to establish thermal continuity of the insulation line is a performance requirement of both parties in order to achieve a typical solution, as shown in Figure 5-5b. The insulation above grade needs to be protected with a surface or coating that is weather resistant and abuse tolerant.

Penetrations of insulation in which metal structural members must protrude from the building in order to support an external shade or construction (balcony, signage, etc.) need to be insulated. In these cases, the insulation should wrap the protruding metal piece when it is within the indoor cavity, and an additional length of insulation should be provided on its connection in each direction in order to prevent excessive heat transfer from the metal into the internal wall cavity. It should be noted that a façade consultant can model these types of situations to advise on the various lengths and thicknesses of insulation that would be needed to limit adverse impacts from condensation within the wall cavity.

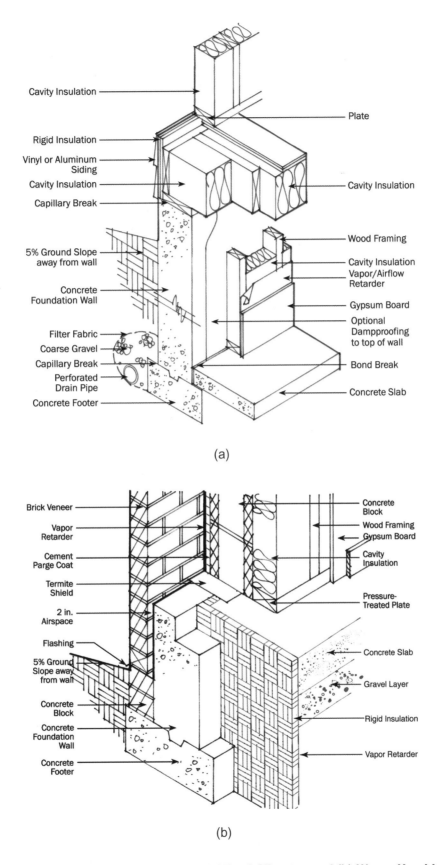

Labels for (a):
Cavity Insulation
Plate
Rigid Insulation
Vinyl or Aluminum Siding
Cavity Insulation
Capillary Break
Cavity Insulation
5% Ground Slope away from wall
Wood Framing
Cavity Insulation
Vapor/Airflow Retarder
Gypsum Board
Concrete Foundation Wall
Optional Dampproofing to top of wall
Filter Fabric
Coarse Gravel
Capillary Break
Perforated Drain Pipe
Concrete Footer
Bond Break
Concrete Slab

(a)

Labels for (b):
Brick Veneer
Concrete Block
Vapor Retarder
Wood Framing
Gypsum Board
Cement Parge Coat
Cavity Insulation
Termite Shield
2 in. Airspace
Flashing
Pressure-Treated Plate
5% Ground Slope away from wall
Concrete Slab
Concrete Block
Gravel Layer
Concrete Foundation Wall
Rigid Insulation
Concrete Footer
Vapor Retarder

(b)

Figure 5-3   (EN21) Moisture Control for (a) Mixed Climates and (b) Warm, Humid Climates

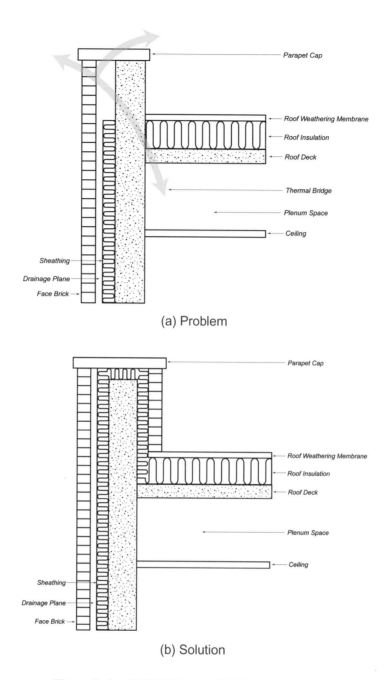

(a) Problem

(b) Solution

Figure 5-4 (EN22) Thermal Bridges—Parapets

EN23   *Thermal Bridging—Fenestration* (Climate Zones: all)

A typical fenestration situation where thermal bridging arises is at the detailing of how a piece of well-insulated glazing abuts the opaque façade, whether it be through a metal mullion system or whether it just frames into the wall. Windows that are installed out of the plane of the wall insulation are an example of this construction (shown in Figure 5-6a).

The normal solution is not to rebuild the wall but to blow hot air against the window to increase the interior surface temperature of the frame and glazing, which increases the temperature difference across the glazing and reduces the interior film coefficient thermal resistance from 0.68 to 0.25 h·ft^2·°F/Btu.

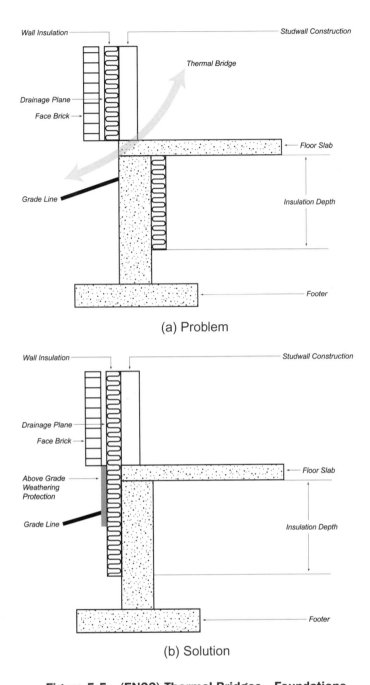

Figure 5-5 (EN22) Thermal Bridges—Foundations

Careful specification is also necessary to ensure that the framing of the glazed units also incorporates a thermal break. Installing the fenestration outside of the plane of the wall insulation defeats the thermal break in the window frame. Fenestration should be installed to align the frame thermal break with the wall thermal barrier (see Figure 5-6b). This will minimize the thermal bridging of the frame due to fenestration projecting beyond the insulating layers in the wall.

In colder climates, it is essential to select a glazing unit to avoid condensation and frosting. This requires an analysis to determine internal surface temperatures, since glass is a higher thermal conductor as compared to the adjacent wall in which it is mounted. There is a risk of condensation occurring on the inner face of the glass whenever the inner surface temperature approaches the room dew-point temperature.

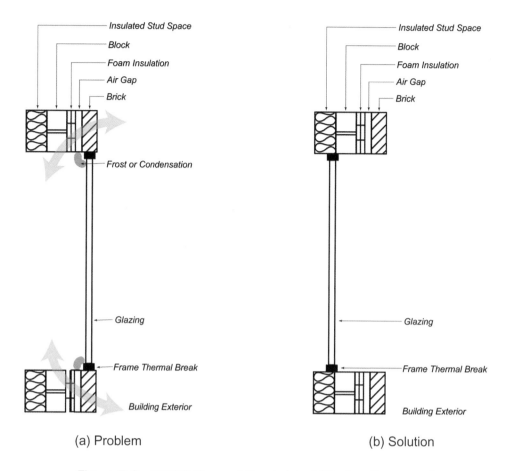

Figure 5-6 (EN23) Thermal Break (a) at Window Frame and (b) in Window Frame Aligned with Wall Insulation

VERTICAL FENESTRATION

Good Design Practice

EN24   *Fenestration Descriptions* (Climate Zones: all)

Fenestration refers to the light transmitting areas of a wall or roof, utilized as either view windows or daylighting fenestrations, but also includes glass doors and glass block walls. Vertical fenestration includes sloped glazing if it has a slope equal to or more than 70° from the horizontal. If it slopes less than 70° from the horizontal, the fenestration falls in the skylight category. This means that clerestories, roof monitors, and other such fenestration fall in the vertical category.

The recommendations for vertical fenestration specify the U-factor, solar heat gain coefficient (SHGC), and the whole window visible transmittance (VT). Specific descriptions of representative vertical fenestration products that would comply with these recommendations for each climate zone are presented in Table 5-2.

The recommendations regarding VT and SHGC shall be characterized by the following:

- Fenestration orientation
- Whether the fenestration is a daylighting fenestration or view window
- ASHRAE climatic zone

Table 5-2 Vertical Fenestration Descriptions

CZ	U-Factor	SHGC	VT	Glass and Coating	Gas	Spacer	Frame
1	0.50	0.26	0.40	Low-e semi-reflective	Air	Metal	Thermally improved
1	0.57	0.63	0.66	Double clear	Air	Metal	Thermal break
1–2	0.64	0.64	0.66	Double clear	Air	Metal	Thermally improved
2	0.43	0.24	0.40	Low-e semi-reflective	Air	Metal	Thermal broken
2	0.45	0.50	0.63	Low-e double	Air	Metal	Thermal broken
3	0.41	0.23	0.40	Low-e semi-reflective	Air	Insulated	Thermal broken
3	0.39	0.49	0.63	Low-e double	Argon	Insulated	Thermal broken
3	0.59	0.27	0.30	Low-e reflective	Air	Metal	No break
3	0.57	0.63	0.66	Double clear	Air	Metal	Thermal broken
4	0.37	0.35	0.59	Selective Low-e double	Argon	Insulated	Thermal broken
4	0.39	0.49	0.63	Low-e double	Argon	Insulated	Thermal broken
4–5	0.44	0.36	0.59	Selective Low-e double	Air	Metal	Thermal broken
4–5	0.43	0.50	0.63	Low-e double	Air	Insulated	Thermal broken
5	0.45	0.50	0.63	Low-e double	Air	Metal	Thermal broken
5–6	0.33	0.34	0.59	Selective Low-e double	Argon	Insulated	Thermally isolated
5–6	0.34	0.48	0.63	Low-e double	Argon	Insulated	Thermally isolated
6	0.41	0.36	0.59	Selective Low-e double	Air	Insulated	Thermal broken
6	0.43	0.50	0.63	Low-e double	Air	Insulated	Thermal broken
7–8	0.33	0.34	0.59	Selective Low-e double	Argon	Insulated	Thermally isolated
7–8	0.34	0.48	0.63	Low-e double	Argon	Insulated	Thermally isolated
8	0.24	0.40	0.54	LowE 2 Lites Triple	2 Argon	Insulated	Thermally isolated

Note: SHGC = solar heat gain coefficient; VT= visible transmittance

The orientation of the fenestration shall be determined by the following:

- Fenestrations that are located within 30° of true north or south shall be considered north or south facing.
- Fenestrations that are located within 60° of true east or west shall be considered east or west facing.

View Windows. All fenestrations shall be considered view windows (as opposed to daylighting fenestrations) if the fenestration is located at a height below 7 ft above finished floor (AFF) and is *not* classified as a daylighting fenestration.

Daylighting Fenestrations. Windows below 7 ft AFF can be considered daylighting fenestrations if they are

- north-facing, below 7 ft AFF, and designed to reduce contrast (uniformity illuminance ratio less than 10:1 within the intended daylighted space); or
- south-, east-, or west-facing, below 7 ft AFF, and have a VT below 0.30.

All fenestrations not considered daylighting fenestrations must comply with the solar heat gain coefficients (SHGC) restrictions and glass amounts delineated in Table 5-3. This table represents a maximum of the product of the SHGC times the view window-to-floor area ratio (VFR).

If the fenestration is a daylighting fenestration, the minimum and maximum prescriptive fenestration-to-floor area ratio (FFR) for each individual room/space should be used. The floor area shall be defined as the intended daylighted space. Not all areas (e.g., the projection screen area) within an individual room/space within a school may want to be daylighted. If the VT values vary significantly (over 10%) from those listed, it will be necessary to conduct a separate daylighting simulation to accurately account for the deviation.

Table 5-3   Effective Solar Heat Gain by Climate Zone

	Component	Orientation	CZ 1	CZ 2	CZ 3	CZ 4	CZ 5	CZ 6	CZ 7	CZ 8
View Fenestration	Maximum VFR	East/west	5%	5%	5%	5%	5%	5%	5%	5%
		North	7%	7%	7%	7%	7%	7%	7%	7%
		South	7%	7%	7%	7%	7%	7%	7%	7%
	Maximum SHGC	East/west	0.25	0.25	0.25	0.40	0.42	0.42	0.45	0.45
		North	0.62	0.62	0.62	0.62	0.62	0.62	0.62	0.62
		South	0.25	0.50	0.75	0.75	0.75	0.75	0.75	0.75
	Effective solar heat gain	East/west	0.0125	0.0125	0.0125	0.0200	0.0210	0.0210	0.0225	0.0225
		North	0.0434	0.0434	0.0434	0.0434	0.0434	0.0434	0.0434	0.0434
		South	0.0175	0.0350	0.0525	0.0525	0.0525	0.0525	0.0525	0.0525

Note: Effective solar heat gain by space = maximum SHGC × VFR.

The recommendations for view windows are listed in Chapter 4 by climate zone. To be useful and consistent, the U-factors for windows should be measured over the entire window assembly, not just the center of the glass. Look for a label that denotes the window rating is certified by the National Fenestration Rating Council (NFRC). The selection of high-performance window products should be considered separately for each orientation of the building and for daylighting and viewing functions.

To meet the SHGC recommendations for view windows in Chapter 4, use the SHGC multipliers for permanent projections, as provided in Table 5-4. These multipliers allow for a higher SHGC for vertical fenestration with overhangs. For an overhang with a projection factor greater than 0.5, the recommended SHGC can be increased by 64%. For example, the recommended SHGC in climate zone 1 is 0.25. For an overhang with a projection factor of 0.5, a SHGC of 0.4 is acceptable.

EN25   *View Window-to Floor Area Ratio (VFR)* (Climate Zones: all)

The VFR is the percentage resulting from dividing the total view window area by the total floor area of the individual room/space. This differs from the daylighting fenestration-to-floor area ratio (DFR), which considers just the floor area to be the intended daylighted space.

The total of the view windows and daylighting fenestrations divided by overall floor area of the space/room shall not, in any case, exceed the percentages delineated for each climate zone in Table 5-3. A reduction in the view fenestration will also save energy, especially if glazing is significantly reduced on the east and west facades. The smallest glazed area should be designed that is still consistent with needs for view, daylighting, and passive solar strategies.

WINDOW DESIGN GUIDELINES FOR THERMAL CONDITIONS

Uncontrolled solar heat gain is a major cause of energy use for cooling in warmer climates and thermal discomfort for occupants. Appropriate configuration of windows according to the orientation of the wall on which they are placed can significantly reduce these problems.

EN26   *Unwanted Solar Heat Gain Is Most Effectively Controlled on the Outside of the Building* (Climate Zones: all)

Significantly greater energy savings are realized when sun penetration is blocked before it enters the windows. Horizontal overhangs at the top of the windows are most effective for south-facing facades and must continue beyond the width of the windows to adequately shade them. Vertical fins can be problematic in schools from the perspective of vandalism. Consider louvered or perforated sun-control devices, especially in primarily overcast and colder climates, to prevent a totally dark appearance in those environments.

EN27   *Operable versus Fixed Windows* (Climate Zones: all)

Operable windows offer the advantage of personal comfort control and beneficial connections to the environment. However, individual operation of the windows not in coordination with the

Table 5-4 SHGC Multipliers for Permanent Projections

Projection Factor	SHGC Multiplier (All Other Orientations)	SHGC Multiplier (North-Oriented)
0–0.10	1.00	1.00
>0.10–0.20	0.91	0.95
>0.20–0.30	0.82	0.91
>0.30–0.40	0.74	0.87
>0.40–0.50	0.67	0.84
>0.50–0.60	0.61	0.81
>0.60–0.70	0.56	0.78
>0.70–0.80	0.51	0.76
>0.80–0.90	0.47	0.75
>0.90–1.00	0.44	0.73

Source: ASHRAE (2004) Table 5.5.4.4.1

HVAC system settings and requirements can have extreme impacts on the energy use of a building's system. Advanced energy-efficient buildings with operable windows should strive for a high level of integration between envelope and HVAC system design. First, the envelope should be designed to take advantage of natural ventilation with well-placed operable openings. Second, the mechanical system should use interlocks on operable windows to ensure that the HVAC system responds by shutting down in the affected zone if the window is opened. The window interlock zones need to be designed to correspond as closely as possible to the HVAC zone affected by the open window. See HV29 for more information.

Warm Climates

EN28   *Building Form and Window Orientation* (Climate Zones: ❶ ❷ ❸ ④)

In warm climates, north- and south-facing glass can be more easily shielded and can result in less solar heat gain and glare than do east- and west-facing glass. During site selection, preference should be given to sites that permit elongating the building in the east-west direction and that permit orienting more windows to the north and south. A good design strategy avoids areas of glass that do not contribute to the view from the building or to the daylighting of the space. If possible, configure the building to optimize north- and south-facing walls and glass by elongating the floor plan on an east-west axis. Since sun control devices are less effective on the east and west facades, the solar penetration through the east- and west-facing glazing should be minimized. This can be done by reducing the area of glazing or, if the glass is needed for view or egress, by reducing the SHGC. For buildings where a predominantly east-west exposure is unavoidable, more aggressive energy conservation measures will be required in other building components to achieve an overall 50% energy savings.

EN29   *Glazing* (Climate Zones: ❶ ❷ ❸ ④)

For north- and south-facing windows, select windows with a low SHGC and an appropriate VT (see EN24). Certain window coatings, called *selective low-e*, transmit the visible portions of the solar spectrum selectively, rejecting the nonvisible infrared sections. These glass and coating selections can provide a balance between VT and solar heat gain. Window manufacturers market special "solar low-e" windows for warm climates. For buildings in warm climates that do not use a daylight design, north and south view windows should be limited to values no higher than those recommended in Table 5-3. East- and west-facing windows in warm climates should be selected for an SHGC no higher than 0.25. All values are for the entire fenestration assembly, in compliance with NFRC procedures, and are not simply center-of-glass values. For warm climates, a low SHGC is much more important for low-energy use than the window assembly U-factor. Windows with low SHGC values will tend to have a low center-of-glass U-factor because they are designed to reduce the conduction of the solar heat gain absorbed on the outer layer of glass through to the inside of the window. Structural performance, hurricane impact-resistant requirements in coastal areas, and durability must also be considered since they will affect fenestration product selection and the resulting energy performance. This is particularly true when schools are used as designated storm shelters.

EN30   *Obstructions and Planting* (Climate Zones: all)

Adjacent taller buildings and trees, shrubs, or other plantings effectively shade glass on south, east and west facades. For south-facing windows, remember that the sun is higher in the sky during the summer, so shading plants should be located high above the windows to effectively shade the glass. Also, be careful to not block south light that is being counted on for daylighting or passive heating. The glazing of fully shaded windows can be selected with higher SHGC ratings without increasing energy use. The solar reflections from adjacent building with reflective surfaces (metal, windows, or especially reflective curtain walls) should be considered in the design. Such reflections may modify shading strategies, especially on the north facade.

Cold Climates

EN31   *Window Orientation* (Climate Zones: ⑤ ⑥ ❼ ❽)

Only the south glass receives much sunlight during the cold winter months. If possible, maximize south-facing windows by elongating the floor plan in the east-west direction, and relocate windows to the south face. By facing the glazing south and not extending it too low to the floor, it is easy to implement overhangs and simple sun-control devices that allow for passive heating when desired but prevent unwanted glare and solar overheating in the warmer months. Glass facing east and west should be significantly limited. Areas of glazing facing north should be optimized for daylighting and view. During site selection, preference should be given to sites that permit elongating the building in the east-west direction and that permit orienting more windows to the south.

EN32   *Passive Solar* (Climate Zones: ⑤ ⑥ ❼ ❽)

Passive solar energy-saving strategies should be limited to office spaces or spaces other than classrooms, such as lobbies and circulation areas, unless those strategies are designed so that occupants are not affected by direct beam radiation. To use passive solar heating, the solar radiation must be diffused as it enters into the classrooms. Consider light-colored blinds, blinds within the fenestration, or light shelves to control solar heat gain. In spaces where glare is not an issue, the usefulness of the solar heat gain collected by these windows can be increased by using hard, massive, darker colored floor surfaces, such as tile or concrete, in locations where the transmitted sunlight will fall. These floor surfaces absorb the transmitted solar heat gain and release it slowly over time to provide a more gradual heating of the structure. Consider higher SHGC, low-e glazing with optimally designed exterior overhangs.

EN33   *Glazing* (Climate Zones: ⑤ ⑥ ❼ ❽)

Higher SHGCs are allowed in colder regions, but continuous horizontal overhangs are still necessary to block the high summer sun angles.

DAYLIGHTING

GENERAL RECOMMENDATIONS

DL1   *General Principles* (Climate Zones: all)

Daylighting is an essential component of the most energy-efficient and sustainable school design. Properly designed daylighting uses sunlight to offset electrical lighting loads, saving

Benefits of Daylighting

Smith Middle School

The benefits of daylighting are documented in a study conducted by Rensselaer Polytechnic Institute at the well-daylighted Smith Middle School in Chapel Hill, NC, that was released in February of 2010 (Figueiro and Rea 2010). The research indicated that students in daylighted environments were receiving more short-wave blue light than students exposed to florescent fixtures. This impacted the circadian cycle of students exposed to daylighting and allowed students to have better sleep patterns and receive more sleep each night. For decades it has been observed that students in daylighted environments have had higher attendance records. This study identifies daylighting as a significant factor in why students in these types of environments are healthier and more alert.

energy and reducing cooling loads. From a student and teacher productivity standpoint, classrooms (particularly special-needs classrooms) derive the most benefit from daylighting. A recent study by Rensselaer Polytechnic Institute (RPI) concluded that 8th-grade students receiving daylighting were positively impacted (Figueiro and Rea 2010).

Daylighting must provide controlled, quality lighting. For daylighting to save energy, it must do a better job of lighting the space than electric lighting alone. Otherwise, occupants will persist in the habit of walking into a space and turning on the lights. Develop a daylighting strategy that will provide superior lighting for at least 60% of the hours of school operation. From an energy-use perspective, an inadequate daylighting strategy may not result in savings because the electric lights will not be turned off. However, it is also critical that daylighting strategies do not employ excessive fenestration areas. More is not necessarily better. Even though the daylighting contribution may increase, so will the cooling loads. To ensure optimum balance between maximizing daylighting and reducing cooling loads, the daylighting strategy should designed to provide the great majority of lighting needs no less than 50% of the time, but no more than 75% of the time.

If designed correctly, a daylighting strategy can reduce the following:

- Electricity for lighting and peak electrical demand
- Cooling energy and peak cooling loads
- Maintenance costs associated with lamp replacement

Cooling loads can be reduced by providing just the right amount of daylighting in a school. Using fewer lights results in reduced lighting loads. The lumens per watt (efficacy) of a well-designed daylighting system are higher than that of electric lighting sources. In other words, daylighting produces less heat to meet the same lighting need. However, to achieve this reduced cooling, the following criteria must be met:

- No more solar radiation can be allowed to enter the building during peak cooling times than is required to meet the lighting design criteria.
- Overhangs and other shading devices must be properly sized to control solar radiation during peak cooling times.
- Electric lights must be automatically dimmed or turned off through the use of photosensors.

Fenestrations are considered daylighting fenestrations if they comply with the minimum and maximum DFRs listed in Table 5-5 *and* meet the following criteria:

- Are located at 7 ft AFF or greater, are designed to reduce contrast (uniformity illuminance ratio less than 10:1 within the daylighted space), and incorporate design elements that block direct beam radiation from reaching any location (during normal operational hours) that is below 5 ft AFF and within the intended daylighted space
- Are north facing, below 7 ft AFF, and are designed to reduce contrast
- Are south, east, or west facing; below 7 ft AFF; and have a VT below 0.30

Prescriptive daylighting strategies include the following sidelighting and toplighting options:

- South facing (within 30° of south), sidelighting strategies include fenestrations
  - at 7 ft AFF and higher and located above light shelves (both interior and exterior),
  - at 7 ft AFF and higher and incorporate blinds-between-glazing, or
  - that incorporate glazing systems with VT below 0.30 (including those utilizing fiber-filled or aerogel).
- North-facing (within 30° of north), sidelighting strategies include fenestrations above or below 7 ft AFF that are designed to reduce contrast.
- South-facing (within 30° of south) roof monitors with vertical glazing (within 20° of vertical) with geometry that prohibits direct beam radiation from entering an intended daylighted space.
- North-facing (within 30° of north) roof monitors with vertical glazing (within 20° from vertical).
- Skylights, in combination with sidelighting strategies, with proportional DFRs equal to or less than that listed within the daylighting section.
- Tubular daylighting devices, in combination with sidelighting strategies, with proportional DFRs equal to or less than that listed within the daylighting section.

DL2   *Consider Daylighting Early in the Design Process* (Climate Zones: all)

The most economic and effective daylighting strategies are well integrated into the design from structural, mechanical, electrical, and architectural standpoints. In designing good daylighting, the many interrelated aspects of the school's architecture, landscape, and engineering must be considered. When daylighting systems are optimized to reduce peak cooling loads, mechanical cooling equipment can be scaled back because overall cooling loads are reduced. This will allow for proper trade-offs between the daylighting and the sizing of the cooling system.

When properly integrated, common architectural components may serve dual functions, which reduces first costs. For example, white single-ply roofing can serve as a waterproofing membrane and generally reflect solar radiation but also increase radiation into the vertical glazing in roof-monitors. Only a comprehensive, well-thought-out approach will provide a low-cost system that achieves the desired benefits.

The opposite is true of nonintegrated designs. If the daylighting system is designed and bid as an alternate to a design with no daylighting, the daylighting strategy probably will not be as cost effective or resource efficient. If the designer thinks that the daylighting components have a good chance of being eliminated, he or she will be less likely to risk designing a smaller mechanical cooling system for fear of having to pay to redo the design.

The best way to guarantee a low-cost daylighting strategy is to integrate daylighting early in the schematic design phase. With a good schematic design cost estimates that reflect the added daylighting components and the reduced cooling equipment and multiuse of building components, the designer will see that the net daylighting costs are very reasonable.

DL3   *Space Types* (Climate Zones: all)

When designing a school to reduce energy consumption by at least 50%, daylighting the majority of all well-utilized spaces should be a high priority. In order of potential impact on students, teachers, and staff, the classrooms and resource rooms are the most important spaces to daylight, followed by media centers and administrative spaces. Note that while daylighting in media centers is encouraged, no specific DFR recommendations have been included in this Guide because media center designs vary considerably. In terms of the biggest impact on energy savings, the highly utilized gymnasiums and multipurpose spaces tend to produce the greatest financial benefit. While cafeterias are occupied by large numbers of people during lunch periods only, they require good lighting by the cafeteria staff for a much longer portion of the day and should be considered for daylighting. These spaces are many times utilized for end-of-grade testing and, because of this, require good glare, contrast, and direct beam radiation protection. Specific design guidelines are provided within this document for the following typical spaces:

- Classrooms and resource rooms
- Gymnasium/multipurpose spaces
- Cafeterias
- Exterior administrative offices

The Guide assumes that you are daylighting these spaces at a minimum.

When incorporating daylighting strategies in other types of spaces that tend to vary considerably, depending upon the designer and program needs, conduct daylighting simulations that simulate

- multiple points (at varying heights, depending upon the work plane) within the particular space and
- hourly, daily, monthly, and yearly contributions.

DL4   *How to Select Daylighting Strategies* (Climate Zones: all)

For this Guide, prescriptive daylighting strategies are presented for classrooms and resource rooms; gymnasiums or high-ceiling, multipurpose spaces; cafeterias; and exterior administrative offices. For each strategy, there are several options and variations, depending on climate and orientation. These strategies are designed to provide the recommended illuminance for these spaces over 60% of the occupied daytime hours.

The strategies are based on all the spaces being oriented so the daylighting fenestrations face either north or south. Although daylighting can be achieved for other orientations, the recommendations in this document do not apply. The patterns are summarized below, and more specific information is provided in DL20 through DL41.

Table 5-5 Acceptable DFR Ranges by Climate Zone

Measure	Orientation	VT*	CZ 1		CZ 2		CZ 3		CZ 4		CZ 5		CZ 6		CZ 7		CZ 8	
			Min	Max	Min	Max	Min	Max	Min	Max	Min	Max	Min	Max	Min	Max	Min	Max
Light shelf	S	0.80	6%	9%	6%	9%	7%	10%	7%	10%	7%	10%	8%	11%	10%	13%	10%	13%
BBG[1]	S	0.50	7%	9%	7%	9%	8%	10%	8%	10%	8%	10%	9%	11%	11%	13%	11%	13%
North, High	N	0.80	9%	12%	9%	12%	10%	13%	10%	13%	10%	13%	11%	14%	13%	16%	13%	16%
Roof[2] Monitor	S	0.80	5%	7%	5%	7%	6%	8%	6%	8%	6%	8%	7%	9%	9%	11%	9%	11%
	N	0.80	6%	8%	6%	8%	7%	9%	7%	9%	7%	9%	8%	10%	10%	12%	10%	12%
Fiberfill	S	0.30	9%	14%	9%	14%	10%	15%	10%	15%	10%	15%	12%	17%	14%	18%	14%	18%
Aerogel	S	0.20	11%	15%	11%	15%	12%	16%	12%	16%	12%	16%	14%	17%	16%	19%	16%	19%
Tubular Skylight	Horizontal	0.50	2%	5%	2%	5%	3%	5%	3%	5%	3%	5%	4%	5%	4%	5%	4%	5%
Skylight	Horizontal	0.50	2%	5%	2%	5%	3%	5%	3%	5%	3%	5%	4%	5%	4%	5%	4%	5%

1 Visible Transmittance values are for center-of-glass; BBG = blinds between glass.
2 DFRs on the lower end of the range for roof monitors should be used for gyms and high ceiling spaces while DFRs on the higher end of the range should bused for classrooms.

Classrooms, Resource Rooms, and Administrative Offices with Sidelighting Only. Variations of this are provided for north-facing, and one for south-facing, classrooms. South-facing classrooms are assumed to have overhangs to protect against excessive gain in the warmer months and light shelves to bounce daylighting deeper into the space.

Within these sidelighting variations, prescriptive strategies are provided for the following:

- South-facing light shelves utilizing glazing above the light shelf with 80% center-of-glass visible transmittance (VT)
- High, south-facing glazing on the exterior wall with blinds between glazing and a combined 50% center-of-glass VT
- High, south-facing, fiber-filled glazing with 30% center-of-glass VT
- High, south-facing, aerogel-filled glazing with 20% center-of-glass VT
- High, north-facing glazing with 80% center-of-glass VT

Classrooms with Toplighting Only. This single-strategy solution utilizes a south-facing roof monitor positioned in the center of the space and coupled with light baffles to bounce and filter light.

Classrooms with a Combination of Sidelighting and Toplighting. This daylighting pattern combines the sidelighting solutions for south- or north-facing classrooms, described in the first bullet above, with top lighting at the back of the classrooms. The toplighting may be provided by either skylights, tubular daylighting devices, or roof monitors, depending on climate and other design constraints. If horizontal skylights or tubular daylighting devices are utilized, no more than one-third of the combined contribution should come from the horizontal fenestration strategies.

Gymnasiums, Multipurpose Rooms, or Cafeterias with Roof Monitors. This option incorporates south-facing roof monitors.

Gymnasiums, Multipurpose Rooms, or Cafeterias with a Combination of Toplighting and Sidelighting. Four variations of this daylighting pattern are provided:

- South-facing roof monitors (80% center-of-glass VT) and high, south- and north-facing fiber-filled glazing with 20% VT
- South-facing roof monitors (80% center-of-glass VT) and high, south- and north-facing aerogel-filled glazing with 20% VT
- Skylights or tubular daylighting devices and high south- and north-facing, fiber-filled glazing with 20% VT with no more than one-third of the combined contribution coming from the horizontal fenestration strategies

Examples of Daylighting Strategies in K-12 School Spaces

Classroom and Gymnasium with Baffles Inside South Facing Monitor

Cafeterias and Multipurpose Rooms with Roof Monitors

Libraries/Media Centers Using South-Facing Roof Monitors with Baffles

- Skylights or tubular daylighting devices and high south- and north-facing aerogel-filled glazing with 20% VT with no more than one-third of the combined contribution coming from the horizontal fenestration strategies

When determining the appropriate DFR values in strategies employing multiple daylighting systems, multiply the DFR of the particular daylighting system times the square footage of floor area times the percent contribution expected from each daylighting system. For example, if daylighting a 10,000 ft^2 gymnasium in climate zone 3 with a combination of 70% south-facing roof monitors and 30% south-facing fiber-fill sidelighting select, as a minimum:

$$6\% \text{ DFR} \times 10,000 \text{ ft}^2 \times 70\% = 420 \text{ ft}^2 \text{ of roof monitor glazing}$$

and

$$10\% \text{ DFR} \times 10,000 \text{ ft}^2 \times 30\% = 300 \text{ ft}^2 \text{ of fiber-fill glazing}$$

DL5   *Recommended Daylighting Fenestration-to-Floor Area Ratios (DFR)*
(Climate Zones: all)

For visual connection to the outdoors, provide view windows below 7 ft AFF. East- and west-facing glass should be minimized, and shading should be provided on the south side. Overhangs and light shelves are not needed on north-facing view glass (see EN24 and EN26 for more information). Glazing above 7 ft AFF is designed to provide daylighting and should be sized according to the DFR in Table 5-5. This basic guidance will help you determine the right amount of daylighting fenestration for a given system. These numbers can be fine tuned by using daylighting analysis particular to the climate and the actual space configuration and use. These rules assume a center-of-glass VT of the vertical daylighting fenestration ranging from 20% to 80%, depending upon strategy used. For horizontal daylighting fenestration (skylights or tubular daylighting devices), a 50% VT is assumed. Further details about each daylighting strategy are provided in DL20–41.

The recommendations regarding DFRs for each optional daylighting strategy are included in Table 5-5.

DL6   *View Windows Separate from Daylighting Strategy* (Climate Zones: all)

When designing daylighting systems, the view windows must be separated from the daylighting fenestrations. To maximize energy efficiency and avoid discomfort, the daylighting glazing is sized and typically placed above 7 ft to provide good quality lighting to the space, independent of the view glass. The exception would be the use of fenestration strategies that incorporate very low VT characteristics. Additional view windows should be added in classrooms, resources rooms, cafeterias, and administrative offices but only for view and ventilation. The larger the view windows are, the lower the energy performance of the building.

Windows on the east and west should be minimized, as they cause excessive cooling loads and are not effective for heating because of the sun angles.

Visual comfort is strongly affected by window location, shading, and glazing materials. Well-designed windows can be a visual delight, but poorly designed windows can create a major source of glare.

In schools, wall space is precious. As a result, view windows often serve as display areas. Additionally, these windows are almost always accompanied by user-operated window treatments (blinds or shades) that can readily be closed by teachers and students. Although view windows are recommended to provide a visual connection with the outdoors, they should not be considered as a contributor to daylighting. Even if they are not covered by artwork or blinds, they have limited benefit, lighting only the spaces very close to the window. Daylighting fenestration should ideally include only that which is located above door height, about 7 ft. It is best to design daylighting around roof monitors; high, south-side light shelf apertures; or high, north glass transom windows.

DL7   *Lighting Design Criteria* (Climate Zones: all)

Design the daylighting system to provide enough but not too much lighting. Classroom daylighting systems should be designed to meet the following criteria:

- 45 to 50 fc of average illumination for general instruction
- 30 to 50 vertical fc on the teaching wall (non-audio-visual [AV] mode)
- 7 to 15 fc on the teaching wall of average illumination for AV mode
- Uniformity illuminance ratio not in excess of 8:1
- Glare illuminance ratio not in excess of 20:1

The same criteria for lighting quality and quantity apply to electric lighting and daylighting. When the criteria cannot be met with daylighting, electric lighting will meet the illuminance design criteria. The objectives are to maximize the daylighting and to minimize the electric lighting. To maximize the daylighting without oversizing the fenestration, in-depth analysis may be required.

For sunny climates, designs can be evaluated on a sunny day at the summer solar peak. For cloudy climates, a typical cloudy day should be used to evaluate the system. Typically, the DFR percentage will increase for less sunny climates. Daylighting can still work for a school in a cloudy climate. Cloudy climates can produce diffuse skies, which create good daylighting conditions and minimize glare and heat gain.

DL8   *Use Daylighting Analysis Tools to Optimize Design* (Climate Zones: all)

While the enclosed prescriptive guidelines can be utilized effectively early in the design process to better insure that the 50% energy reduction goal is realized, more comprehensive daylighting and whole-building energy simulations conducted by the design team are also recommended. To more accurately simulate daylighting contributions in these spaces or other spaces not specifically listed in the tables, each of these additional typical spaces should be analyzed for multiple locations and changing light levels on any hourly, daily, monthly, and yearly basis (see CHPS [2006a] for a list of available tools). At a minimum, daylighting should be evaluated for multiple design conditions, including sunny and cloudy conditions, the summer and winter solstices, the peak cooling day, the equinox, and three times during the day: 9:00 a.m., noon, and 3:00 p.m. The analysis tool should be able to predict illumination and surface brightness for a grid of points within the space and to calculate performance during all hours of operation.

Annual savings will have to be calculated with an annual whole-building energy simulation tool after the daylighting design tools have been used to determine the foot candles in the classrooms and the window sizes have been appropriately sized. Current daylighting analysis tools do not help with heating and cooling loads or other energy uses. They predict only illumination levels and perhaps electric lighting use.

DL9   *Building Orientation* (Climate Zones: all)

Cost-effective daylighting starts with good orientation. For classrooms and most other spaces, the vertical facades that provide daylighting should be oriented within 15° (maximum 30°) of either north or south. Sidelighted daylighting solutions can be developed for other orientations, but they are beyond the recommendations provided in this document and typically are less effective. Orientation is less important if toplighting is used as the primary daylighting pattern, since roof monitors can be rotated on the roof. However, even with roof monitors, the main axis of the building should still be within 15° (maximum 30°) of north/south or east/west. East and west glass is problematic from a solar heat gain perspective and provides nonuniform daylighting.

When positioning the building on the overall site, make sure that the daylighting apertures are not shaded by adjacent buildings, trees, or elements of the school building (self shading). Also consider ambient noise levels when selecting the type of daylighting system to incorporate.

DL10   *Ceiling Height* (Climate Zones: all)

For all daylighted classrooms, a minimum 10 ft ceiling height is recommended. When daylighting must be provided entirely from sidelighting, a higher ceiling is recommended at the perimeter wall, and the ceiling should be sloped when possible. See DL20–28 for additional information.

DL11   *Outdoor Surface Reflectance* (Climate Zones: all)

Consider the reflectance of the roofs, sidewalks, and other surfaces in front of the glazing areas. The use of lighter roofing colors can increase daylighting concentration and, in some cases, reduce the glass area needed for roof monitors or clerestories. However, a light-colored walkway in front of view windows should be carefully considered. Although a light-colored surface may improve daylighting, depending on the design of the facade it may also cause unwanted reflections and glare.

DL12   *Eliminate Direct Beam Radiation* (Climate Zones: all)

An essential component of any good daylighted school design is the elimination of uncontrolled, direct beam radiation onto the work plane. This is critical for all classrooms, libraries, media centers, and administrative spaces, but less critical for some gymnasiums, multipurpose rooms, and corridors. Use strategies that bounce, redirect, and filter sunlight so that direct radiation does not directly enter space. A good test is to evaluate sun angles at 9:00 a.m., noon, and 3:00 p.m. on the equinox and at the summer solar peak and make sure that there is no direct solar radiation on the work plane (typically a surface 30 in. above the floor, perhaps less for lower elementary grades) inside a band of 4 ft from the edges of the walls. If this criterion to eliminate direct beam radiation is met, interior shades may not be necessary, except to darken the space for AV purposes. If this criterion is not met, the daylighting contribution will be negatively impacted because interior shades will be needed to reduce solar heat gain and glare. With advances in AV technology, including flat screens, high-lumen LCD projectors, and the incorporation of intentionally shaded projection screen areas within the classroom, it is now possible to allow the seating area within the classroom to benefit from daylighting while still creating a darker projection area.

The purpose of shading, filtering, baffling, and/or reflecting solar radiation is to prevent direct solar penetration into the space, which can be a source of glare and excess heat gain, or to limit the amount of radiation entering the space. Various strategies can be implemented in order to better control the incoming radiation including:

- *External shading strategies* that optimize the amount of direct sun that reaches the glazing. These include major building and architectural elements, such as overhangs, soffits, trellises, awnings, and external light shelves. This method, if sized correctly, is the most effective, as it prevents excess solar heat gain and glare.
- *Shading, filtering, or reflecting strategies that are integral to the glazing* and are used to reject unwanted, excessive solar gain. These include glazings that employ advantageous colorations (absorption), reflectivity, and selective transmissions, as well as opaque elements integral to the glazing, such as fritted patterns, fiber-fill, aerogel or blinds-between-glazing panels.
- *Internal shading methods* for filtering and controlling solar gain that has already entered the space. These include baffles, louvers, rolling shades, blinds, and internal light shelves.

The success of daylighted schools depends on how occupants interact with the daylighting system. This is particularly true for blinds or shades that are available for adjustment. Occupants

Shading Strategy Examples

External Light Shelves

Exterior light shelves can serve to bounce additional radiation through higher daylighting apertures while shading lower view glazing. Interior light shelves used in sidelighting daylight strategies and baffles employed in south-facing roof monitors are key elements in blocking direct beam radiation.

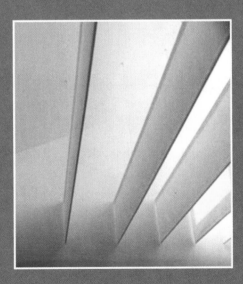

(Left) Translucent Ceiling Baffles and (Right) Translucent Interior Light Shelf

are motivated to close the blinds but not to reopen them, and they tend to adjust blinds for the long term. If blinds are left closed, the daylighting potential will not be realized. If temporary darkening of a specific space it is not functionally required, do not install shades or blinds on the daylighting glass. Unnecessary blinds will result in reduced performance, increased first costs, and higher long-term maintenance expenses.

DL13 *Daylighting Control for Audio-Visual (AV) Projection Activities* (Climate Zones: all)

If a classroom or multipurpose room requires darkening for AV or other functions, consider motorized roller shades or motorized vertical blinds for apertures that are out of reach. This may seem to result in higher maintenance costs, but such controls can have the opposite effect. The mechanical stress placed on manual operators by students and teachers (because of uneven cranking) limits the effective life of these devices. The inconvenience associated with the process also results in a number of shades being left closed. Motorized shades, which cost more up front, will provide greater ease of operation and result in a better-performing daylighting design. Some motorized devices can also be programmed to reset in the open position at the beginning of each day.

Some teachers still use overhead projectors, but most new schools use TV monitors or liquid crystal display (LCD) projectors. These teaching tools often require that the light level at the specific location of the screen wall be as low as 7 fc for optimum contrast. Slightly higher levels (7 to 15 fc) should still provide acceptable light levels for the visual aids, but the reduced

Compatibility between Daylighting and Audiovisual Projection

Daylighted Classroom with Audio-Visual in Use

It is possible to allow full daylighting in the main seating area of the classroom while still retaining a darker light level at the projection screen and/or TV monitor locations. One approach is to design the space to intentionally darken the screen area without affecting the rest of the classroom. Locating television screens in a corner away from windows will minimize glare on the screen.

contrast will make them slightly harder for the students to read. If the light levels on the projection screen area are to exceed 15 fc, high-lumen projectors (3000+ lumens) and intentionally shaded screen areas should be utilized, and screens should be selected that are intended for use in daylighted spaces.

Whiteboards need sufficient light (about 30 fc) with an illuminance ratio not in excess of 8:1. Whiteboards have a specular surface and should be carefully located so there is no reflected glare from either daylighting apertures or lighting fixtures. Since the whiteboard is typically in the same location as the projection screen, separate control of the teaching surface light is essential. To address both needs, intentionally darken the area of the teaching wall that has the screen and then use electric lighting to enhance the wall when the whiteboard is used.

DL14   *Interior Finishes for Daylighting* (**Climate Zones: all**)

Select light colors for interior walls and ceilings to increase light reflectance and reduce lighting and daylighting requirements. Minimum surface reflectances are shown in Table 5-6. The color of the ceiling, walls, floor, and furniture have a major impact on the effectiveness of the daylighting strategy. When considering finish surfaces, install light colors (white is best) to ensure the daylight is reflected throughout the space.

Consider a ceiling tile or surface that has a high reflectivity. Make sure that the ceiling tile light reflectance includes the fissures within the acoustical tiles, as these irregularities affect the amount of light absorbed. Do not assume that the color of a tile alone dictates its reflectance. When selecting a tile, specify a minimum reflectivity. Most manufactures will list the reflectance as if it were the paint color reflectance. The commissioning authority (CxA) should verify the reflectance.

DL15   *Calibration and Commissioning* (**Climate Zones: all**)

Even a few days of occupancy with poorly calibrated controls can lead to permanent overriding of the system and loss of savings. All lighting controls must be calibrated and commissioned after the finishes are completed and the furnishings are in place. Most photosensors require daytime and nighttime calibration sessions. The photosensor manufacturer and CxA should be involved in the calibration. Document the calibration and commissioning settings and plan for future recalibration as part of the school maintenance program.

DL16   *Dimming Controls* (**Climate Zones: all**)

For most spaces in a school, dimming-type daylighting controls are recommended. In all regularly occupied daylighted spaces, such as classrooms, gyms, and offices, continuously dim rather than switch electric lights in response to daylight to minimize occupant distraction. Specify dimming ballasts that dim to at least 20% of full output with the ability to turn off when daylighting provides sufficient illuminance. Provide a means and a convenient location to override daylighting controls in spaces that are intentionally darkened to use overhead projectors or slides. The daylighting control system and photosensor should include a 15-minute

Table 5-6   Minimum Reflectance

Location	Minimum Reflectance
Walls above 7 ft	70%
Ceiling	70% (preferably 80%–90%)
Light wells	70%
Floors	20%
Furniture	50%
Walls below 7 ft	50%

time delay or other means to avoid cycling caused by rapidly changing sky conditions, and a 1-minute fade rate to change the light levels by dimming. Automatic multilevel daylight switching may be used in not regularly occupied environments like hallways, restrooms, lounges, and lobbies if they are daylighted.

DL17   *Photosensor Placement and Lighting Layout* (Climate Zones: all)

Correct photosensor placement is essential. Consult daylighting references or work with the photosensor manufacturer for proper location. Mount the photosensors in a location that closely simulates the light level (or can be set by being proportional to the light level) at the work plane. Depending on the daylighting strategy, photosensor controls should be used to dim particular logical groupings of lights. Implement a lighting fixture layout and control wiring plan that complements the daylighting strategy. In sidelighted classrooms, locate luminaires in rows parallel to the window wall, and wire each row separately. Because of the strong difference in light that will occur close to and away from the window, having this individual control by bank will help balance out the space. In a space that has a roof monitor, install one photosensor that controls all the perimeter lights and a second that controls all the lights within the monitor well. See EL14 for more details on electric lighting for gymnasiums.

DL18   *Photosensor Specifications* (Climate Zones: all)

Photosensors used for classrooms should be specified for the appropriate illuminance range (indoor or outdoor) and must achieve a slow, smooth linear dimming response from the dimming ballasts.

In a *closed-loop* system, the interior photocell responds to the combination of daylight and electric light in the daylighted area. The best location for the photocell is above an unobstructed location such as the middle of the classroom. If using a lighting system that provides an indirect component, mount the photosensor at the same height as the luminaire or in a location that is not affected by the uplight from the luminaire.

In an *open-loop* system, the photocell responds only to daylight levels but is still calibrated to the desired light level received on the work surface. The best location for the photosensor is inside the skylight/roof monitor well.

DL19   *Select Compatible Light Fixtures* (Climate Zones: all)

First consider the use of indirect lighting fixtures that more closely represent the same effect as daylighting. Indirect lighting spreads light over the ceiling surface, which then reflects the light to the task locations; with the ceiling as the light source, indirect lighting is more uniform and has less glare.

In addition, insist on compatibility between ballast, lamps, and controls. Be sure that the lamps can be dimmed and that the dimming ballasts, sensors, and controls will operate as a system.

CLASSROOM SIDELIGHTING STRATEGIES

DL20   *Sidelighting Patterns* (Climate Zones: all)

The sidelighting patterns shown in Figure 5-7 through 5-11 are appropriate for south- and north-facing classrooms within 30° of true. Sidelighting strategies can be used in classrooms on any floor; Figure 5-7 shows several sidelighting options for a two-floor school. DL21–28 provide further information on sidelighting strategies.

DL21   *South-Facing Classrooms—Configuration of Apertures* (Climate Zones: all)

The choice of fenestration and the placement of the apertures are critical. If uncontrolled, direct beam radiation enters the classroom window. It can create glare and the teacher will simply close the blinds and negate the daylighting strategy.

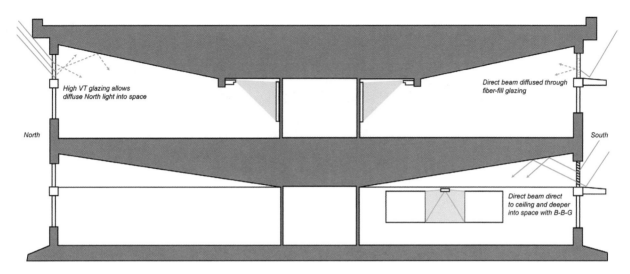

Figure 5-7   (DL20) Classroom Sidelighting Strategies

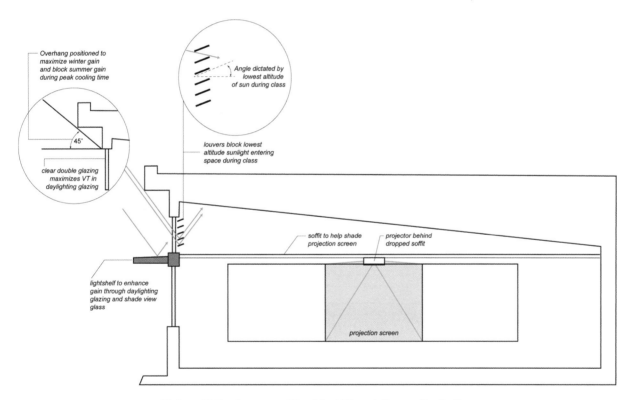

Figure 5-8   Louvers Blocking Direct Beam Radiation

A light shelf is recommended for south-facing walls. The daylighting fenestration above the light shelf should be as continuous as possible; the daylighting fenestration is typically 3 to 5 ft high. The window should be positioned as close to the ceiling as possible within structural constraints. As shown in Figure 5-8, louvers can be positioned to block all radiation and reflect sunlight up to the ceiling during typical class hours.

An overhang should be positioned over the daylighting aperture and sized with the light shelf to prevent direct sun from entering the space. Set the cutoff angle of the light shelf or

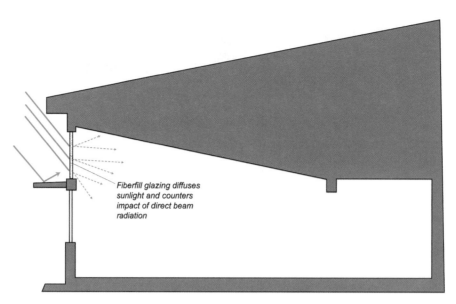

Figure 5-9 (DL 21) Fiber-Filled Glazing Diffuses Sunlight

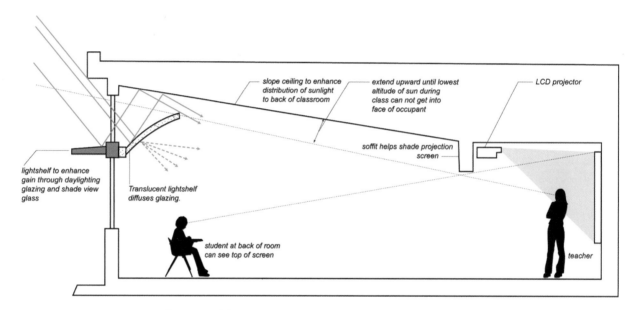

Figure 5-10 (DL21) Translucent Interior Light Shelf

louvers to eliminate direct sun penetration at the back of the space during normal school hours. (See Figure 5-8).

Alternatives to interior light shelves include fiber-filled glazing to diffuse incoming sunlight (Figure 5-9) or the addition of mini-blinds between panes of glass to redirect sunlight up to the ceiling, with the addition of a third pane in cold climates (see Figure 5-11). For these alternatives, the interior portion of the light shelf may be eliminated, but the outer portion is still needed to shade view glass.

Another option would be to incorporate a translucent interior light shelf that, when sloped up toward the ceiling, has the advantage of allowing sunlight to be filtered through the light shelf itself or bounced up to the ceiling. Unlike horizontal interior light shelves, the design allows all direct beam radiation to be intercepted. As shown in Figure 5-10, sunlight is intercepted and either filtered through the translucent light shelf or reflected deeper into the space.

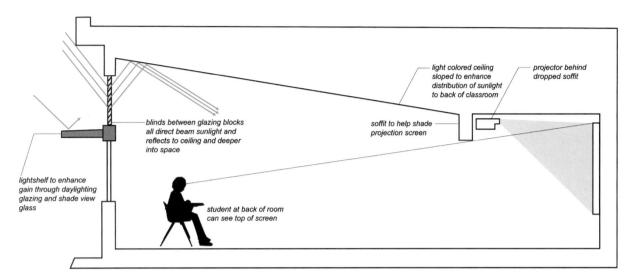

Figure 5-11   (DL22) Light Shelf Utilizing Blinds between Panes of Glazing

For north-facing classrooms, a light shelf is not needed because its benefits are related to the reflection of direct solar radiation, and north facades experience little direct solar gain.

DL22   *South-Facing Classrooms—Glazing Area and Fenestration Type* **(Climate Zones: all)**

The area of the daylighting aperture for a south-facing light shelf application should be in the range of 70 ft^2 to 120 ft^2 for a typical 1000 ft^2 classroom. This recommendation is based on glazing with a center-of-glass VT of 80%. Glazing with a lower visible transmittance may be used, but the aperture should be increased to maintain the same equivalent visible aperture. If the high daylighting fenestration incorporates blinds-between-glass, the VT is typically 50%, while fiberfill applications are 30% and aerogel-filled glazing is 20%. Where windows are used specifically for daylighting, consider the use of uncoated clear glass or low-e coated clear glass with a high VT. A larger daylighting aperture with a lower VT has the advantage of providing the same amount of daylight but with less glare and contrast. The disadvantage is that the costs associated with all of the components of the daylighting system typically are higher.

As an alternative to interior light shelves, consider horizontal blinds located between glazings. As shown in Figure 5-11, blinds between glass both block all direct beam radiation and reflect incoming sunlight up to ceiling. The horizontal blinds should be highly reflective and have either flat or slightly curved blades. Because of potential dirt buildup and maintenance, the blinds should be placed between panes of glazing. If this option is used, consider the transmission of the blinds and increase the glazing area accordingly.

Most shades that are available today are operable and can be closed. However, if the space does not need to be temporarily darkened, the internal blinds should be directed up to the ceiling and fixed at the recommended cutoff angle for light shelves (see Figure 5-8). By fixing the angle and not allowing the occupants to operate the blinds, there will be less opportunity to override the daylighting benefits. If the internal blinds do need to be operated for darkening purposes, provide two fixed positions: the one just described and a second "closed" position.

DL23   *View Glazing and VTs* **(Climate Zones: all)**

The view windows below 7 ft do not require high light transmission glazing, so center-of-glass VT values between 0.25 and 0.75 are acceptable, depending on the orientation and climatic zone. Higher center-of-glass VT values are preferred in predominantly overcast climates. Center-of-glass VT values below 0.35 may appear noticeably tinted and dim and may degrade luminous quality and views. However, lower VT values should be used for higher DFRs. Lower VT values may also be appropriate for other conditions of low sun angles or light-colored ground cover. See EN24 for specific recommendations that consider SHGC and VFR.

Thermal comfort can also be compromised by poor fenestration choices, especially for view glazing, which is closer to occupants. Poorly insulated windows contribute to uncomfortable indoor temperatures, but windows with low U-factors keep glass surface temperatures closer to the interior air temperature and improve thermal comfort. In addition, east-west windows and unshaded south windows (if they cannot be avoided) can increase cooling loads.

In all cases, windows should be made of high-quality construction, incorporate thermal breaks, and include appropriate glazing for the particular application.

Carefully consider the visible light, solar transmission, and insulation qualities of the particular daylighting glazing system; place particular emphasis on how much additional glazing will be needed to achieve the same VT. If the design is to cost-effectively address energy and create a good daylighting strategy, the size of the daylighting apertures needs to be minimized and the transmission maximized.

The desirable color qualities of daylighting are best transmitted by neutral-colored tints that alter the color spectrum to the smallest extent. In particular, avoid dark green and bronze glazing. To the greatest extent possible, avoid the use of reflective glass or low-e coatings with a highly reflective component, even for view glass. These reduce the quality of the view and the mirrored effect is unpleasant to occupants after dark.

DL24 *South-Facing Classrooms—Make Light Shelf Durable and Reflective* (Climate Zones: all)

Select durable materials for interior and exterior light shelves and, if they are reachable, design them to carry the weight of a person. Aluminum exterior light shelves are a good compromise between good reflectance with little or no maintenance and cost. Incorporate white finishes on the top of interior light shelves. Aluminized acrylic sheets applied to the top of the interior shelf allows light to bounce further back into spaces and can improve performance in deeper rooms without toplighting. It is critical if interior light shelves are utilized that they are designed to block all direct beam radiation that may create negative consequences.

DL25 *North-Facing Classroom—Configuration of Apertures* (Climate Zones: all)

The daylight glazing should extend as close as possible to the ceiling. Window area below door height of about 7 ft should be considered as view glazing and not considered as a contributor to daylight. The daylighting glazing should be as continuous as possible along the facade. If continuous fenestration cannot be provided for structural or other reasons, the windows should be placed in the corners of the space with the opaque wall for shear or structure located in the center of the wall. This will light the walls perpendicular to the daylighting wall and provide better illuminance ratio and surface brightness.

From a daylighting perspective, high north glazing can be a good option into spaces up to a distance of 1.5 to 2.0 times the height of the top of the window. As with north-facing roof monitors, more glazing is required than for a south light shelf to achieve the same annual contribution, so the energy performance is not quite as good. The most significant advantage is that controlling direct beam radiation is not usually a problem.

Often, when implementing a daylighting strategy in classrooms that face both north and south, the designer is confronted with the challenge of establishing a common ceiling height. South side light shelves generally require less glazing than high, north transom apertures unless blinds between the glass or a south-facing fenestration with a lower VT are used, in which case the height of the south aperture will closely match the height of north transom glazing. To maintain a common ceiling height, also consider some of the lower view glass on the north as an integral part of your daylighting strategy. Because blinds would typically not be needed on the north to block direct beam radiation, it is logical to include some lower view glass. The big drawback is that the window area could still be used as a display board, which blocks the light.

DL26   *North-Facing Classroom—Glazing Area and Fenestration Type*
(Climate Zones: all)

For high glazing (above 7 ft AFF) with a center-of-glass VT of 80%, an area of 90 to 160 ft^2 is recommended for a typical 1000 ft^2 classroom. If glazing with a lower center-of-glass VT is used, the area should be increased accordingly. Because of the lack of direct beam radiation on the north, light shelves provide no benefit and should not be used. Assuming that lower north side view glass is considered in your daylighting strategy, it would be advisable to use low-e glass in this case for comfort and sacrificing the 10% to 20% reduction in visible light benefit.

DL27   *South- and North-Facing Classrooms—Sloped Ceilings* (Climate Zones: all)

When daylight can be provided only from the side, the ceiling should be sloped down to the back wall. A sloped ceiling can achieve a higher window head, which will result in greater daylighting penetration into the space. The slope will also provide a brighter ceiling.

By sloping the ceiling from the outside wall to the back of the space, it is often possible to encroach into the ceiling cavity space just at the window area, not increase floor-to-floor dimensions, and still have enough space for ductwork.

DL28   *South- and North-Facing Classrooms—Recognize the Limits of Side Daylighting*
(Climate Zones: all)

Sidelighting is an effective strategy for daylighting spaces in rooms with tall ceilings. For rooms with low ceilings, effective daylight can be provided only for spaces within 15 to 20 ft from the window. To daylight the whole classroom, consider rear wall washing skylights, tubular daylighting devices, or roof monitors to supplement the sidelight.

CLASSROOM TOPLIGHTING STRATEGIES

DL29   *Classroom Toplighting Pattern* (Climate Zones: all)

This Guide provides one option for toplighting. Other options may be explored for specific school applications; however, within this Guide the use of skylights and tubular daylighting devices should only be used as a means to supplement sidelighting strategies that would provide for at least two-thirds of the daylighting contribution.

Roof monitors that incorporate vertical south glazing and properly sized overhangs and interior baffles have the following advantages:

- Create uniform lighting throughout the space
- Can be used to daylight spaces far from the perimeter of the building .
- Create passive heating benefits, allowing more radiation to enter the space in the colder months
- Create a more diffuse, filtered lighting strategy
- Reduce glare and contrast

The limitation of roof monitors is that they can be used only in single-story designs or on the top floors of multistory designs. Figure 5-12 shows a cross section for a typical roof monitor setup.

DL30   *Sizing the Roof Monitors* (Climate Zones: all)

For a 1000 ft^2 classroom, the well opening of the roof monitors (considering requirements associated with mechanical ductwork space and dropped areas over the teaching wall) should be maximized. The key to sizing the south-facing glazing in the monitor is to provide the desired level of daylighting illumination at the summer solar peak on a clear day. Size the glazing and the overhangs so that daylighting provides the required illumination (see Table 5-5) during the summer peak cooling condition. With south-facing glazing, this strategy will result in more daylight entering the space during other times of the year, when the sun has a lower

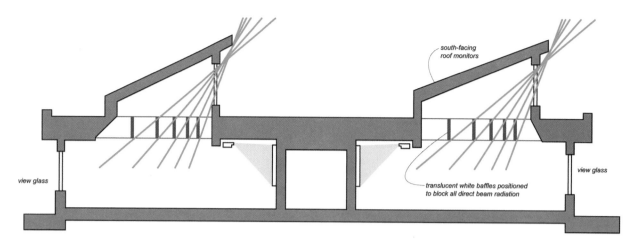

Figure 5-12 (DL29) Classroom with South-Facing Monitors

altitude. If it is south-facing, the glazing area is typically 25% less than if it is north-facing to provide the same annual daylighting contribution.

A fully daylighted 1000 ft² classroom should have a 6% to 13% monitor DFR, with 80% center-of- glass VT for the daylighting fenestration. Glazing with a lower light transmission may be used, but the aperture should be increased to maintain the same effective visible aperture area (fenestration area × VT). Where glazing is used specifically for daylighting, consider the use of uncoated clear glass or low-e coated clear glass with a high VT. A larger daylighting aperture with a lower VT has the advantage of providing the same amount of daylight but with less glare and contrast. The disadvantage is that the costs associated with all the components of the daylighting system are typically higher.

To provide optimal levels the following process can be used:

- Determine the target lighting level (recommended illuminance).
- Multiply that level by 1.5, which equals the targeted maximum (solar noon) daylight illuminance level in the warmest month that the school is occupied.

DL31   Overhang for Roof Monitor (Climate Zones: all)

Assuming the school is in a location that has a winter heating requirement, consider placing the overhang the same as if designing a passive solar building. Start by placing the outer point of the overhang at an angle of about 45° from horizontal above the head of the window. This will allow most of the solar gain to enter during the winter, even at noon when the altitude is low.

By moving the overhang in and out and simulating these conditions during peak cooling times (as well as with annual simulations), you will be able to determine the correct, optimum location. The overhang should not allow any more radiation entering the space during peak cooling times than is necessary to deliver the required light levels. If during peak cooling time the space has higher foot candle levels than is necessary, this will increase your cooling loads.

Design the south-facing monitor to capture passive heating in the winter months. This will help offset the heat not being provided when electric lights are off. Do not overextend the overhang. It will negatively impact the daylighting contribution as well as the passive heating benefit.

DL32   Use Light-Colored Roofing in Front of Monitors (Climate Zones: all)

Specify a light-colored roofing material to reflect additional light into the glazing. A white single-ply roofing material (aged reflectance of 69%) typically provides the best long-term reflectance (Akbari et al. 2005). This compares to a black ethylene propylene diene monomer (EPDM) of 6%, a gray EPDM of 23%, or a light-colored rock ballast of 25%.

Using Baffles in Roof Monitors

South-Facing Roof Monitor

Fire-retardant, UV-resistant baffles within a South-facing roof monitor block all direct beam radiation at any solar altitude. Light-colored translucent baffles reflect the sunlight into the space and help eliminate contrast from one side of the baffle to the other.

Interior View of Translucent Baffles Inside Roof Monitor

When white single-ply roofing is placed directly in front of the south-facing roof monitors, the glazing area in the monitors can be reduced by up to 20% because of the additional reflected radiation entering the monitor.

The white color also provides an overall benefit of reflecting solar radiation that would otherwise be absorbed and reradiated downward into the conditioned space. Energy savings also result as a benefit of a lowered cooling load.

DL33   *Use Baffles to Block Direct Beam Radiation and Diffuse Light* (Climate Zones: all)

In the roof monitor light well assemblies, white baffles should hang parallel to the glass and be spaced to ensure that no direct beam light enters the space. The spacing and depth of the baffles should be determined so that when standing inside the room looking out, the occupants cannot see the sky. This will ensure that no direct beam light can strike the work plane. Baffles should have the following characteristics:

- Fire retardant and UV resistant
- Light-colored and translucent to reflect the sunlight into the space and help eliminate contrast from one side of the baffle to the other

DL34   *Minimize Contrast at Well-Ceiling Intersection* (Climate Zones: all)

At the bottom of the light well, contrast is significantly reduced if there is a transition between the vertical and the horizontal planes. A 45° angled plane is good, but a curved transition is even better. To achieve this curved effect, many designers now use fiber-reinforced plaster curved sections that nicely receive gypsum board.

DL35   *Address the Monitor Design* (Climate Zones: all)

To help reduce conductive gains and losses, the walls and ceiling of the roof monitor should be insulated and should incorporate appropriate insulation and moisture barriers as recommended in EN2–4 and EN6–7.

Make sure that the colors used within the monitor well are very light. White is best. Darker colors will result in a considerable loss in efficiency (see Figure 5-13).

Also consider acoustic issues. If acoustical ceiling material is used, make sure that the light reflectance and the acoustical sound absorption are both high. Often manufacturers, in presenting the light reflectance of an acoustical tile, will specify the paint color. Remember to account for the reduced light reflectance caused by the fissures in the tile.

DL36   *Let the Heat Stratify* (Climate Zones: all)

A key to achieving the desired cooling reductions is to rely on the stratification of heat within the monitor. Do not attempt to remove this heat by placing supply and return grilles in this area, but instead allow the heat to stratify. This benefit is often overlooked in designing daylighted spaces and comparing one strategy to another.

DL37   *Minimize the Depth of the Ceiling Cavity* (Climate Zones: all)

The depth of the well is very important. The deeper the well, the harder it is for the radiation to reflect down into the space. For example, in a 20 × 20 ft square sky well that is 7 ft deep and has 70% reflectance, the loss in effectiveness will be 50% (see Figure 5-13).

CLASSROOM SIDELIGHTING PLUS TOPLIGHTING STRATEGIES

DL38   *Classroom Sidelighting Plus Toplighting Pattern* (Climate Zones: all)

This daylighting pattern is appropriate for one-story buildings or for the top floor of a multi-story school. It combines the sidelighting recommendations of the previous pattern, supplying at least two-thirds of the benefit, with small interior skylights, tubular daylighting devices, or

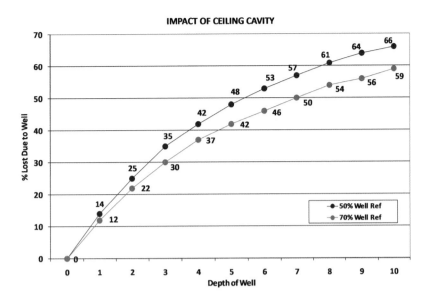

Figure 5-13 (DL37) Impact of Ceiling Cavity with 50% and 70% Reflectance in the Well

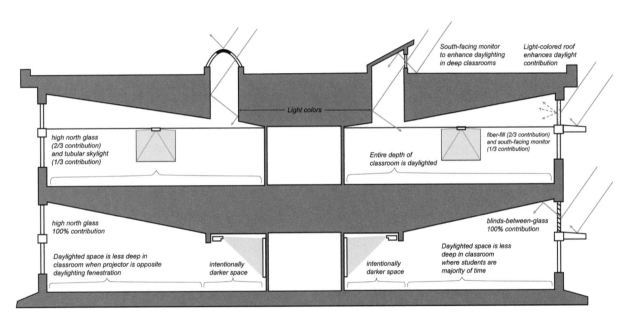

Figure 5-14 (DL 35) Sidelighting Enhanced with Toplighted Skylights or Roof Monitors

roof monitors to balance daylighting across the space. Figure 5-14 shows a cross section for this pattern. See DL4 for recommendations for implementing this type of daylighting strategy.

GYM TOPLIGHTING STRATEGIES

DL39   Gym Toplighting Overview (Climate Zones: all)

For spaces with high ceilings, such as gymnasiums, or for larger spaces, such as multipurpose rooms, cafeterias, and commons, a basic daylighting design that uses toplighting is recommended. Toplighting has the distinct advantage of providing useful daylight under most conditions and allows for almost any orientation of the space.

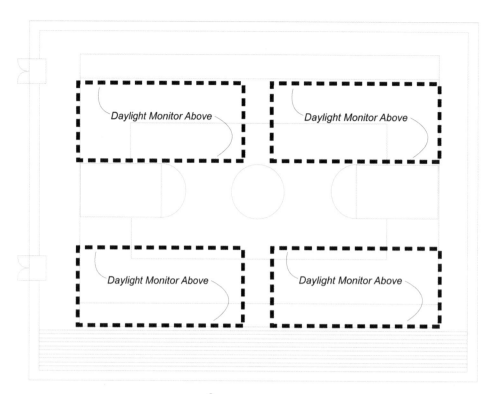

Figure 5-15   (DL 41) Typical 7600 ft² Gymnasium Floor Plan with Four Roof Monitors

DL40   *Gym Toplighting Sizing* (**Climate Zones: all**)

For those performing daylighting calculations using a daylighting program, the optimum day-lighting performance will generally be achieved when the maximum average light level reached under winter conditions is no more than about 200 fc, and there is never any direct sun penetration. In the warmer peak cooling months, footcandle levels should average no more than 1.5 times the design footcandle level. This will produce, between 9:00 a.m. and 3:00 p.m, use-ful daylight ranging from about 30 fc in the summer to 200 fc in the winter if south-facing roof monitors are used.

The following process can be used to provide optimal levels:

•   Determine the target lighting level (recommended illuminance).
•   Multiply that level by 1.5, which equals the targeted maximum (solar noon) daylight illu-minance level in the warmest month that the school is occupied.

DL41   *Gym Toplighting Using South-Facing Roof Monitors* (**Climate Zones: all**)

A south-facing clerestory can be employed to create good uniformity with very low DFR (5% to 9% of the floor area), but it must be carefully designed with an overhang to shade direct summer sunlight and interior baffles to diffuse direct sunlight and prevent glare.

Figures 5-15 and 5-16 show typical toplighted gymnasium floor plans employing south-facing roof monitors.

DL42   *Gym Toplighting in Combination with North- and South-Facing Sidelighting* (**Climate Zones: all**)

Often the optimum strategy for daylighting a large gymnasium involves a combination of roof monitors and sidelighting. In this case, refer to the DL4 when determining the appropriate DFR values to be employed.

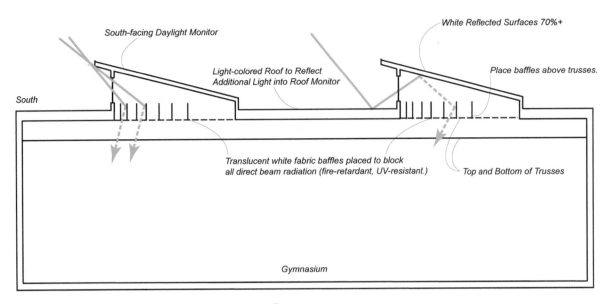

Figure 5-16   (DL 41) Typical 7600 ft² Gymnasium Floor Plan with Four Roof Monitors

REFERENCES AND RESOURCES

Akbari, H., A.A. Berhe, R. Levinson, S. Graveline, K. Foley, A.H. Delgado, and R.M. Paroli. 2005. Aging and weathering of cool roofing membranes. Paper Number 58055, Lawrence Berkeley National Laboratory, Berkeley, CA. http://repositories.cdlib.org/cgi/viewcontent.cgi?article=3574&context=lbnl.

ASHRAE 2004. ANSI/ASHRAE/IESNA Standard 90.1-2004, *Energy Standard for Buildings Except Low-Rise Residential Buildings*. Atlanta: American Society of Heating, Refrigerating and Air-Conditioning Engineers.

ASHRAE 2009. *ASHRAE Handbook—Fundamentals*. Atlanta: American Society of Heating, Refrigerating and Air-Conditioning Engineers.

ASHRAE. 2010a. ANSI/ASHRAE/IES Standard 90.1-2010, *Energy Standard for Buildings Except Low-Rise Residential Buildings*. Atlanta: American Society of Heating, Refrigerating and Air-Conditioning Engineers.

CHPS. 2006a. *High Performance Schools Best Practices Manual Volume II—Design*. Sacramento, CA: The Collaborative for High Performance Schools. pp. 205, 208. http://www.triumphmodular.com/resources/documents/chps/CHPS_II_2006_locked.pdf.

CHPS. 2006b. Criteria for high performance schools. The Collaborative for High Performance Schools, Sacramento, CA. http://www.chps.net/dev/Drupal/node/212.

Evans, B. 1997. Daylighting design. In *Time Saver Standards for Architectural Design Data*, Ed., D. Watson. Columbus, OH: McGraw-Hill.

Figueiro, M.G., and M.S. Rea. 2010. Lack of short-wavelength light during the school day delays dim light melatonin onset (DLMO) in middle school students. *Neuroendocrinology Letters* 31(1):92–96. http://http://node.nel.edu/?node_id=9849.

IESNA. 1996. *EPRI Lighting Controls—Patterns for Design*. New York: Illuminating Engineering Society of North America.

IESNA. 1997. E*PRI Daylight Design: Smart & Simple*. New York: Illuminating Engineering Society of North America.

LBNL. 2011. Tips for daylighting with windows. Lawrence Berkeley National Laboratories, Berkeley, CA. http://windows.lbl.gov/daylighting/designguide/designguide.html.

NBI. 2003. Advanced Lighting Guidelines. New Buildings Institute, White Salmon, WA. http://http://www.algonline.org/.

ELECTRIC LIGHTING

INTERIOR LIGHTING

Goals for School Lighting

Energy-efficient lighting systems in schools can be designed with or without daylighting. However, to achieve at least a 50% reduction in energy consumption, controlled daylighting will likely be provided in classrooms, resource rooms, gymnasiums, multi-purpose rooms, cafeterias, media centers, and the majority of administrative spaces

Good Design Practice

EL1   *Light-Colored Interior Finishes* (Climate Zones: all)

For electrical lighting to be used efficiently, spaces must have light-colored finishes. Ceiling reflectance should be at least 80% (preferably 90%), which in general means using smooth white acoustical tile or ceiling paint. The average reflectance of the walls should be at least 50%, which in general means using light tints or off whites for the wall surface, as the lower reflectance of doors, tack surfaces, and other objects on the walls will reduce the average. Floor surfaces should be at least 20%, for which there are many suitable surfaces.

In addition, take the shape and finish of the ceiling into account. A flat painted or acoustical tile ceiling without fissures or holes (but retaining good acoustical properties) is the most efficient; sloping ceilings are somewhat less efficient, and exposed roof structures, even if painted white, may significantly reduce the effective ceiling electric light reflectivity. Lighting systems with indirect components are recommended, but if the ceiling cavity includes exposed structures or exposed ductwork, a higher percentage of downlight may be required. Make sure the ceiling and all components are painted a high-reflectance white.

EL2   *Color Rendering Index* (Climate Zones: all)

The Color Rendering Index (CRI) is a scale measurement identifying a lamp's ability to adequately reveal color characteristics of objects and people. The scale maximizes at 100, with 100 indicating the best color rendering capability. All lamps recommended in this guide are rated at 80 CRI or greater.

EL3   *Color Temperature* (Climate Zones: all)

The color temperature is a scale identifying a lamp's relative warmth or coolness—the higher the color temperature, the bluer the source. A majority of the lamps in use today are either 3500, 4100, or 5000 K (absolute temperature) fluorescent lamps. Preliminary studies (Boyce et al. 2001) show that higher-color temperature light at the 5000 K end instead of the 3500 K end may provide better visual acuity; however, 5000 K lamps may produce an artificially cool-looking building at night. The higher 4100 K or 5000 K color temperatures will also match the daylight from windows and skylights more closely than will the lower, 3500 K color temperature.

Create a purchasing plan to buy only one color temperature lamp to maintain color consistency during spot and/or group relamping.

EL4   *Linear Fluorescent Lamps and Ballasts* (Climate Zones: all)

To achieve the lighting power density (LPD) recommendations in Chapter 4, high-performance T-8 lamps and high-performance electronic ballasts are used for general lighting.

T8 High-Performance Lamps. High-performance T-8 lamps are defined, for the purpose of this Guide, as having a lamp efficacy of 90+ nominal lumens per watt, based on mean lumens divided by the cataloged lamp input watts. Mean lumens are published in lamp catalogs as the reduced lumen output that occurs at 40% of the lamp's rated life. High-performance T-8s also are defined as having a CRI of 81 or higher and 94% lumen maintenance. The high performance

Table 5-7 Commonly Manufactured 4-foot T8 lamps

T8 Lamp Description	Lamp Series	CCT	Watts	Average Lumens		MLPW
				Initial	Mean	
F032\730	700	3000	32	2800	2613	82
F032\735	700	3500	32	2800	2613	82
F032\741	700	4100	32	2800	2613	82
F032\750	700	5000	32	2700	2515	79
F032\830	800	3000	32	2950	2801	88
F032\835	800	3500	32	2950	2801	88
F032\841	800	4100	32	2950	2801	88
F032\850	800	5000	32	2817	2677	84
F032\830\HL	800	3000	32	3100	2937	92
F032\835\HL	800	3500	32	3100	2937	92
F032\841\HL	800	4100	32	3100	2937	92
F032\850\HL	800	5000	32	3008	2848	89
F032\830\30W	800	3000	30	2850	2718	91
F032\835\30W	800	3500	30	2850	2718	91
F032\841\30W	800	4100	30	2850	2718	91
F032\850\30W	800	5000	30	2783	2653	88
F032\830\28W	800	3000	28	2725	2599	93
F032\835\28W	800	3500	28	2725	2599	93
F032\841\28W	800	4100	28	2725	2599	93
F032\850\28W	800	5000	28	2667	2509	90
F032\830\25W	800	3000	25	2458	2344	94
F032\835\25W	800	3500	25	2458	2344	94
F032\841\25W	800	4100	25	2458	2344	94
F032\850\25W	800	5000	25	2383	2273	91

Note: Dark shaded lamps comply with the 90+ mean lumens per watt (MLPW).

lamp is available in 32 W rapid start and 30, 28, and 25 W instant start lamps. Table 5-7 lists the corrected color temperature (CCT), watts, average lumens, and mean lumens per watt (MLPW) of the commonly manufactured 4 ft T8 lamps.

Ballasts. The ballast factor (BF) is a measure of the relative light output of the ballast. A BF of 1.0 would mean that the ballast is driving the lamp to produce 100% of the rated lamp lumens. Light output and wattage are related—the lower the BF the lower that wattage and the lower the light output. Normal BF ballasts are in the 0.85 to 1.0 range, with most at 0.87 or 0.88. Low BF ballasts, with BF below 0.85, can be used to reduce the light output and wattage of the system when the layout of the fixtures will overlight the space. High BF ballasts, with BF above 1.0, can be used to increase the light output of the lamp in areas where the fixture layout will underlight the space—wattage will go up proportional to the BF.

Ballast efficacy factor (BEF) is a term used to compare the efficiency of different lamp/ballast systems. BEF is [(BF ·100)/ballast input wattage)]. Unfortunately, the calculated BEF changes due to the number of lamps the ballast drives, so for this guide we will modify the BEF by multiplying the calculated BEF by the number of lamps to generate a BEF-P (ballast efficacy factor—prime).

Instant-Start Ballasts. High-performance electronic instant start ballasts are defined, for the purpose of this Guide, as having a BEF-P of 3.15 or greater.

For energy-saving T8 lamps, the BEF-P for 30 W systems is 3.3 or greater, for 28 W systems is 3.6 greater, and for 25 W systems is 3.9 or greater.

BEF-P Calculation

From a lamp catalog, the 2-lamp ballast with 32 W lamps uses 55 W and has a BF of 0.87.

$$BEF = (0.87 \cdot 100)/55 = 1.58$$

$$BEF\text{-}P = 1.58 \cdot 2 = 3.16, \text{ which passes.}$$

Instant-start T-8 ballasts provide the greatest energy savings options and are the least costly option. Additionally, the parallel lamp operation allows one lamp to operate even if the other burns out.

Caution: Instant-start ballasts may reduce lamp life when controlled by occupancy sensors or daylight switching systems. However, even if the rated lamp life is reduce by 25%, if due to the occupancy sensor the lamp is off more than 25% of the time, then the socket life (the length of time before the lamps are replaced) will be greater. If extended socket life is desired, consider program rapid start ballasts.

Program Rapid Start Ballasts. High-performance electronic program rapid start ballasts are defined, for the purpose of this Guide, as having a BEF-P of 3.00 or greater. While program rapid start ballasts are normally recommended on occupancy sensor controlled lamps due to increased lamp life, they use approximately 5% more power than instant start ballasts do. For this Guide, program rapid start ballasts are not used to achieve the LPD in Chapter 4. Program rapid start ballasts may be used as long as the LPDs in Chapter 4 are not exceeded.

Caution: Using program rapid start ballasts will result in slightly higher power consumption with the same light level. The wattage and light levels will need to be reduced in other areas to meet the LPD recommendations in Chapter 4.

Dimming Ballasts. High-performance dimming ballasts are defined, for the purpose of this Guide, as having a BEF-P of 3.00 or greater. Dimming ballasts are used along with daylight controls in all open office spaces.

T5 Lamps and Ballasts. T5HO and T5 lamps have initial lumens per watt that compare favorably to the high-performance T8. In addition to energy, T5s use fewer natural resources (glass, metal, phosphors) than a comparable lumen output T8 system. However, when evaluating the lamp and ballast at the "mean lumens" of the lamps, T5HO lamps perform more poorly. On instant start ballasts, high-performance T8s are 13% more efficient than T5s.

Cautions: Since T5s have higher surface brightness, they should not be used in open-bottom fixtures. Without highly reflective ceilings, it may be difficult for indirect lighting systems to achieve the LPD recommendation in Chapter 4 and maintain the desired light levels.

All fluorescent lamps are temperature sensitive and will produce lower light levels in cold and hot environments. This is more critical is specifying the new energy saving T8, T5, and T5HO lamps.

EL5　*Compact Fluorescent* (Climate Zones: all)

To achieve the LPD recommendations in Chapter 4, compact fluorescent lamps (CFLs) can be used for a variety of applications, such as utility lighting, downlighting, and wall washing. Suitable lamps include twin tube, multiple twin tube, and long twin tube lamps. Only pin-based CFLs are included in this group, since a screw-based lamp can be replaced with an incandescent lamp and is therefore not compliant with most energy codes. Suitable luminaires have integral hard-wired electronic ballasts.

Because the efficacy of CFLs is only 30 to 60 MLPW, they should not be used for general lighting in most space types. To meet the efficacy requirements of this Guide, some CFL and ballast combinations must be avoided (see Table 5-8).

Table 5-8 System Efficacy for CFL-Ballast Systems

Lamp Type	Electronic Ballast (4-Pin Lamp) Program Start Except [†]	
	Wattage	System Efficacy
5–13 W twin tube	13 W only	52–57
10–26 W double twin tube	13 W	57[†]
	18 W	52
	26 W	53
13–42 W triple and quad twin tube and most twist tube lamps	13 W	53[†]
	18 W	53
	26 W	55
	32 W	51
	42 W	57
2D	28 W	63
Long twin tube	18 W	46
	24/27 W	61
	36/39 W	64
	40 W	60

▨ Does not meet efficiency criteria   Meets 50 MLPW efficacy criteria for utility and special lighting

† Instant start

EL6 *Metal Halide* (Climate Zones: all)

To achieve the LPD recommendations in Chapter 4, metal halide lamps may be used for general lighting in large spaces, outdoor lighting, and for accent lighting and wall washing in low wattages. In the metal halide family there are two primary types: ceramic metal halide (CMH) lamps and quartz metal halide (QMH) lamps. Both types are high-intensity discharge lamps in which intense light energy is generated inside an arc tube made either of ceramic or quartz glass. The two types are comparably efficient. CMH lamps have very good color in the warm (3000 K) and neutral (4000 K) ranges; QMH lamps' color rendering quality is mediocre except in high color temperature lamps (5000 K and above).

All lamps 400 W and below are now "pulse start" rather than "probe start" and can be operated on either magnetic ballasts or more efficient electronic ballasts. Just recently, electronic ballasts have become practical for indoor use of pulse start metal halide.

The apparent high efficacy of metal halide lamps is often offset by their high rate of lumen depreciation. Because MLPW takes lumen depreciation into account, the type of ballast plays a significant role in system efficacy. As a result, a number of lamps and ballasts do not meet the efficacy criteria, as shown in a partial list in Table 5-9.

Cautions: Metal halide lamps require a warm up time and a restrike time of up to 15 minutes if turned off during operations. Therefore, a supplemental emergency source is required that will provide light during the restrike time.

Color consistency in appearance (color temperature) may be a problem as QMH lamps age, especially if used in an indirect luminaire.

EL7 *Light-Emitting Diode (LED) Lighting* (Climate Zones: all)

LED lighting is gaining in popularity and acceptance as an interior lighting option. Every day, more interior LED products are being offered, and technology in this area is advancing rapidly.

While this technology continues to develop, lighting designers should be aware of both the advantages and disadvantages of its use in interior spaces. Some items to consider are increased operating temperatures, varying color temperatures, lower installed wattage, and varying control parameters.

Table 5-9 System Efficacy for Metal Halide Lamp-Ballast Systems

Lamp	Magnetic Ballast	Electronic Ballast (Minimum Efficacy, Some Ballasts Will Be Higher)
35/39 W CMH	43	53
50 W QMH	33	40
70 W CMH	45	51
100 W CMH	51	60
150 W CMH	59	67
175 W QMH	62	66
400 W QMH	71	75
400 W CMH	72	76

Does not meet efficacy criteria   Meets 50 MLPW efficacy criteria for utility and special lighting   Meets 75 MLPW efficacy criteria for general lighting

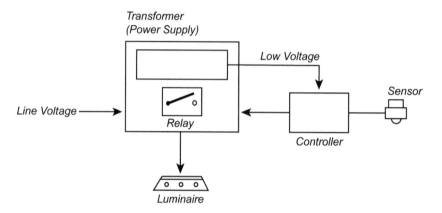

Figure 5-17   (EL8) Occupancy-Sensing Control

EL8   Occupancy Sensors (Climate Zones: all)

Use occupancy sensors in all classrooms, offices, mechanical rooms, restrooms, and special-use spaces like music practice rooms. Manual ON/automatic OFF sensors offer greater energy savings than do standard automatic ON/automatic OFF devices. Partial ON sensors (e.g., where lights turn on automatically to a 50% light level and the occupant has to manually turn on the remaining 50% light level) offer even greater energy savings.

Occupant should not be able to override the automatic OFF setting in any application, even if it is set for manual ON. Unless otherwise recommended, factory-set occupancy sensors should be set for medium to high sensitivity with a 15-minute time delay (the optimum time to achieve energy savings without excessive loss of lamp life). Review the manufacturer's data for proper placement and coverage. Figure 5-17 shows a typical occupancy-sensing control setup.

The two primary types of occupancy sensors are *passive infrared* (PIR) and *ultrasonic*. PIR sensors can see only in a line of sight and should not be used in rooms where the user cannot see the sensor (e.g., storage areas with multiple aisles, restrooms with stalls). Ultrasonic sensors can be disrupted by high airflow and should not be used near air duct outlets. Dual-mode sensors that combine PIR with another technology such as ultrasound or audible noise should be considered for problem areas. The best solutions use both technologies.

Cautions:

- Motion sensors should not be used with high-intensity discharge (HID) lamps because of warm-up and restrike times.
- Fluorescent lamps and CFLs should use program start ballasts if short ON/OFF cycles are expected.

ASHRAE/IES Standard 90.1-2010 Occupancy Sensor Requirements

Occupancy sensors are required in Standard 90.1-2010 in the following spaces:

- Classrooms, conference rooms, meeting rooms, and training rooms, employee lunch and break rooms, storage and supply rooms between 50 ft^2 and 1000 ft^2, rooms used for document copying and printing, office spaces up to 250 ft^2, restrooms, and dressing/locker rooms

Standard 90.1-2010 requires that occupancy sensors shall either be manual ON or shall be controlled to automatically turn the lighting on to not more than 50% power, except in public corridors and stairwells, restrooms, primary building entrance areas and lobbies, and areas where manual ON operation would endanger the safety or security of the room or building occupant(s) where full automatic ON is allowed.

- In classrooms, consider a timer bypass for the motion sensor to prevent lights flashing when only the teacher is present and working quietly.
- The greatest energy savings are achieved with manual ON/automatic OFF occupancy sensors or automatic ON to 50% light level. This avoids unnecessary operation when electric lights are not needed and greatly reduces the frequency of switching.
- Confirm that the occupancy sensor is set to manual ON operation during installation. Many manufacturers ship sensors with default setting of automatic ON.

EL9   *Multilevel Switching or Dimming* (Climate Zones: all)

Specify luminaires with multiple lamps to be factory wired for inboard-outboard switching or in-line switching or dimming. The objective is to have multiple levels of light uniformly distributed in the space. Avoid checkerboard patterns of turning every other fixture off in medium and large spaces. In open office and large, open areas avoid nonuniform switching patterns unless different areas of the large space are used at different times or for different functions.

EL10   *Exit Signs* (Climate Zones: all)

Use LED exit signs or other sources that use no more than 1.5 W per face. The selected exit sign and source should provide the proper luminance to meet all building and fire code requirements.

EL11   *Circuiting and Switching* (Climate Zones: all)

In addition to the customary general lighting of classrooms, lighting and controls must now take into account the requirements of video images. For cost and other practical reasons, most classrooms will use a low-cost video projector connected to a personal computer, laptop, DVD, cable, or VCR. Teachers will use a combination of video and computer-generated images ranging from software slide shows to recorded programs and streaming Internet to teach classes at all levels. New schools design should anticipate substantial daily classroom time in which the lights are dimmed and video replaces the whiteboard as the principal teaching medium.

This creates two substantially different "scenes":

- A *bright scene* in which classic qualities of classroom lighting and daylighting are appropriate. Light levels of 30 to 70 fc at every point, reasonably even surface brightness, and a cheerful feeling are the result of this type of design.
- An *AV scene* in which the electric lighting and daylighting are controlled to limit ambient light on the screen to less than 15 fc. This permits the average projector to achieve an acceptable image contrast on an ordinary pull-down screen when it is properly sized for the room. Darkened ceilings and upper walls are essential, and daylighting must be controlled

or eliminated. Use of darkening is not required if good daylighting designs are employed that intentionally dim the projection screen area.

There is a distinct chance that once shades are put in place for AV, they will be left there all day, effectively preventing daylighting. The preferred solution is to educate teachers about the importance of daylighting. An alternative and more foolproof solution is to use electrically operated shades that automatically retract when lights are turned on for the bright scene; unfortunately, this is considered too expensive for most projects. Another approach, designing the room for AV concurrent with daylighting, is very difficult to do and forces very specific architectural decisions that some projects cannot include. The California Public Interest Energy Research program addressed this situation and contains a number of reports and research data (PIER 2005).

For most other spaces in an education facility, the controls for switching and dimming the lighting system should *not* be readily accessible. The controls should be located in a supervised location or one that is accessible to the building staff only. General-use spaces such as corridors should be controlled by a time-of-day scheduling system and may be integrated with daylight harvesting. For gymnasiums and multipurpose rooms, consider a modern preset dimming or control system, especially if touch-screen control and other modern AV interfaces are planned.

For assembly spaces and some larger classrooms, the room needs to be equipped with an emergency lighting system that can produce at least 1 fc, on average, along the path of egress. In general, the best way to do this is to power some of the lighting from an emergency source, which must be either an emergency generator or a battery backup system that can provide egress lighting for at least 90 minutes. The controls must be designed so that if a power emergency occurs, the proper lights are illuminated regardless of setting. This often requires the use of automatic transfer relay or other mechanism that bypasses room controls during a power emergency. Transfer relays must be listed for use in emergency circuits.

EL12   *Electrical Lighting Design for Schools* (Climate Zones: all)

The 0.7 W/ft^2 LPD represents an average LPD for the entire building. Individual spaces may have higher power densities if they are offset by lower power densities in other areas. Refer to the Chapter 4 recommendation tables for a complete list of LPDs for a space-by-space method of achieving the overall 0.7 W/ft^2 goal.

EL13   *Classroom Lighting* (Climate Zones: all)

Classrooms are typically designed for a single lighting scene in which conventional classroom lighting levels are maintained, and the lights are turned off for AV uses. However, classroom lighting design is changing rapidly because of advances in technology. The approach addressed in this Guide is to design classrooms with multiple lighting scenes: one for general lighting and at least one additional scene where stray lighting is controlled to permit maximum AV screen contrast. This approach specifically addresses classrooms where advanced teaching technology (computers, video, computer projection, etc.) are to be used, but is appropriate for all classroom types.

For best results, provide a flat, white acoustical tile or gypsum board ceiling at least 9 ft 6 in. above the finished floor with a direct/indirect suspended lighting system. By using a classroom lighting system designed for this application, including energy-efficient ballasts and controls (see EL4, EL8, and EL9), the lighting system, including supplemental whiteboard lighting, can operate at an LPD lower than 0.8 W/ft^2. Choosing among the many options includes considering the grade level, teaching technology, budget, and whiteboard relevance.

Classroom lighting can be accomplished by using luminaries with indirect distribution, direct distribution, or a combination of both. These options include the following:

- *Direct* distribution in which all of the light is radiated downward. Direct lighting systems tend to have high efficiency but can produce light of fair-to-poor visual comfort if not selected properly. Uniformity and shadowing problems can also result from direct lighting.

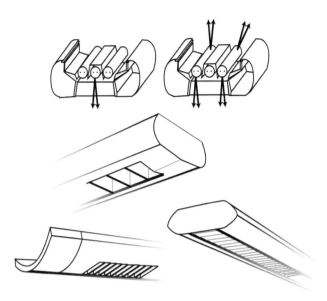

Figure 5-18   (EL13) Variations on Classroom Lighting Systems

- *Indirect* distribution in which all the light is radiated upward and, in turn, reflected downward by the ceiling. Indirect lighting systems are generally less efficient than direct lighting systems but usually produce light of superior quality, visual comfort, and uniformity.
- *Direct/indirect* distribution in which approximately equal (40%–60% to 60%–40%) amounts of light are radiated downward and upward. In general, direct/indirect lighting is used to provide comfortable but efficient illumination in spaces of medium room cavity ratios, such as libraries and offices.
- *Semi-indirect* distribution in which a modest amount of light is directed downward (10% to 40%) and a larger amount of light is directed upward (60% to 90%). In general, semi-indirect lighting is used in large spaces, such as open office areas and classrooms, to provide comfortable lighting with relatively high efficiency.
- *Semi-direct* distribution in which a modest amount of light is directed upward (10% to 40%) and a larger amount of light is directed downward (60% to 90%). In general, semi-direct lighting is used in spaces with very high ceilings, low-reflectance ceiling surfaces, and open structures that result in poor ceiling cavity reflectance.

For best results, classroom lighting systems should have separate semi-indirect and direct lighting components. See Figure 5-18 for variations of classroom direct/indirect lighting systems.

Lack of visual comfort has been identified as a major complaint about almost all direct lighting systems. The principal cause of discomfort is the contrast between a very bright luminaire and a comparatively dark adjacent ceiling. There is no way that a direct luminaire, including the so-called "recessed indirect" basket luminaires, can produce indirect light onto the ceiling to reduce this contrast. Totally indirect luminaires do provide a soft, glare-free lighting quality, but do not provide three-dimensional modeling and sparkle for visual interest. Therefore, suspended luminaires that provide a combination of indirect and direct distribution should generally be used. Low ceiling applications are the exception.

Current products offer a wide range of quality, performance, and appearance. For projects on tight budgets, formed steel indirect luminaires are sufficiently inexpensive and efficient to compete with parabolics and many other types of lay-in direct lighting. For projects with slightly higher budgets, designers can choose from a variety of attractive, high-performance lighting systems.

These lighting systems are typically suspended 15 to 18 in. from the ceiling, depending on the specific luminaire. If the ceiling is not at least 9 ft 6 in., special consideration should be made.

Pendant indirect or direct/indirect lighting systems are particularly well suited for integration with daylight systems, since both approaches require higher ceilings and secondary reflective surfaces. In daylighted rooms, pendant systems should be run parallel to the primary windows or daylight source so they can be switched or dimmed in response to daylight gradients. In a classroom, three rows of pendants will allow a more gradual response to daylight than two rows. Daylight controls can then switch or dim each row separately. This would be the preferred choice if the budget allows.

For classrooms in which advanced teaching technology such as video and computer projection are to be used, the lighting system should provide multiple scenes—one for general lighting and at least one in which stray light is controlled to permit maximum screen contrast. This approach may also be used for all classroom types and is valid in primary classrooms where the ability to create a darkened room, such as for student calming and story time, is desired. Pendant luminaires equipped with optical controls or dimming ballasts allow relatively precise low light level settings. The general lighting system should not exceed 0.8 W/ft^2, and the highly controlled lighting system should use less, with switching to prevent simultaneous use.

This system lends itself to three principal control scenes, as follows:

- *Night, general lighting scene.* All general lighting system lamps are ON.
- *Daytime, general lighting scene.* General lighting system lamps are affected by available daylight, either switching or dimming. Switched daylighting scenes can be created by switching luminaire rows or rows of lamps.
- *Any time, low-level scene.* General lighting lamps are OFF, controlled downlight lamps are ON or ON with manual dimming controls. In a single-lamp direct/indirect system, dimming to low level with extinguishing of luminaire closest to the screen is encouraged.

Acceptable performance can also be achieved with a direct/indirect luminaire with dimming, provided that the row of luminaires closest to the screen is switched off in the AV mode.

The key to achieving a suitable design is to reduce the ambient light level on the projection screen to a maximum of 15 vertical fc. If the daylighting strategy does not employ an effective strategy to intentionally darken the projection area, shades may be necessary. However, given that most teachers prefer to keep their students in well-lighted seating when viewing videos, strategies must be employed that allow the projection screen area to be kept darker while the seating area remains well lighted (see DL13). The solution of creating a dropped soffit in front of the screen works in both daylighted and non-daylighted classrooms where simply switching off the lights in the front half of the classroom still fails to reduce light levels.

As the use of the teaching board evolves, it remains an important part of education at all levels. There seems to be a correlation between illumination of the teaching surface and retention of information. If the teaching board (white board) is used, additional lighting—with either normal lighting or in a dimmed setting for the rest of the room—serves as a significant "attractor," which aids in the learning process. Energy use is about the same, but the slightly more expensive system with board light (see Figure 5-19) is recommended for improved student attention during board activities.

To coordinate with a ceiling-mounted computer video projector, two rows of luminaires are recommended for classrooms up to about 30 ft wide, as shown in Figure 5-20. (For larger classrooms, consider these principles and make the necessary adjustments.)

Caution/Low Ceiling Solutions: If a ceiling is lower than 9 ft and suspended fixtures may be accessible to students, recessed lighting systems should be considered. The most efficient recessed lighting systems use T5 lamps with special lenses and reflectors to minimize glare. Troffers are more efficient than pendant lighting systems in low ceiling applications, but produce light that is less comfortable and makes AV integration more difficult. The use of stepped

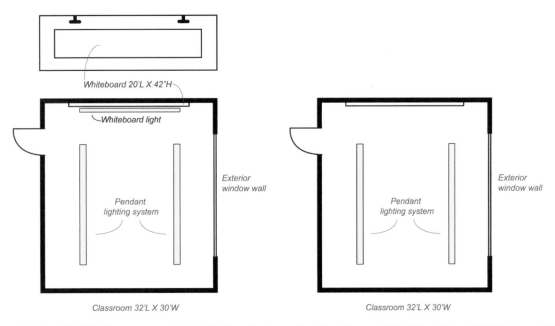

Figure 5-19 (EL13) Recommended Lighting System (Left) with and (Right) without Whiteboard Light

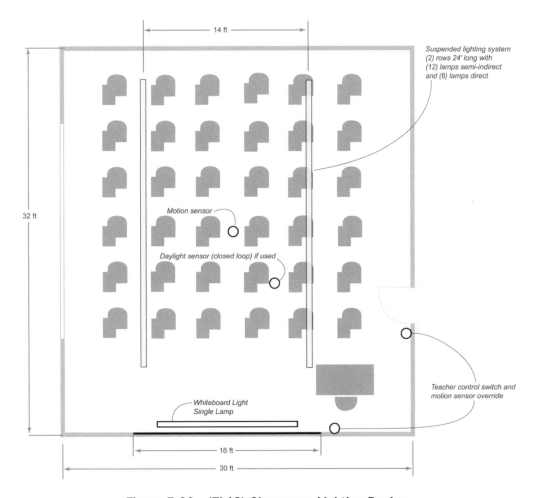

Figure 5-20   (EL13) Classroom Lighting Design

or full dimming ballasts is recommended, and for better AV integration, switch the back of the room separately from the front.

EL14 *Gym Lighting* (Climate Zones: all)

Most school gyms are simple, high bay structures with open trusses or bar joists. Whenever possible, a combination of daylighting and electric lighting is desirable, but electric lighting may be the principal design solution because of the extended hours of operation of this space.

Daylighting design is especially well suited to the high ceilings and large open space of gymnasiums and multipurpose rooms. Roof monitors or north and south, filtered glazing systems (fiber-filled, blinds-between-glazing, or aerogel with VLT below 30) that effectively block direct beam radiation from entering and reaching the playing area are preferred. See DL40–41 for further gym/multipurpose room daylighting guidance. In daylighting gymnasiums and multipurpose spaces, it is essential that a dimmable lighting strategy be employed on lights that would be utilized during typical daytime uses (gym classes). It is reasonable to consider ON-OFF strategies for additional, supplemental lighting that may be employed during night-time competitions (typical in high school gymnasiums where games are filmed).

For electric lighting, high bay luminaires are easily attached to the structure, with the luminaires suspended within the "truss space" so that the bottom of the luminaire is flush with the lowest beam or truss member. In the rare instance where the gym has a finished ceiling, recessed lighting might be considered, but basic high bay lighting systems are by far the most common approach. The height of the gym space's ceiling is a major factor in the choice of gym lighting systems. Most gyms will have a room cavity ratio of about 2.5. By comparing the coefficient of utilization of luminaires being considered, an efficient lighting system can be selected. For most gyms, luminaires with spacing-to-mounting height of less than 1.4 is appropriate.

Fluorescent systems that use multiple T5HO or T8 lamps are preferred for ordinary gyms and other high-ceiling spaces. Superior color, elimination of flicker, and the ability to turn lights on and off (or dim if daylighted) as needed are major advantages over HID systems. The added cost of the fluorescent system is offset by much lower energy use, estimated to be as much as 50% less if the multiple light level (lamp switching) capability of a fluorescent system is used. Systems that use multiple CFLs also provide these benefits, although without the high efficacy of the linear fluorescent lamps. It is recommended that fluorescent high bays be provided with wire guards to prevent lamps from being hit by flying objects.

In general, metal halide high bay lighting systems tend to be more appropriate when ceilings are especially tall, such as in large high school gymnasiums and field houses. Long lamp life and a minimum number of luminaires keep costs down. The color of metal halide is suitable for television and everyday use. The long warm up and restrike periods of metal halide lighting are drawbacks, since switching lights off regularly is not recommended for these systems. If employing them, be certain to use pulse-start lamps.

A separate dimmable fluorescent lighting system is highly recommended for two reasons:

- It is an instant-on/instant-off system. This feature is especially important if metal halide lights are accidentally extinguished, as they will require a 5 to 10 minute cool-off and restrike delay.
- A dimmable system can make the gym more appealing for social events and can serve as a "house" lighting system for many of the gym's performance and entertainment uses.

Cautions: Lighting quality is a crucial issue in gym spaces. Avoiding direct view of an extra bright light source, such as a metal halide lamp, high output lamp, or skylight, can be especially critical in a gymnasium where athletes must scan for the ball and react quickly. Even though a luminaire may normally be out of the line of sight, it can still create a devastating glare to a volleyball or basketball player. Consult IES RP-6-01 (R2009), *Sports and Recreational Area Lighting* (IES 2009) for fixture placement.

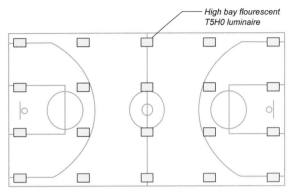

PATTERN 1 GYM
(20) 320 watt Pulse Start metal halide fixtures
Electronic ballast
50 footcandles maintained at 0.86 W/SF
60 footcandles maintained on court

PATTERN 2 GYM
(20) Gym-rated flourescent high bay fixtures
         each with (6) F54T5HO lamps
(2) or (3) electronic ballast total 360 watts
60 footcandles maintained at 0.90 W/SF
70 footcandles maintained on court

Figure 5-21   (EL14) Gym Lighting Patterns

Table 5-10   Gym Lighting Systems

Applications	Lighting Systems	Lamp Watts (Fixture input Watts)	Spacing Area (Approx. Grid)	Notes
PATTERN 1 HID lighting	CMH or QMH metal halide lamp with proper electronic ballast. Note: high frequency electronic for QMH, and low frequency electronic for CMH.	250 (275) 320 (345) 350 (370) 400 (425)	306 (17 × 18 ft) 383 (19 × 20 ft) 411 (20.5 × 20 ft) 472 (21.5 × 22 ft)	Mounting height at least 20 ft AFF. Set lamp height for proper spacing criterion (<1.1).
PATTERN 2 High bay fluorescent T5HO	T5HO with high bay reflector system and ballast designed for at least 60°C ambient temperature and 80°C case temperature in a properly designed luminaire with spacing criterion of <1.3	(4) T5HO with BF = 1.0 IS ballast (226 W) (6) T5HO with BF = 1.05 IS ballast (344 W)	251 (16 × 15 ft 9in.) 382 (19 × 20 ft)	Mounting height at least 20 ft AFF. Choose reflector for proper spacing criterion (<1.1).

Choose luminaires with shields to protect lamps from inadvertent damage by sports equipment.

Switching and dimming of the lighting system should not be readily accessible. Locate controls in a supervised location.

Consider a modern preset dimming or control system, especially if touch-screen control and other modern AV interfaces are planned.

Typical gym lighting systems and patterns are shown in Figure 5-21 and Table 5-10.

EL15   *Lighting for a Multipurpose Room* (Climate Zones: all)

Because multipurpose rooms often serve as cafeterias, study halls, social gathering spots, special event spaces, community meeting halls, and AV facilities, the lighting and controls must provide proper operation for every intended use of the room.

Multipurpose rooms can be successfully daylighted, either from high clerestories or roof monitor toplighting. However, near-blackout capability for the daylight system is often necessary in this type of space for AV use and special events, so operable shades or blinds are highly recommended. If daylighting can be reduced in the stage or projection screen area to 5 to 7 fc, most reduced light functions, including stage performances, can operate effectively. A small amount of sunlight can be a cheerful presence in a multipurpose room used as a cafeteria, as long as the light can be blocked if required (see DL39–41 for further multipurpose room day-lighting guidance). It is also possible to utilize higher lumen projectors that will allow the foot-candle level at the projection screen to increase to 15 to 25 fc and, in turn, allow the main portion of the multipurpose space to also increase.

At a minimum, a multipurpose room should have at least two independent lighting systems:

- A general lighting system that provides 20 to 30 fc of uniform illumination with standard fluorescent lamps.
- A dimmable "house" lighting system that supports AV and social uses of the room, producing no more than 5 fc.

In addition, theatrical lighting may be added to illuminate specific stage or performance locations. The lighting used for performance only is exempt from the LPD recommendations.

For the general lighting system, consider one of the types previously suggested for class-room lighting. If suspended luminaires are chosen, be careful to locate luminaires so as not to interfere with AV and other uses of the room. If the room will be used for any sports or games, all lighting systems should be protected from damage.

For the house lighting system, consider recessed or surface downlights. Halogen lighting is recommended for its superior color, inexpensive dimming, and good light control. Luminaires should use standard infrared halogen parabolic aluminized reflector lamps or T6 lamps. The lighting beam patterns should overlap at head height to provide excellent uniformity for a variety of functions. Black baffles or cone trims are recommended for AV applications. The house lighting system should be laid out to prevent light from striking walls or screens. Some general lighting systems might also serve as the house lighting system if properly laid out and equipped with electronic dimming ballasts. But most general lighting systems generate too much diffuse light, even when dimmed, for AV use and some social functions.

In general, two separate lighting systems, one being a dimmed halogen system, is initially the most cost effective. A single fluorescent lighting system with dimming mechanism is usually more costly and less flexible.

A control system that activates the general lighting system according to a calendar program and employs motion sensing for off hours should be used. Rooms with plentiful daylight should have automatic daylight stepped switching or dimming to reduce electric lighting during the day. A manual override switch should be provided. Manual dimming of the house lighting system should be provided along with an interlock switch to prevent simultaneous operation of both general and house lighting. Consider placing the lighting in zones that have individual manual override switches to permit an unoccupied zone to be deactivated.

Figures 5-22a and 5-22b show a typical multipurpose room with two lighting schemes. Figure 5-22a shows pendant-mounted luminaires and Figure 5-22b shows recessed troffers. Both schemes have a separate system of downlights to serve as house lights for social and AV use.

Cautions: Switching and dimming of the lighting system should not be readily accessible. Locate controls in a supervised location.

Consider a modern preset dimming or control system, especially if touch-screen control and other modern audio/video interfaces are planned.

EL16   *Lighting for a Library or Media Center* (Climate Zones: all)

Library spaces tend to be among the most expensive to light. These recommendations provide a good balance between cost, energy efficiency, and good lighting practice.

A control system that activates the general lighting system according to a calendar program and uses motion sensing for off hours should be used. In areas with plentiful daylight, use automatic daylight switching or dimming to reduce electric lighting during the day. In addition, in areas such as reference stacks that are less frequently used, consider providing individual motion sensors or digital time switches for stack aisles that are connected to dimming ballasts

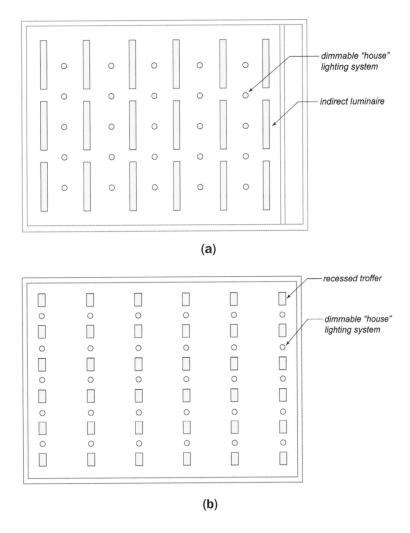

(a)

(b)

Figure 5-22   (EL15) Multipurpose Room (a) Indirect/Direct Lighting and (b) Direct Lighting Options

to produce low light levels (but not completely off) until the aisle is occupied. Individual reading and study rooms should use motion sensors. Personal motion sensors and plug strips should be used in study carrels, especially those with fixed computers.

The library or media center is a multipurpose space with a variety of uses; therefore, it is an excellent space to consider a task ambient lighting system. Daylight is an good option for providing basic ambient light in a library. Reading areas and storytelling niches especially benefit from gentle daylight and view windows. With thoughtful daylight design, only the task lighting at checkout desks or stack areas needs to be on during the day. In addition, these can be connected to occupancy sensors to reduce their hours of operation.

Provide lighting for a library as follows:

- A lighting system with standard fluorescent lamps that provide 20 to 50 fc of general illumination in casual reading, circulation, and seating areas.

- Overhead task lighting at locations such as conventional card files and circulation desks. In libraries where these tasks have been computerized, the general lighting system will provide proper illumination without overhead task lighting.

- Task lighting (LEDs, CFLs, or linear fluorescent lamps) at carrels and other obvious task locations.

- Stack lights with T8 or T5 lamps in areas where stack locations are fixed and locate general overhead lighting in areas with high-density stack systems.
- Special lighting for media rooms, as required.

The general lighting system may be one of the types previously suggested for classroom lighting (EL12). With adequate ceiling height, suspended lighting systems are preferable. Overhead lighting systems for task locations should also be selected from among choices suitable for classrooms or offices. The general lighting system can be designed to become more concentrated in task areas such as circulation desks, thus minimizing the number of luminaire types. Alternately, this may be an area where supplemental specialty luminaires are added for the additional benefit of navigating through the space.

Task lighting at carrels and other locations should be selected according to architecture and finish details. Common options include the following:

- Undershelf task lights with high color rendering T8 or T5 lamps
- Table or floor lamps equipped with CFLs up to 40 W
- LED task lighting

Stack lighting should use luminaires that are specifically designed for lighting stacks. There are several choices but generally a single continuous T-8 or T-5 lamp system will provide adequate illumination. Where the stack locations need flexibility (stacks relocated or placed off axis), an indirect lighting system or a linear stack light mounted from the stacks will provide the most flexibility.

Media rooms for video monitoring and editing, sound monitoring and editing, distance learning, and video teleconferencing have special requirements. Lighting must be designed to meet those specific needs, and lighting controls must be provided to enable the room to be used for the varying needs.

Figure 5-23a shows a typical library lighting design. The design illustrates general lighting that uses troffers, table lights for study desks, task lights at kiosks, and stack lights. Using high ballast factor two-lamp troffers, this design works at an overall power density of 0.9 W/ft^2. Increasing stack lights to a high ballast factor increases overall connected power to 0.9 W/ft^2. The stacks to the right on the plan are half height. Figure 5-23b shows an indirect/direct lighting option for a library.

Cautions: Switching and dimming of the lighting system should not be readily accessible. Locate controls in a supervised location.

If the library has computers for research or card catalog searches, special care should be taken to avoid glare on the computer monitors from light fixtures or windows.

Undercabinet task lights should be specified carefully. Avoid traditional inch light systems with magnetic ballasts that use twin tube CFLs and old-style linear lamps such as the F6T5 (9 in.), F8T5 (12 in.), and F13T5 (21 in.) models. Use tasks lights that employ modern F14T5 (22 in.), F21T5 (34 in.), F28T5 (46 in.), F17T8, F25T8, or F32T8 lamps. Always use electronic ballasts, and consider dimming for all task lights.

Desk lamps and table lamps with linear fluorescent lamps, hardwired CFLs, or LEDs should be used. Medium based screw-in CFLs are not a good choice for new projects, since they can be replaced with incandescent lamps and therefore do not comply with most energy codes.

EL17 *Corridor Lighting* (Climate Zones: all)

Corridor lighting in schools must provide lighting for wall-mounted lockers and information boards in addition to the normal corridor function. Vertical illuminance is important for these tasks, and the corridor lighting system should provide light at high angles. In corridors with lockers, luminaires should be aligned parallel to the corridor walls to provide good quality light and to make light useful for lockers. Illuminating the corridor walls should be the primary objective.

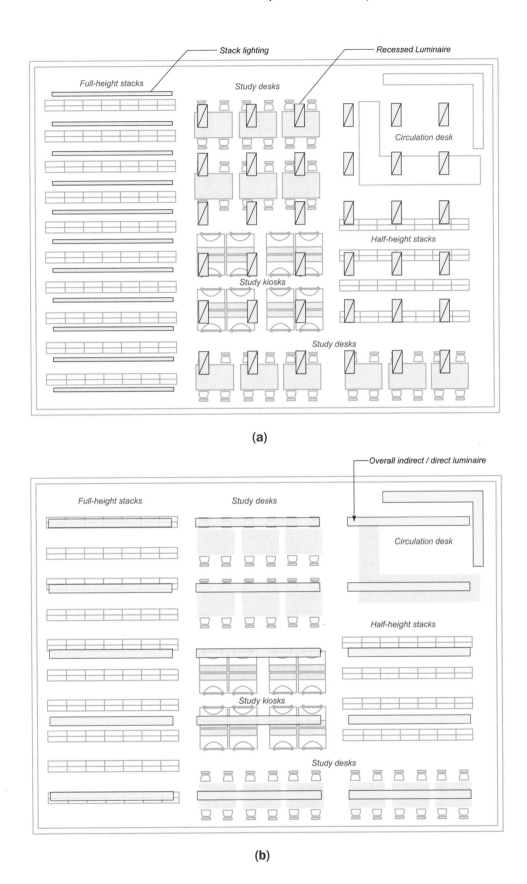

(a)

(b)

Figure 5-23 (EL16) (a) Typical Library Lighting Design and (b) Library Indirect/Direct Lighting Option

Given the choices of luminaires, an attractive solution that is suitable for any type of corridor ceiling construction, including indoor and outdoor corridors, acoustical tile or gypsum board ceilings, etc., should be possible.

Because the ceiling space above interior corridors is often utilized for mechanical systems and because corridors require lower footcandle levels and are not as frequently occupied, daylighting of interior corridors is typically not as cost effective as of other spaces. However, it is critical that the corridor lighting strategy be compatible with the daylighted spaces that lead from the corridor. A good example of this transitional problem is a corridor in which the lenses of the fixtures are visually exposed. To a person walking down this corridor, it appears as if the hall space, even though it is lighted to one-third footcandle of the classroom level, may appear better lighted than the daylighted classroom that contains a softer feeling, full-spectrum diffuse light.

Several lighting systems are available:

- With high ceilings, a suspended lighting system similar to classroom or library lighting may be used with an indirect or indirect/direct distribution.
- Interior corridors may use recessed indirect luminaires that should be oriented with the lamp along the corridor long axis. This design is suited for all ceiling types.
- As an alternative, especially in schools where vandalism is a concern, use surface ceiling wraparound luminaires, preferably vandal resistant or high-abuse types or vandal-resistant recessed fixtures.
- Exterior corridors should use surface-mounted wraparounds or ceiling-mounted, high-abuse luminaires. In some cases, wall-mounted, high-abuse luminaires may be acceptable.

Luminaires should use T5 or T8 lamps and electronic ballasts. Outdoor corridors and corridors with plentiful daylight should use automatic daylight switching or dimming to reduce electric lighting by day. Figure 5-24 shows typical lighting options for corridors.

Cautions: Ensure that the luminaires are not overly "institutional" in appearance. If required by the application, choose one of many modern "rough service" luminaires that are attractive and durable.

In general, recessed downlights have insufficient vertical illumination to provide good service in corridors. However, recessed downlights that use CFLs or LEDs may be preferred for lobbies and similar applications where a dressier appearance is desired.

Switching of the lighting system should not be readily accessible. In general, switching should use an automatic time of day control system with motion sensor override during normally off hours, but make certain that the controller is easily programmed for days on and off, holiday schedules, etc.

In addition, provide automatic daylighting controls, including dimming or switching off lights in corridors having windows, skylights, or other forms of natural lighting.

EL18 ***Lighting for Offices and Teacher Support Rooms*** **(Climate Zones: all)**

The main office is another multifunction space. Administrative staff provides services including reception for visitors, reporting/record keeping (classroom lists, attendance records), support for the principal, support for the teaching staff, and care for students when a nurse is not on site. As with most office workers today, computer work comprises a significant part of the day and the lighting system must provide high-quality light. The lighting system should provide some light on the vertical walls to help the space feel more open.

In some schools the offices are located in the interior of the building and do not have windows to the exterior. However, because of the amount of time that these spaces are occupied throughout the year and during the work day, daylighting should be a high priority.

- With high ceilings, a suspended lighting system similar to the classroom or library lighting may be used with an indirect or indirect/direct distribution.

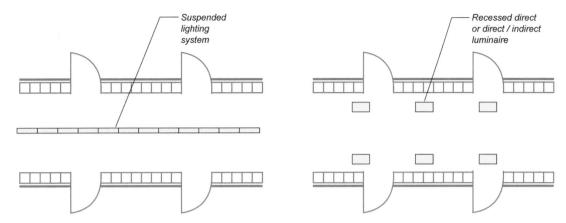

Suspended lighting system

Recessed direct or direct / indirect luminaire

Figure 5-24 (EL17) Corridor Lighting Options

- For lower-ceiling office spaces, recessed indirect systems should be considered, as they provide visual comfort for the workers and light on the upper wall surfaces.
- For support areas, recessed fluorescent lens troffers with at least 78% fixture efficiency and with T8 premium lamps and electronic ballasts should be used.

Where offices are located on an exterior wall and daylight strategies are being implemented, the approach to daylighting control is similar to that for the classroom.

For teacher support areas (making copies, work preparation) where computers are not in use, troffer lighting systems generally offer excellent efficiency but with some loss of visual comfort. They make excellent use of the low cost, widely used T8 lamp system. Systems operating at about 0.6 W/ft^2 will generate 30 to 50 fc maintained average with very good uniformity. Separate task and ambient systems may create a more comfortable atmosphere.

For non-dimming applications, luminaire light and power can be varied by choice of ballast factor. Use the information in EL2 and specify ballasts accordingly.

Cautions: Lens troffer lighting systems are low cost, but their inexpensive appearance can be a drawback. Suspended lighting systems provide a high degree of cost effectiveness and improved appearance in most applications.

Recessed parabolic fixtures with a 45° cutoff provide glare control but will not provide light on the upper walls. This makes the office space seem dark.

EL19   *Lighting for Locker Areas and Restrooms* (Climate Zones: all)

These types of spaces are historically the most abused interior portions of school buildings. Durable lighting is unfortunately less attractive and less integrated than other lighting types.

Daylight is a welcome addition to any locker area or restroom. The high light levels from daylight promote good maintenance. For privacy and security reasons, daylight is often best provided in these spaces via diffusing roof monitors or diffusing glazing systems. Often these spaces can be designed to need no additional electric light during the day.

This Guide generally recommends fluorescent luminaires that use standard T8 lamps or CFLs. These luminaires are part of a relatively new generation of "vandal resistant" or "rough service" lights that are considerably more attractive than previous products. These luminaires should be specified with UV-stabilized, prismatic polycarbonate lenses for maximum efficiency and resistance to abuse. Tamper-resistant hardware is also recommended.

Wall-mounted rough-service lights include the following:

- Linear lights that use T8 or T5 lamps and electronic ballasts.
- Rectangular, oval, and round luminaries that can be equipped with CFL and LED (low-wattage HID lamps can also be used in these luminaries but are not recommended).

- Recessed ceiling lights are generally troffers that use the polycarbonate lens and tamper-resistant hardware, as well as more robust components. These luminaires are available in 1 × 4 ft, 2 × 2 ft, and 2 × 4 ft versions with standard T5 or T8 lamps and electronic ballasts.

For showers, use either surface or recessed luminaires designed for CFLs. Due to the long warm up and restrike times, HID lamps should not be used. In either case, luminaires should be listed for wet applications. In general, choose luminaires that are attractively styled to prevent an overly institutional appearance. For interior spaces that do not have daylighting, controls should perform in one of the following ways:

- Continuously on during normal school hours, with a night/emergency light on all the time
- Continuously on during normal school hours, with both a night/emergency light on at all times and a motion sensor override for full lighting during off hours

EL20 *Twenty-Four Hour Lighting* (Climate Zones: all)

Night lighting or lighting left on twenty-four hours to provide emergency egress needs when the building is unoccupied should be designed to limit the total lighting power to 10% of the total LPD. It should be noted that most jurisdictions also allow the application of occupancy-sensor controls on egress lighting to further reduce electricity associated with lighting an unoccupied building.

REFERENCES AND RESOURCES

Boyce, P.R., Y. Akashi, C.M. Hunter, and J.D. Bullough. 2003. The impact of spectral power distribution on the performance of an achromatic visual task. *Lighting Research and Technology* 35(2):141–156.

CHPS. 2006. Criteria for high performance schools. The Collaborative for High Performance Schools, Sacramento, CA. http://www.chps.net/dev/Drupal/node/212.

IES. 2009. IES RP-6-01 (R2009), *Sports and Recreational Area Lighting*. New York: Illuminating Engineering Society of North America.

IESNA. 2000. *IESNA RP-3-2000, Lighting for Educational Facilities*. New York: Illuminating Engineering Society of North America.

IESNA. 2011. *IESNA Handbook 10th Edition*. New York: Illuminating Engineering Society of North America.

PIER. 2005. Pier lighting research program. Public Interest Energy Research program, State of California. http://www.archenergy.com/lrp/index.htm.

EXTERIOR LIGHTING

Good Design Practice

With the publication of ASHRAE/IES Standard 90.1 (ASHRAE 2010), exterior LPDs are now calculated using five lighting zones, as shown in Table 5-11. These range from lighting zone 0, which includes undeveloped areas within national parks, state parks, forest land, rural areas, and other undeveloped areas, to lighting zone 4, which includes high-activity commercial districts in major metropolitan areas as designated by the local jurisdiction. Most school buildings will fall into lighting zone 2.

Cautions: Calculate LPD only for areas that you intend to light. In this Guide, areas that are lighted to less than 0.1 fc are assumed not to be lighted and cannot be counted in the LPD allowance. For areas that are intended to be lighted, design with a maximum-to-minimum ratio of illuminance no greater than 30 to 1. Therefore, if the minimum light level is 0.1, then the maximum level in that area should be no greater than 3 fc.

For parking lot and grounds lighting, do not increase luminaire wattage in order to use fewer lights and poles. Increased contrast makes it harder to see at night beyond the immediate

Table 5-11   Exterior Lighting Zones

Lighting Zone	Description
0	Undeveloped areas within national parks, state parks, forest land, rural areas, and other undeveloped areas as defined by the authority having jurisdiction
1	Developed areas of national parks, state parks, forest land, and rural areas
2	Areas predominantly consisting of residential zoning, neighborhood business districts, light industrial with limited nighttime use and residential mixed use areas
3	All other areas
4	High activity commercial districts in major metropolitan areas as designated by the local jurisdiction

fixture location. Flood lights and wall packs should not be used, as they cause hazardous glare and unwanted light encroachment on neighboring properties.

Limit poles to 20 ft mounting height and use luminaires that provide all light below the horizontal plane to help eliminate light trespass and light pollution.

EL21   *Exterior Lighting Power—Parking Lots and Drives* (Climate Zones: all)

Limit exterior lighting power to 0.10 W/ft^2 for parking lot and drives in lighting zones 3 and 4 or 0.06 W/ft^2 in lighting zone 2. Calculate only for paved areas, excluding grounds that are lighted to less than 0.1 fc.

Use LED parking lot fixtures with a bi-level switching driver that will reduce its power between noon and 6:00 a.m. as per the recommendations in Chapter 4 of this Guide.

Cautions: Parking lot lighting locations should be coordinated with landscape plantings so that tree growth does not block effective lighting from pole-mounted luminaires.

Parking lot lighting should not be significantly brighter than lighting of the adjacent street. Follow IESNA RP-33-1999 (IESNA 1999) recommendations for uniformity and illuminance recommendations.

EL22   *Exterior Lighting Power—Walkways* (Climate Zones: all)

Limit exterior lighting power to 0.08 W/linear foot for walkways less than 10 ft wide and 0.16 W/ft^2 for walkways 10 ft wide or greater, plaza areas, and special feature areas in lighting zones 3 and 4 or 0.07 W/linear foot for walkways less than 10 ft wide and 0.14 W/ft^2 for walkways 10 ft wide or greater, plaza areas, and special feature areas in lighting zone 2. Exclude grounds that are lighted to less than 0.1 fc.

EL23   *Decorative Façade Lighting* (Climate Zones: all)

Avoid use of decorative façade lighting. If façade lighting is desired, limit the lighting power to 0.075 W/ft^2 in lighting zones 3 and 4 or 0.05 W/ft^2 in lighting zone 2 for the area intended to be illuminated to a light level no less than 0.1 fc.

Façade lighting that is installed is assumed to be programmed to turn off between the hours of midnight and 6 a.m. This does not include lighting of walkways or entry areas that may also light the building.

EL24   *Sources* (Climate Zones: all)

- All parking lot fixtures should utilize LED light sources.
- All grounds and building lighting should utilize pulse-start metal halide, fluorescent, LED, or compact fluorescent amalgam lamps with electronic ballasts.
- Standard high-pressure sodium lamps are not recommended due to their reduced visibility and poor color-rendering characteristics.

- Incandescent lamps are only recommended when used on occupancy sensors for lights that are normally off.
- For colder climates, fluorescent and CFL luminaires must be specified with cold temperature ballasts. Use CFL amalgam lamps.

EL25   *Controls* (Climate Zones: all)

Use photocell or astronomical time switches on all exterior lighting. If a building energy management system is being used to control and monitor mechanical and electrical energy use, it can also be used to schedule and manage outdoor lighting energy use.

Incorporate a time clock when the building is unoccupied to turn off exterior lighting not designated for security purposes. Design the total exterior lighting power (for parking, facades, building grounds, entry lights) to be reduced to a maximum of 25% of the design level when no occupants are present between midnight and 6 a.m.

REFERENCES AND RESOURCES

ASHRAE. 2010. ANSI/ASHRAE/IES Standard 90.1-2010, *Energy Standard for Buildings Except Low-Rise Residential Buildings*. Atlanta: American Society of Heating, Refrigerating and Air-Conditioning Engineers.

IES. 2011. *IES Lighting Handbook*, 10th ed. New York: Illuminating Engineering Society.

IESNA. 1999. IESNA RP-33-1999, Lighting for Exterior Environments. New York: Illuminating Engineering Society.

PLUG LOADS

EQUIPMENT AND CONTROL GUIDELINES

PL1   *General Guidance* (Climate Zones: all)

Plug loads in a school are diverse and represent many different types of energy consumption loads. They can be typical "plug in" equipment, such as copy machines, vending machines, refrigerators, coffee machines, etc. Plug loads also include office and classroom technology, such as computers, printers, interactive whiteboards, server equipment, TV head-end equipment, etc. Plug loads can even represent energy loads such as elevators, security cameras and monitors, transformer losses, portable heaters, fire alarm systems, temperature control systems, and ejection pumps. It is important to understand and account for all plug loads when energy modeling for a school. Kitchen equipment energy usage is addressed independent of plug loads in this Guide.

Plug loads provide a significant opportunity to contribute to overall building energy savings. Without accounting for kitchen loads, they may consume 10%–20% of the school's energy, depending on climate zone and relative efficiencies of the other building systems. As the HVAC and lighting systems become more energy efficient, the plug-load percentage of total building energy will increase unless energy reduction strategies are addressed.

Many plug loads constitute a continuous energy load. These may include servers, refrigeration equipment, security, etc., that cannot be avoided. Other plug loads can be deactivated to conserve energy when a school is not occupied. A school that has a typical 180 day, 8 a.m. to 3 p.m. calendar schedule is largely unoccupied approximately 75% of the year. This compounds the effect unregulated plug loads have on annual energy.

PL2   *Computer (Information Technology) Equipment* (Climate Zones: all)

School computer equipment considerations need to include the main distribution frame (MDF) room; intermediate distribution frame (IDF) rooms; classroom computers; interactive white boards; and television, intercom, and security systems. The MDF and IDF room energy consumption can be significant, and the energy usage is constant. To reduce the energy consumption of this equipment in off-peak hours, the school's technology coordinator should be included in the design process. The technology design should evaluate opportunities for the servers, television system, and intercom system to be off when the school is unoccupied. Computer systems should have network control with power.

Computer systems should have network control with power-saving modes and be controlled during unoccupied hours. The server equipment should be selected with energy consumption as a priority.

The use of laptops (or tablets) in lieu of workstation computers should be considered to minimize energy usage. A laptop computer uses significantly less power than a workstation computer. Some school districts are now eliminating computer rooms and switching to a mobile cart approach. This requires a wireless network to support laptops but allows any classroom to become a computer room. It also provides a first cost savings opportunity by eliminating the building square-footage requirement of the computer room. The mobile carts can be recharged at night at off-peak electrical rates to provide additional energy savings.

Eliminate unnecessary equipment and consolidate printing equipment to minimize the number of required devices. Use of multifunction devices that provide printing, copying, and fax operations reduce power demand from multiple devices.

PL3   *Staff and Occupant Equipment Control* (Climate Zones: all)

Copiers, vending machines, fax machines, classroom computers, coffee makers, and drinking fountains consume power constantly when left unregulated. To reduce this load potential, consider controlling the top outlet of each classroom duplex outlet to deactivate the power on a set time schedule or via occupancy sensor. The occupancy sensor may be the same used to control the lighting in the room.

Vending machines, especially soda machines, can be a large consumer of energy if left uncontrolled. Vending machines should be de-lamped and equipped with occupancy sensor controls for cooling operation if applicable. ENERGY STAR™ rated vending machines include this type of control or can be retrofitted with add-on equipment. The soda vending machine efficiency can be improved by limiting the refrigeration compressor start/stops to a maximum of one every three hours. This will provide greater compressor run time and improve efficiency.

Vending machines without refrigeration, copy machines, coffee machines, water coolers, and other similar equipment can have their power circuits controlled through a contactor interfaced to the buildings occupied/unoccupied schedule. A local override switch can activate the circuit if operation is needed outside occupied hours.

A personal appliance policy should be created for the school district, and constant energy-awareness training for equipment and appliances should be conducted. A school energy team consisting of students, parents, administrators, faculty, and facility staff are another effective tool to educate occupants through their participation on the team.

PL4   *Phantom/Parasitic Loads* (Climate Zones: all)

A VCR that has been flashing the default time since it was installed in a classroom is a prime example of an electronic device that consumes energy when switched off. This use of electrical energy is classified as a *phantom* or *parasitic load*, are also known as *standby power* or *leaking electricity*. Phantom loads usually coincide with any electronic or electrical device or appliance. Equipment with electronic clocks or timers or remote controls, portable equipment and office equipment with wall cubes (e.g., a small box that plugs into an AC outlet to charge cell phones or provide power to computers) all have phantom loads. Phantom loads can consume up to 5% of an electrical plug load.

Table 5-12   Recommendations for Efficient Plug Load Equipment

Equipment/Appliance Type	Purchase Recommendation	Operating Recommendation
Desktop computer	ENERGY STAR only	Implement sleep mode software.
TV/VCR	Purchase with flat screens with sleep modes	Many of these items are only used during peak times and should be unplugged with occupancy sensors.
Laptop computer or tablet—Use where practical to minimize energy use	ENERGY STAR only	Implement sleep mode software.
Computer monitors	ENERGY STAR flat-screen monitors only	Implement sleep mode software.
Printer	ENERGY STAR only	Implement sleep mode software.
Copy machine	ENERGY STAR only	Implement sleep mode software.
Fax machine	ENERGY STAR only	Implement sleep mode software.
Water cooler	ENERGY STAR only	N/A
Refrigerator	ENERGY STAR only	N/A
Vending machines	ENERGY STAR only	Delamp display lighting.
TV/VCR	ENERGY STAR only	

The best, most direct way to control phantom loads is to unplug items such as TVs and VCRs when they are not in use. In lieu of directly unplugging these item, they can be plugged into a power strip that is switched off at the end of each day, over the weekend, and during holidays and vacations. Occupancy sensor-controlled plug strips can also be used to power down these items. Items can also be plugged into the occupancy-controlled outlet (See PL3). Good education can encourage occupants to plug the majority of their appliances into the power-controlled plugs.

PL5   *ENERGY STAR Appliances/Equipment* (Climate Zones: all)

A school board policy should be established that requires all electrical equipment and appliances placed in a school to have the ENERGY STAR label (where there is an ENERGY STAR rating for the equipment or appliance). See the ENERGY STAR Qualified Products page for a list of qualified ENERGY STAR products (DOE 2011).

The recommendations presented in Table 5-12 for the purchase and operation of plug load equipment are an integral part of this Guide.

PL6   *Electrical Distribution System* (Climate Zones: all)

Distribution transformer efficiency should be considered on all projects. The Energy Policy Act of 2005 established minimum energy efficiency standards for low-voltage, dry-type distribution transformers and specifies that any such transformer manufactured after January 1, 2007 "shall be the Class I Efficiency Levels for distribution transformers specified in Table 4-2 of the 'Guide for Determining Energy Efficiency for Distribution Transformers' published by the National Electrical manufacturers Association." These specifications are referred to by the U.S. Department of Energy as "TP-1" (NEMA 2002).

CSL-3 (Candidate Standard Level 3) transformers are an alternate to TP-1 transformers. Transformers are normally rated at 35% loading. At this loading condition, a CSL-3 is 98.6% efficient versus 98% for TP-1. Transformers often operate at a much lower loading condition where the efficiency gap widens. At 3% loading, the CSL-3 is 92.59% efficient versus 88.66% for a TP-1.

K-12 schools are normally designed with either a 120/208 V three-phase service or 277/480 V three-phase service. Elementary schools are typically 120/208 V and middle/high schools are typically 277/480 V. When the 277/480 V service is provided, 120/208 V dry step-down transformers are placed in key locations in the building to provide power to the electrical outlets. Installing CSL-3 versus TP-1 transformers offers an additional energy-savings strategy. The potential energy savings should be compared to the first costs to ensure the project life-cycle goals are maintained.

REFERENCES AND RESOURCES

DOE. 2011. Find ENERGY STAR products. U.S. Department of Energy, Washington, D.C. http://www.energystar.gov/index.cfm?c=products.pr_find_es_products.

NEMA. 2002. NEMA TP-1-2002, *Guide for Determining Energy Efficiency for Distribution Transformers*. Rosslyn, VA: National Electrical Manufacturers Association.

KITCHEN EQUIPMENT

EQUIPMENT AND DESIGN GUIDELINES

KE1   *General Guidance* (Climate Zones: all)

K-12 kitchens range from those with just a few appliances to a complete cooking kitchen with walk-in refrigeration. In addition, some school districts use a central kitchen to prepare food and then transport meals to the schools shortly before the serving period. A typical school kitchen includes significant refrigeration equipment, such as a walk-in freezer, walk-in cooler, ice machine, pass-through refrigerators, and milk coolers.

Despite the wide range of appliances in the kitchens and cafeterias and the resulting energy intensity of a particular building, the appliance selection process and best practices design strategies apply to all food service facilities. To impact the energy consumption of the kitchen, it is best to include the food service manager in the design process. Opportunities to conserve energy include the following:

- Select cooking appliances that reduce radiant heat loss to the kitchen by eliminating high-heat producing appliances, such as broilers, griddles, and ranges, and replacing them with combination oven-steamers (combi oven), tilting skillets, convection ovens, microwaves, or appropriate lighter duty appliances.
- Select appliances that minimize idle energy use.
- Select exhaust hood styles that reduce exhaust air and make-up airflow.
- Select walk-in freezers and coolers with high-performance thermal envelopes and refrigeration systems. The refrigeration system should comply with Section 312 of the Energy Independence and Security Act of 2007 (DOE 2011b).
- Select ENERGY STAR equipment as a minimum standard for designs that include any of the eight appliance categories currently available. For other categories, refer to publications from Consortium for Energy Efficiency (CEE 2011) and the Food Service Technology Center (FSTC 2011).
- Shut down the coolers and freezers during long periods when the school kitchen will not be used, such as summer break. Move any remaining food to one school in the district and shut down the refrigeration equipment in the rest. Design the refrigeration system for easy shut down during these periods, and make sure that shutting down the system causes no mold problems.

KE2   *Energy-Efficient Kitchen Equipment* (Climate Zones: all)

Select energy-efficient appliances, including dishwashers, solid-door freezers, fryers, hot-food holding cabinets, ice machines, refrigerators (solid and glass door), and steamers. In addition, select low-flow hot-water fixtures to minimize both water use and energy use.

The Commercial Kitchens Initiative (CKI) and ENERGY STAR Web sites provides good lists of efficiency strategies and ENERGY STAR rated commercial kitchen equipment (CEE

2011; DOE 2011a). The goal of the CKI is to provide clear and credible definitions in the marketplace as to what constitutes highly efficient energy and water performance in cooking, refrigeration, and sanitation equipment and to help streamline the selection of products through a targeted market strategy.

A number of resources are available from the Food Service Technology Center (FSTC 2011) with links and guidance on efficient design for commercial kitchens. The FSTC is the industry leader in commercial kitchen energy efficiency and appliance performance testing and has developed over 35 standard test methods for evaluating commercial kitchen appliance performance.

Note that there are only eight categories of commercial kitchen equipment in the ENERGY STAR program. There are over 35 ASTM standard performance test methods that provide a recognized method to test the capacity, performance, and energy use of appliances. Using a specification that requires the manufacturer to provide test results from an ASTM test method assures that appliances submitted for approval during construction meet the project's design energy goals. Table 5-13 lists appliances with ASTM performance test method standards (ASTM 2011).

KE3 *Exhaust and Ventilation Energy Use* (Climate Zones: all)

Design exhaust ventilation systems with proper layout of cooking equipment and proper hood design to minimize total airflow while still providing sufficient exhaust flow. After minimizing ventilation needs, consider variable-speed exhaust hood flow systems. The design and specifications of a kitchen hood system, including the exhaust hood, ductwork, exhaust fan, and makeup air need to be addressed by the food service consultant and/or the mechanical engineer, which requires sufficient collaboration and communication between these two disciplines. Additional opportunities include makeup air energy recovery using dedicated makeup air units with desiccant or flat plate heat exchangers. Energy recovery from grease-laden exhaust air is usually too expensive, especially if the exhaust and makeup air designs have been optimized.

The following commercial kitchen ventilation design guides provide additional guidance for energy efficiency:

- *Design Guide 1: Selecting and Sizing Exhaust Hoods* (SCE 2004) covers the fundamentals of kitchen exhaust and provides design guidance and examples.
- *Design Guide 2: Optimizing Makeup Air* (CEC 2002) augments Design Guide 1, with an emphasis on the makeup air side of the equation.
- *Design Guide 3: Integrating Kitchen Exhaust Systems with Building HVAC* (SCE 2009) provides information that may help achieve optimum performance and energy efficiency in commercial kitchen ventilation systems by integrating kitchen exhaust with building HVAC.
- *Design Guide 4: Optimizing Appliance Positioning and Hood Performance* (PG&E 2011) discusses the influence of appliance positions under a hood on the exhaust requirements.

KE4 *Minimize Hot-Water Use* (Climate Zones: all)

FSTC publishes a hot-water system design guide for commercial kitchens that provides key information to restaurant designers and engineers on how to achieve superior performance and energy efficiency with their systems. The design guide *Improving Commercial Kitchen Hot Water System Performance: Energy Efficient Water Heating, Delivery and Use* (Fisher-Nickel 2010) reviews the fundamentals of commercial water heating and describes the design process, including the following topics:

- Reducing hot-water use of equipment while maintaining performance
- Increasing the efficiency of water heaters and distribution systems
- Improving hot-water delivery performance
- Incorporating "free heating" technologies, such as waste heat recovery and solar preheating

Table 5-13   Commercial Food Service Appliance ASTM Standard Test Methods

ASTM #	Appliance Type
F1275-03	Griddles
F1361-05	Open deep fat fryers
F1484-05	Steam cookers
F1496-99(2005)	Convection ovens
F1521-03	Standard test methods for performance of range tops
F1605-95(2001)	Double sided griddles
F1639-05	Combination ovens
F1695-03	Underfired broilers
F1696-96(2003)	Standard test method for energy performance of single rack hot-water Sanitizing, door-type commercial dishwashing machines
F1704-05	Standard test method for capture and containment performance of commercial kitchen exhaust ventilation systems
F1784-97(2003)	Pasta cookers
F1785-97(2003)	Steam kettles
F1786-97(2004)	Braising pans
F1787-98(2003)	Rotisserie ovens
F1817-97	Conveyor ovens
F1920-98(2003)	Rack conveyor, hot-water sanitizing, commercial dishwashing machines
F1964-99(2005)	Pressure and kettle fryers
F1965-99(2005)	Deck ovens
F1991-99(2005)	Chinese (wok) ranges
F2022-00	Booster heaters
F2093-01	Rack ovens
F2140-01	Hot food holding cabinets
F2141-05	Self-serve hot deli cases
F2142-01	Drawer warmers
F2143-04	Refrigerated buffet and preparation tables
F2144-05	Large open vat fryers
F2237-03	Upright overfired broilers
F2238-03	Rapid cook ovens
F2239-03	Conveyor broilers
F2324-03	Pre-rinse spray valves
F2379-04	Powered open warewashing sinks
F2380-04	Conveyor toasters
F2472-05	Staff served hot deli cases
F2473-05	Water bath rethermalizers
F2474-05	Standard test method for heat gain to space performance of commercial kitchen ventilation/appliance systems
F2519-05	Standard test method for grease particle capture efficiency of commercial kitchen filters and extractors
F2644-07	Commercial patio heaters

KE5   *High-Efficiency Walk-in Refrigeration Systems* (Climate Zones: all)

Energy efficiency improvements for walk-in refrigeration systems were included in the 2007 amendments to the Energy Policy and Conservation Act. Walk-in boxes that have 3000 ft^2 or less of floor area are subject to the regulations. The important improvements for all walk-ins manufactured after January 1, 2009, are as follows:

- Automatic door closers (to ensure complete closure when door is within 1 in. of full closure).
- Strip curtains or spring-hinged doors (to minimize infiltration whiles doors are open).
- Insulation ratings of at least
  a. R-25 for walk-in cooler walls, ceiling, and doors;
  b. R-32 for walk-in freezer walls, ceiling, and doors; and
  c. R-28 for walk-in freezer floors.
- Electronically commuted motors (ECMs) or three-phase motors for evaporator fans rated at 1 hp or less
- PSC or ECM or three phase motors for condenser fans rated at 1 horsepower or less.
- High-efficacy internal lighting sources (e.g., 40 lumens per watt or less, including ballast, unless on a timer that shuts lights off after 15 minutes).

Energy performance metrics are still being defined and may be published by the Department of Energy in 2012.

Energy efficiency improvements on the refrigeration side include variable volume compressors, staged compressors, floating-head pressure controls, liquid pressure amplifiers, subcooling liquid refrigerant, and evaporative condensers. Consider the following system technologies, as recommended by National Resources Canada (NRC 2011), but note that they may not have additive effects on reducing energy use if combined. Estimated savings for these technologies are shown in Table 5-14.

- *Floating-head pressure controls* applied to systems with outdoor air-cooled condensers take advantage of low air temperatures to reduce the amount of work for the compressor by allowing the head pressure to vary with outdoor conditions. This reduces compressor load and energy consumption and can extend compressor life. The technology is standard on many new systems and can be added to existing systems.
- *Liquid pressure amplifiers* are small refrigerant pumps that reduce capacity loss at low head pressures when outdoor temperatures are cool by raising the liquid line pressure. Using liquid pressure amplifiers on air-cooled systems increases efficiency as ambient temperature drops.
- *Subcooled liquid refrigerant* results in a lower evaporator temperature and reduces load on the compressor. There are two ways to accomplish this.
  - Using an oversized condenser, or an additional heat exchanger that increases the heat exchange area to the liquid-filled portion of a condenser, can provide additional natural cooling to the condensed refrigerant.

Table 5-14   Refrigeration Technology Savings Estimates and Applications

Technology	Estimated Savings Potential (NRC 2011)	Applicable to New Construction?	Applicable to Retrofit?
Floating-head pressure controls	3% to 10%	Yes	Yes
Liquid pressure amplifier	Up to 20%	Yes	Yes
Subcooled liquid refrigerant			
Oversized condenser	5% to 9%	Yes	No
Mechanical subcooler	Up to 25%	Yes	Yes
Evaporative condensers	3% to 9%	Yes	Yes

- Using a relatively small-capacity mechanical-cooling system or a refrigerant line from a central system, the liquid refrigerant can be cooled further, which increases total system efficiency and cooling capacity.
- *Evaporative condensers* use a wetted filter to cool ambient air as it enters an air-cooled condenser, which increases the condenser capacity and cools the liquid refrigerant, thus reducing compressor load. Note that evaporative media require regular periodic maintenance to assure savings; do not use this technology if maintenance may not be performed on a regular basis.

KE6 *Position Hooded Appliances to Achieve Lower Exhaust Rates* **(Climate Zones: all)**

Research (ASHRAE 2005) sponsored in part by ASHRAE shows that the position of appliances under a hood can make a significant difference in the required exhaust rate—up to 30%. Some key recommendations are as follows:

- Position heavy-duty equipment in the middle of the cook line.
- If a heavy-duty appliance is on the end, a side panel or end wall is imperative.
- Fryers and broilers should not be placed at the end of a cook line. Ranges can be located at the end of cook line because under typical operating conditions the plume strength is not as high as that of broilers.
- Locate double-stacked ovens or steamers at the end of the hood. This has a plume control effect that tends to assist capture and containment.

Positioning of appliances requires approval of the kitchen manager and kitchen consultant. If these recommendations are followed, let the kitchen hood manufacturer and design mechanical engineer know why these decisions were made, and reference the ASHRAE research (ASHRAE 2011) or the Food Service Technology Design Guide 4 (PG&E 2011). The resulting design exhaust and makeup air rates should be less than those of a conventional design.

KE7 *Operating Considerations* **(Climate Zones: all)**

Consider the kind and type of food served in the cafeteria and how much energy is consumed to create the menu, including the use of heaters, fryers, refrigerators, coolers, and ice-making machines. Some school systems have discovered opportunities to save energy, without jeopardizing nutritional requirements, simply by adjusting the menu. Examples include establishing one or two days each week on which to serve cold food for breakfast and lunch and consolidating required menu items around minimal equipment usage.

REFERENCES AND RESOURCES

ASHRAE. 2005. Effect of appliance diversity and position on commercial kitchen hood performance. ASHRAE Research Project RP-1202. American Society of Heating, Refrigerating and Air-Conditioning Engineers, Atlanta, GA.

ASTM. 2011. Standards. ASTM International, West Conshohocken, PA. http://www.astm.org/Standard/index.shtml.

CEC. 2002. *Design Guide 2: Optimizing Makeup Air.* California Energy Commission, Sacramento, CA. http://www.fishnick.com/ventilation/designguides.

CEE. 2011. Commercial kitchen initiative. Consortium for Energy Efficiency, Boston, MA. http://www.cee1.org/com/com-kit/com-kit-equip.php3.

DOE. 2011a. Find ENERGY STAR products. U.S. Department of Energy, Washington, D.C. http://www.energystar.gov/index.cfm?c=products.pr_find_es_products.

DOE. 2011b. Energy Independence and Security Act of 2007 prescribed standards. Appliances and Commercial Equipment Standards. U.S. Department of Energy, Washington, DC. http://www1.eere.energy.gov/buildings/appliance_standards/eisa2007.html.

Fisher-Nickel. 2010. *Improving Commercial Kitchen Hot Water System Performance: Energy Efficient Water Heating, Delivery and Use.* Fisher-Nickel, Inc., San Ramon, CA. http://www.fishnick.com/design/waterheating/.

FSTC. 2011. Food service technology center. San Ramon, CA. http://www.fishnick.com/.

NRC. 2011. Business: Industrial walk-in commercial refrigeration introduction. Natural Resources Canada, Ottawa, Ontario, Canada. http://oee.nrcan.gc.ca/industrial/equipment/commercial-refrigeration/index.cfm?attr=24.

PG&E. 2011. *Design Guide 4: Improving Commercial Kitchen Ventilation System Performance by Optimizing Appliance Positioning and Hood Performance.* Pacific Gas and Electric Company, San Francisco, CA. http://www.fishnick.com/ventilation/designguides/CKV_Design_Guide_4_091911.pdf.

SCE. 2004. *Design Guide 1: Selecting and Sizing Exhaust Hoods.* Southern California Edison, Rosemead, CA. http://www.fishnick.com/ventilation/designguides.

SCE. 2009. *Design Guide 3: Integrating Kitchen Exhaust Systems with Building HVAC.* Southern California Edison, Rosemead, CA. http://www.fishnick.com/ventilation/designguides.

SERVICE WATER HEATING

GENERAL RECOMMENDATIONS

WH1   *Service Water -Heating Types* (Climate Zones: all)

This Guide assumes that the service water heating (SWH) equipment uses the same type of fuel as the HVAC system. This Guide does not cover systems that use oil, hot water, steam, or purchased steam for generating SWH. These systems are alternative means that may be used to achieve energy savings, and, where used, the basic principles of this Guide would apply.

The SWH equipment included in this Guide are gas fired or electric water heaters. Natural gas and propane fuel sources are available options for gas-fired units.

Many factors, including availability of service, utility costs, operator familiarity, and the impact of source energy use, go into deciding whether to use gas or electricity. Efficiency recommendations for both types of equipment are provided to allow for choice.

WH2   *System Descriptions* (Climate Zones: as indicated below)

Gas-Fired Water Heater. A water heater with a vertical or horizontal water storage tank. A thermostat controls the delivery of gas to the heater's burner. The heater requires a vent to exhaust the combustion products. An electronic ignition is recommended to avoid the energy losses from a standing pilot.

Electric Resistance Storage Water Heater. A water heater consisting of a vertical or horizontal storage tank with one or more immersion heating elements. Thermostats controlling heating elements may be of the immersion or surface-mounted type.

Electric Resistance Instantaneous Point-of-Use Water Heater. A compact, under cabinet, or wall-mounted-type water heater with insulated enclosure and minimal water storage capacity. A thermostat controls the heating element, which may be of the immersion or surface-mounted type. Instantaneous, point-of-use water heaters should provide water at a constant temperature, regardless of input water temperature.

Heat-Pump Electric Water Heater. Two types of heat-pump water heaters can be used. The first is an air-to-water heat pump with a storage tank, which uses heat rejected from the heat pump as the heat source. Water storage is required because the heat pump is typically not sized for the instantaneous peak demand for service hot water. A heat-pump water heater is best located in a mechanical room that would benefit from the cool air discharged from the evaporator coil.

The second type is a water-to-water heat pump that uses a ground heat exchanger as the source of heat absorption. This is especially helpful for ground-coupled systems in warmer climate zones because it removes heat from the ground loop. A water storage tank is typically used to minimize the heating capacity of the heat pump.

Heat-pump water heaters should have a coefficient of performance of at least 3.0.

WH3 *Sizing* (Climate Zones: all)

The water heating system should be sized to meet the anticipated peak hot-water load. Calculate the hot water demand based on the sum of the building fixture units according to local code.

Local and state plumbing codes for water closets vary. They range from one for every 20–25 elementary female students to one for every 30–45 secondary female students, and from one for every 30 elementary male students to one for every 40–90 secondary male students. Lavatories in the restrooms are generally in the ratio of 1 for every 2 water closets installed in a general restroom. In many elementary schools, wet areas are provided in K-12 classrooms with hot water for hand washing. Some state codes and educational specifications may require sinks with hot water in laboratories, workshops, vocational classrooms, and art rooms.

Hot-water temperature requirements for restrooms and academic areas of a school vary by local and state code within the range of 100°F–120°F. Hot water is also a requirement in the school kitchen with a delivered temperature of 120°F–140°F. Use booster heaters on dishwashers to bring the temperature to the 160°F–180°F required for sanitation.

In elementary schools, showers are normally specified in health/nurse rooms. In secondary schools, showers are normally specified for physical education locker rooms. In larger secondary schools, showers may be required for team sport areas. The temperature of the hot water provided to the showers should be 100°F–110°F.

In designing and evaluating the most energy-efficient hot-water system for a school and the associated life-cycle costs, consider installing tankless water heaters in most locations. Only in areas where large volumes of hot water are required (such as the cafeteria, gymnasium, and culinary vocational classrooms) should large water heaters or smaller circulating hot-water systems be installed.

WH4 *Equipment Efficiency* (Climate Zones: all)

Efficiency levels are provided in the climate-specific tables in Chapter 4 for the four types of water heaters listed in WH2.

The gas-fired storage water heater efficiency levels correspond to condensing storage water heaters. High-efficiency, condensing gas storage water heaters (with an energy factor higher than 0.90 or thermal efficiency higher than 0.90) are alternatives to the use of gas-fired instantaneous water heaters.

For gas-fired instantaneous water heaters, the energy factor (EF) and thermal efficiency (E_t) levels correspond to commonly available instantaneous water heaters.

Electric water heater efficiency should be calculated as $0.99 - 0.0012 \times$ water heater volume (where volume equals zero for instantaneous water heaters).

Instantaneous electric water heaters are an acceptable alternative to high-efficiency storage water heaters. Electric instantaneous water heaters are more efficient than electric storage water heaters, and point-of-use versions will minimize piping losses. However, their impact on peak electric demand can be significant and should be taken into account during design. Where unusually high hot-water loads (e.g., showers or laundry facilities) are present during peak electrical use periods, electric storage water heaters are recommended over electric instantaneous ones.

WH5 *Location* (Climate Zones: all)

The water heater should be close to the hot-water fixtures to avoid the use of a hot-water return loop or of heat tracing on the hot-water supply piping. Where electric resistance heaters are used, consider point-of-use water heaters with a low number of fixtures to eliminate the need for a recirculating loop.

WH6   *Pipe Insulation* (Climate Zones: all)

All SWH piping should be installed in accordance with accepted industry standards. Insulation levels should be in accordance with the recommendation levels in the climate-specific tables in Chapter 4, and the insulation should be protected from damage. Include a vapor retardant on the outside of the insulation.

WH7   *Solar Hot-Water Systems* (Climate Zones: all)

Simple solar systems are most efficient when they generate heat at low temperatures. Because of the high hot-water demands associated with cafeterias, solar hot-water systems are often viewed as important strategies in reducing energy bills. It can be even more cost effective in middle schools and high schools, which have an additional significant load for gym class showers and sports programs.

General suggestions for solar SWH systems include the following:

- It is typically not economical to design solar systems to satisfy the full annual service water heating load.
- Systems are typically most economical if they furnish 50%–80% of the annual load.
- Properly sized systems will meet the full load on the best solar day of the year.
- Approximately 1–2 gal of storage should be provided per square foot of collector.
- 1 ft^2 of collector heats about 1 gal per day of service water at 44° latitude.
- Glazed flat plate systems often cost in the range of $100–$150 per square foot of collector.
- Collectors do not have to face due south. They receive 94% of the maximum annual solar energy if they are 45° east or west of due south.
- The optimal collector tilt for service water applications is approximately equal to the latitude where the building is located; however, variations of ±20° only reduce the total energy collected by about 5%. This is one reason that many collector installations are flat to a pitched roof instead of being supported on stands.
- The optimal collector tilt for building heating (not service water heating) systems is approximately the latitude of the building plus 15°.

Collectors can still function on cloudy days to varying degrees depending on the design, but they perform better in direct sunlight; collectors should not be placed in areas that are frequently shaded.

Solar systems in most climates require freeze protection. The two common types of freeze protection are systems that contain antifreeze and drainback systems.

Drainback solar hot-water systems are often selected in small applications where the piping can be sloped back toward a collection tank. By draining the collection loop, freeze protection is accomplished when the pump shuts down, either intentionally or unintentionally. This avoids the heat-transfer penalties of antifreeze solutions.

Closed-loop, freeze-resistant solar systems should be used when piping layouts make drainback systems impractical.

In both systems, a pump circulates water or antifreeze solution through the collection loop when there is adequate solar radiation and a need for service water heat.

Solar collectors for service water heating applications are usually flat plate or evacuated-tube type. Flat plate units are typically less expensive. Evacuated-tube designs can produce higher temperatures because they have less standby loss, but they also can pack with snow and, if fluid flow stops, are more likely to reach temperatures that can degrade antifreeze solutions.

REFERENCES AND RESOURCES

ASHRAE. 2011. *ASHRAE Handbook—HVAC Applications*. Atlanta: American Society of Heating, Refrigerating and Air-Conditioning Engineers.

HVAC

HVAC SYSTEM TYPES

Although many types of HVAC system could be used in K-12 schools, this Guide assumes that one of the following three system types will be used:

- HV1: Ground-source heat pumps with a dedicated outdoor air system for ventilation
- HV2: Fan coils with a water chiller, a water boiler or electric resistance heat, and a dedicated outdoor air system for ventilation
- HV3: Multiple zone, variable-air-volume (VAV) air-handling units with a water chiller, a dedicated outdoor air system for ventilation, and perimeter or in-floor radiant heat located in the occupied spaces

Unique recommendations are included for each HVAC system type in the climate-specific tables in Chapter 4. In addition, the energy-use targets included in Chapter 3 provide the design team with further flexibility in reaching the 50% energy savings goal. If one of these three HVAC system types is not being used, but the energy use of the selected HVAC system is less than or equal to the energy use target listed in the Chapter 3 tables, the project may still achieve the 50% savings goal.

This Guide does not cover purchased chilled water for cooling, or solar or steam for heating. These and other systems are alternative means that may be used to achieve the energy savings target of this Guide.

HV1 *Ground-Source Heat Pump System* (Climate Zones: all)

In this system, a separate ground-source heat pump (GSHP) is used for each thermal zone. This type of equipment is available in pre-established increments of capacity. The components are factory assembled and include a filter (see HV23), fan, refrigerant-to-air heat exchanger, compressor, refrigerant-to-water heat exchanger, and controls. The refrigeration cycle is reversible, allowing the same components to provide cooling or heating.

Individual GSHPs are typically mounted in the ceiling plenum over the corridor (or some other noncritical space) or in a closet next to the occupied space. The equipment should be located to meet the acoustical goals of the space, permit access for maintenance, and minimize fan power, ducting, and wiring.

In a GSHP system, all the heat pumps are connected via a common water loop (see HV8) to a ground heat exchanger (ASHRAE 1997, 2011b). A GSHP takes advantage of the Earth's relatively constant temperature and uses the ground instead of a cooling tower and boiler to reject or add heat. During the summer, the heat pumps extract heat from the building and transfer it to the ground. When the building requires heating, heat is transferred from the ground into the building. In a perfectly balanced system, the amount of heat stored over a given period of time would equal the amount of heat retrieved. GSHP systems reduce energy usage because they eliminate the need for a cooling tower and boiler, which are required in a conventional water-source heat pump (WSHP) system.

A GSHP system offers several other advantages for a school owner when compared to a conventional WSHP system. The GSHP system often eliminates the need for boilers and cooling towers, which require maintenance that many school systems contract to vendors. The central plant is substantially reduced in size, which lowers building construction costs. The noise source of a cooling tower is removed, along with the hazard of a boiler. These advantages must be evaluated against the added cost of the ground heat exchanger.

A typical ground heat exchanger includes many vertical pipe bores, each 200 to 400 ft deep. An example is shown in Figure 5-25. Multiple vertical pipe bores are circuited together with horizontal piping and typically ganged together in a piping vault. From the vault, supply and return pipe mains are routed to the building and all of the heat pumps. The water may be

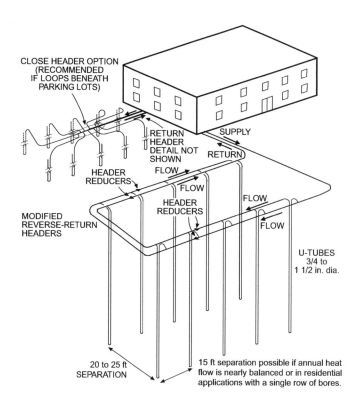

Figure 5-25 (HV1) Vertical Ground Heat Exchanger
Source: ASHRAE (2011b)

recirculated via a central pumping system or a distributed pumping system in which individual pumps are located at each heat pump. For some subsurface conditions, vertical bores may not be the most cost efficient distribution system, and a horizontal ground heat exchanger may be necessary.

Outdoor air (OA) for ventilation is conditioned and delivered by a separate dedicated OA system. This may involve ducting the OA directly to each heat pump, delivering it in close proximity to the heat pump intakes, or ducting it directly to the occupied spaces (see Figure 5-27). Depending on the climate, the dedicated OA unit may include components to filter (see HV23), cool, heat, dehumidify, and/or humidify the OA (see HV4).

The cooling equipment, heating equipment, and fans should meet or exceed the efficiency levels listed in the climate-specific tables in Chapter 4. Efficiency levels listed for ground-source heat pumps are based on "ground loop" test conditions according to ASHRAE/ARI/ISO Standard 13256-1-1998, *Water-Source Heat Pumps Testing and Rating for Performance* (ASHRAE 1998).

Heat pumps should be provided with two-stage or variable-speed compressors to increase part-load efficiency. During part-load conditions, these units operate at a higher efficiency. A typical school operates a majority of the occupied hours at part-load conditions, so these units can increase the overall system performance.

A GSHP system is most appropriate in climate zones 2, 3, 4, 5, and 6, where the summer and winter temperatures are not at the extreme ranges. A properly sized ground heat exchanger can accommodate these variations. While climate zone 6 is heating dominated, a high-performance thermal envelope and the use of heat recovery in the dedicated outdoor air system (DOAS) will reduce the building heating load, making a GSHP feasible. A ground-source heat pump is very efficient when operating in the heating mode. Extending usage into climates with more annual heating hours increases efficiency if appropriate supply water temperature is maintained.

Locating Ground-Source Heat Pumps

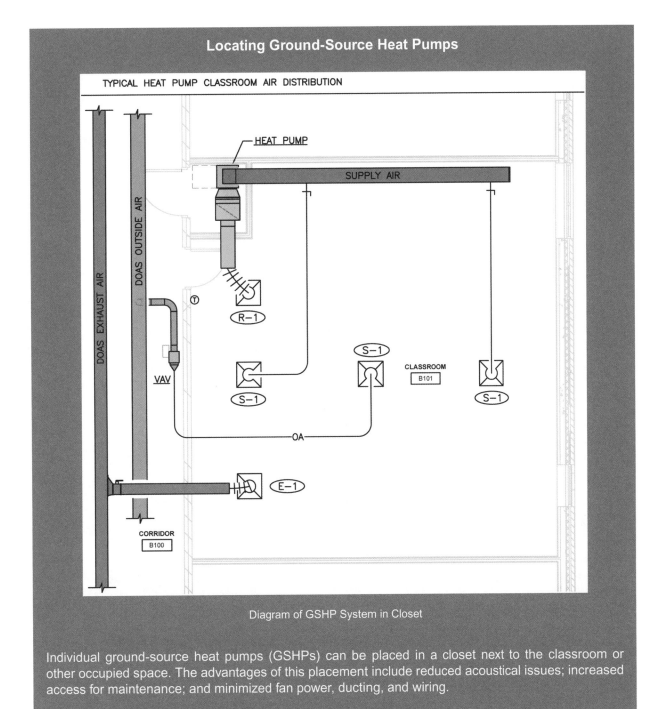

Diagram of GSHP System in Closet

Individual ground-source heat pumps (GSHPs) can be placed in a closet next to the classroom or other occupied space. The advantages of this placement include reduced acoustical issues; increased access for maintenance; and minimized fan power, ducting, and wiring.

A hybrid system can be used to account for the imbalance between heat stored and heat extracted in the extreme climate zones. For example, in a cooling-dominated climate (such as climate zones 1 or 2), a large amount of heat must be rejected to the ground during the cooling season, but a much smaller amount of heat is extracted from the ground during the heating season. This imbalance can cause the temperature of the ground surrounding the ground heat exchanger to increase over time. Conversely, in a heating-dominated climate (such as climate zones 6 or 7), a relatively small amount of heat is rejected to the ground during the cooling season, but a much larger amount of heat must be extracted from the ground during the heating season. In this case, the ground temperature can decrease over time. A hybrid approach

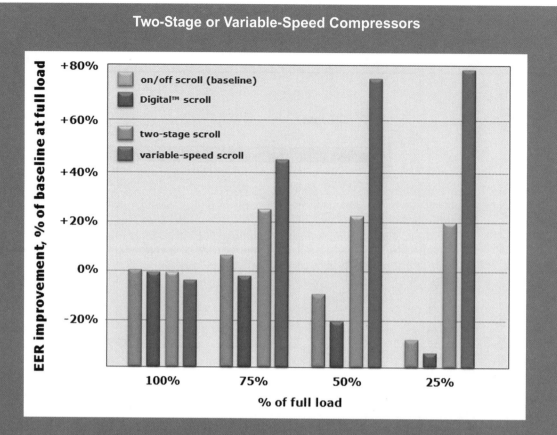

Relative performance of variable-capacity compressors
(4-ton water-source heat pump)

Recently, several equipment manufacturers have developed water-source or ground-source heat pumps that include a two-stage or variable-speed compressor. Compared to the on/off compressor that has historically been used in this type of equipment, a two-stage or variable-speed compressor is better able to match cooling or heating capacity with the changing load in the zone. This typically improves comfort and also results in reduced energy use during part-load conditions, as demonstrated in the chart showing relative performance of variable-capacity compressors.

When combined with a multiple-speed or variable-speed fan, this type of equipment can also result in better part-load dehumidification performance than a traditional heat pump with a constant-speed fan and an on/off compressor. This improvement is due to the reduction in airflow at part load, which allows the heat pump to deliver cooler and therefore drier air to the zone. This can lower indoor humidity levels.

involves adding a cooling tower (or fluid cooler) to the loop for a system that is installed in a cooling-dominated climate, or adding a boiler to a system in a heating-dominated climate.

HV2   *Fan-Coil System* (Climate Zones: all)

In this system, a separate fan-coil unit is used for each thermal zone. The components are factory-assembled and include filters (see HV23), a fan, heating and cooling coils, controls, and possibly OA and return air dampers.

Fan coils are typically installed in each conditioned space, in the ceiling plenum above the corridor (or some other noncritical space), or in a closet adjacent to the space. However, the equipment should be located to meet the acoustical goals of the space, permit access for maintenance, and minimize fan power, ducting, and wiring.

All the fan coils are connected to a common water distribution system (see HV6 and HV7). Cooling is provided by a centralized water chiller. Heating is provided by either a centralized boiler or electric resistance heat. In climate zones 1 and 2, it may be more cost effective to use electric resistance heat in lieu of a hot-water heating system because of minimal heating requirements.

OA for ventilation is conditioned and delivered by a separate dedicated OA system. This may involve ducting the OA directly to each fan coil, delivering it in close proximity to the fan-coil intakes, or ducting it directly to the occupied spaces (see Figure 5-27). Depending on the climate, the dedicated OA unit may include components to filter (see HV23), cool, heat, dehumidify, and/or humidify the outdoor air (see HV4).

The cooling equipment, heating equipment, and fans should meet or exceed the efficiency levels listed in the climate-specific tables in Chapter 4. The cooling equipment should also meet or exceed the part-load efficiency level, where shown.

HV3   *Multiple-Zone, Variable-Air-Volume (VAV) Air Handlers* (Climate Zones: all)

In this system, a central VAV air-handling unit cools recirculated air to serve several individually controlled zones. A dedicated outdoor-air system provides conditioned ventilation air to each zone (Figure 5-26). Each thermal zone has a dual-duct VAV terminal unit. One damper controls outdoor air from the dedicated OA unit to maintain proper ventilation, and the other damper controls cool primary air from the VAV air-handling unit to maintain temperature in that zone.

The components of the VAV air-handling unit include OA and return air dampers (to allow for air-side economizing, when used), filters (see HV23), fans, cooling coil, and controls.

The components of the VAV terminal units include two airflow modulation devices and controls. VAV terminal units are typically installed in the ceiling plenum above the occupied space or above an adjacent corridor. However, the equipment should be located to meet the acoustical goals of the space, permit access for maintenance, and minimize fan power, ducting, and wiring.

All the VAV terminal units served by each air-handling unit are connected to a common air-distribution system. All the air-handling units are connected to a common water distribution system (see HV6 and HV7). Cooling is provided by the centralized water chiller. Heating in the dedicated OA unit is typically provided by an indirect-fired gas burner, a hot-water coil, or an electric resistance heater.

Space heating is typically provided by perimeter (baseboard) or in-floor radiant heat. When hot water is used for heating, all the heating coils along with the water boiler(s) are connected to a common water distribution system (see HV7).

The cooling equipment, heating equipment, and fans should meet or exceed the efficiency levels listed in the climate-specific tables in Chapter 4. The cooling equipment should also meet or exceed the part-load efficiency level, where shown.

HV4   *Dedicated Outdoor Air System (DOAS)* (Climate Zones: all)

Dedicated outdoor air systems (DOASs) can reduce energy use by decoupling the heating, cooling, and dehumidification of OA for ventilation from sensible cooling and heating in the zone. The OA is conditioned by a separate dedicated OA unit that is designed to filter (see HV23), heat, cool, and dehumidify the OA and to deliver it dry enough (at a low enough dew point) to offset space latent loads (Mumma and Shank 2001; Morris 2003). Terminal HVAC equipment, located in or near each space, heats or cools recirculated indoor air to maintain space temperature. Terminal equipment may include fan-coil units, water-source heat pumps,

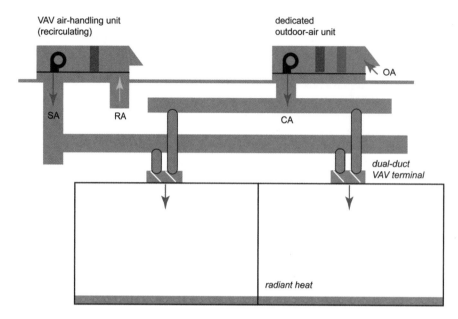

Figure 5-26 (HV3) Multiple-Zone VAV Air Handler with DOAS

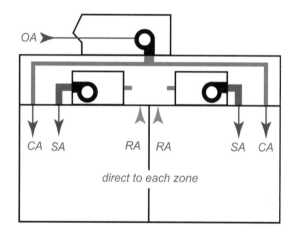

Figure 5-27 (HV4) Recommended DOAS Configuration for GSHPs or Fan Coils

radiant panels, or dual-duct VAV terminals. Dedicated OA systems can also be used in conjunction with multiple-zone, air-handling systems.

Consider delivering the conditioned OA cold (not reheated to a "neutral" space temperature) whenever possible, and use recovered energy to reheat only when needed. Providing cold (rather than neutral) air from the dedicated OA unit offsets a portion of the space sensible cooling loads, allowing the terminal HVAC equipment to be downsized and use less energy (Mumma and Shank 2001; Murphy 2006). In addition, implementing exhaust air energy recovery (see HV5), evaporative cooling, demand-controlled ventilation (see HV15), and temperature reset control strategies (see HV16) can help minimize overall energy use.

GSHPs (see HV1) or Fan-Coils (see HV2). The dedicated OA system should deliver the conditioned OA directly to each zone (Figure 5-27). While other configurations (such as delivering the conditioned OA to the intake or to the supply side of each individual heat pump or fan-coil) are also used, this configuration provides several energy-related advantages (Mumma 2008). For example, this configuration allows the fan in each local HVAC unit to cycle or reduce speed without impacting the delivery of ventilation air, and it maintains a high zone air-distribution

Variable-Air-Volume/Dedicated Outdoor Air System

Typical Classroom Air Distribution

Ramsey Middle School, a 130,000 ft^2 facility completed in 2007, utilizes variable-air-volume (VAV) air-handling units coupled with a dedicated outside air system (DOAS) similar to the system described in HV3.

The school district had traditionally used standard, mixed-air VAV systems. The VAV/DOAS approach was selected to eliminate reheat energy and provide better control of outdoor air throughout the building. Each room is provided with a parallel, fan-powered VAV terminal with a hot-water coil on the return air inlet. The air-handing unit (AHU) supplies air to the inlet air damper of each VAV box at a cold temperature for room cooling purposes. If room heating is required, the inlet damper closes, and the room is heated via the hot-water coil in the VAV box, which eliminates reheat of supply air. The DOAS unit supplies air to a separate shut-off VAV box for distribution of air directly to the room. It is supplied at varying temperatures—colder in the summer months and neutral in the winter months. The DOAS varies airflow using room occupancy sensors and time of day schedules to vary the outdoor airflow delivered to each room.

effectiveness ($E_z = 1.0$) because the air is not delivered at a temperature warmer than the zone, thus avoiding the energy penalty of increasing outdoor airflow during the heating season.

Multiple-Zone, VAV Air Handlers (see HV3). The dedicated OA system should deliver the conditioned OA directly to individual dual-duct VAV terminals that serve each zone (Figure 5-26).

HVAC SYSTEM CONSIDERATIONS

HV5   *Exhaust Air Energy Recovery* **(Climate Zones: all)**

Exhaust air energy recovery can provide an energy-efficient means of reducing the latent and sensible outdoor air cooling loads during peak cooling conditions. It can also reduce the outdoor air heating load in mixed and cold climates. HVAC systems that use exhaust air energy recovery should to be resized to account for the reduced outdoor air heating and cooling loads (ASHRAE 2008c).

When the climate-specific tables in Chapter 4 recommend exhaust air energy recovery, this device should result in an enthalpy reduction of at least 60% for A (humid) or C (marine) climate zones, or a dry-bulb temperature reduction of at least 60% for B (dry) climate zones. Sixty percent reduction shall mean a change in the enthalpy (or dry-bulb temperature) of the outdoor air supply equal to 60% of the difference between the outdoor air and return air enthalpies (or dry-bulb temperatures) at design conditions.

Sensible energy recovery devices transfer only sensible heat. Common examples include coil loops, fixed-plate heat exchangers, heat pipes, and sensible energy rotary heat exchangers (sensible energy wheels). Total energy recovery devices transfer not only sensible heat but also moisture (or latent heat)—that is, energy stored in water vapor in the airstream. Common examples include total energy rotary heat exchangers (also known as *total energy wheels* or *enthalpy wheels*) and fixed-membrane heat exchangers (see Figure 5-28).

An exhaust-air energy recovery device can be packaged in a separate energy recovery ventilator (ERV) that conditions the outdoor air before it enters the dedicated OA unit, or the device can be integral to the dedicated outdoor air unit.

For maximum benefit, the system should provide as close to balanced outdoor and exhaust airflows as is practical, taking into account the need for building pressurization and any exhaust that cannot be ducted back to the energy recovery device.

Exhaust for energy recovery may be taken from spaces requiring exhaust (using a central exhaust duct system) or directly from the return airstream (see HV21).

The energy recovery device should be controlled to prevent the transfer of unwanted heat to the entering outdoor airstream during mild outdoor conditions. In cold climates, follow the manufacturer's recommendations for frost prevention.

HV6   *Chilled-Water System* (Climate Zones: all)

Chilled-water systems with modulating valves should be designed for variable flow and be capable of reducing pump flow rates to 50% or less of the design flow rate. Care should be taken to maintain the minimum flow through each chiller, as defined by the chiller manufacturer.

Small systems with total system pumping power of 10 hp or less may be designed for constant flow and still comply with ASHRAE/IES Standard 90.1, but modulating control valves and VFDs should be used for both energy reduction and controllability reasons.

Piping should be sized to comply with the pipe sizing limitations listed in Table 6.5.4.5 of ASHRAE/IES Standard 90.1 (ASHRAE 2010c). Using a smaller pipe size increases the pressure drop through the pipe, increases the velocity through the pipe, and may cause erosion to occur if velocity is too high. A larger pipe size results in additional pump energy savings but increases the installed cost of the pipe. In systems that operate for longer hours, larger pipe sizes are often very economical.

Energy use and installed costs are typically both reduced by selecting chilled water (CHW) ΔT of 12°F to 20°F rather than the traditional 10°F (ASHRAE 2010c). This will save pump energy, permit the reduction of pipe sizes (reducing installation cost), and minimize pump heat added to the water because of the use of reduced pump horsepower, but it will also affect cooling coil performance. This can be overcome by lowering the chilled-water temperature to deliver the same air conditions leaving the coil. Chilled-water temperature setpoints should be selected based on a life-cycle analysis of pump energy, fan energy, and desired air conditions leaving the coil.

CHW temperatures will vary depending on whether thermal storage is used. If thermal storage is used (see HV30 under "Additional Bonus Savings"), the chiller must be selected for the most extreme temperatures, which typically occur during the charge mode.

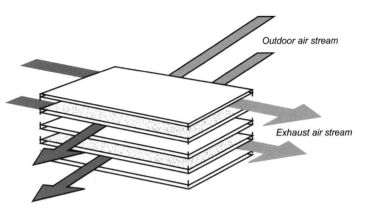

Fixed-plate heat exchanger (crossflow)

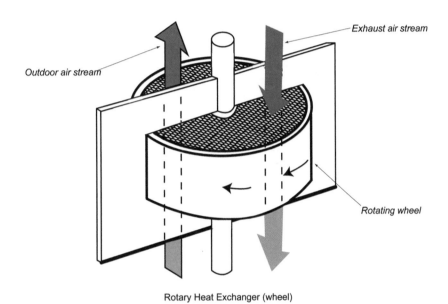

Rotary Heat Exchanger (wheel)

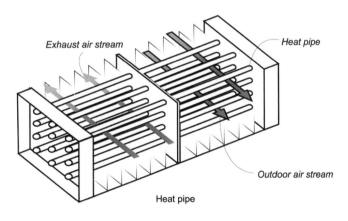

Figure 5-28 (HV5) Examples of Exhaust Air Energy Recovery Devices

HV7 *Water Heating System* (Climate Zones: all)

Condensing boilers can operate at up to 90% efficiency and most models operate at higher efficiency at part load. To achieve higher efficiency levels, condensing boilers require that return water temperatures be maintained below 120°F. Designers should compare boiler efficiency curves, as some condensing boilers do not have high efficiencies until the return water temperatures are very low, while others can be above 90% efficient at low fire with 150°F return water.

High-efficiency boilers fit well with hydronic systems that are designed with ΔTs greater than 20°F (many designers believe that the optimal ΔT is 30°F to 40°F). Higher ΔTs also allow smaller piping and less pumping energy, which reduce first costs. Because condensing boilers work efficiently at part load, VFDs can be used on the pumps to further reduce energy use.

HV8 *Condenser-Water System for GSHPs* (Climate Zones: all)

Condenser-water systems should be designed for variable flow and be capable of reducing pump flow rates to approximately 30% of the design flow rate. Water flow should not be allowed to reduce below pump manufacturers recommendations. Heat pump units should be provided with two-way controls to shut off water flow when the compressor is not operating.

Small systems, with total system pumping power of 10 hp or less, may be designed for constant flow and still comply with ASHRAE/IES Standard 90.1, but modulating control valves and VFDs should be used for both energy reduction and controllability reasons.

Piping should generally be sized for a low pressure drop (see discussion on pipe sizing in HV6).

Pumping systems for condenser-water systems are traditionally variable flow through the use of a "central" pumping system. These pumps are normally located in the primary mechanical room. The central pumps are controlled through a VFD and system water flow varies as building load changes. An alternative is a "distributive" pumping system. Local water pumps are located adjacent to each heat pump unit and operate only when the unit's compressor is operating, thereby varying the system water flow, eliminating the need for a two-way control valve at each heat pump. These systems are usually coupled with a low pressure drop piping system to reduce installed pump horsepower and conserve energy. In the majority of condenser-water systems, this only requires oversizing by one pipe size. The water pumps for a distributive pumping system are normally less than 0.50 hp, so it is important to consider the pump efficiency during selection.

HV9 *Cooling and Heating Load Calculations* (Climate Zones: all)

Accurate sizing of equipment leads to lower equipment costs, lower utility costs, better dehumidification performance, and more comfortable conditions.

Design cooling and heating loads must be calculated in accordance with generally accepted engineering standards and handbooks, such as the methods described in Chapter 18 of the *ASHRAE Handbook—Fundamentals* (ASHRAE 2009a) and ANSI/ASHRAE/ACCA Standard 183 (ASHRAE 2007b). Safety factors should be applied cautiously to prevent oversizing of equipment. Oversized cooling equipment has limited ability to reduce capacity at part-load conditions, which causes short cycling of compressors. This in turn limits the system's ability to dehumidify (see HV13). It can also result in large changes in supply air temperature, which may affect occupant comfort.

Cooling and heating loads of OA, as well as accurate lighting and plug loads, must be included in the load calculations. Separate load calculations should be performed on each thermal zone type, and on each occupancy/activity zone type.

HV10 *Ventilation Air* (Climate Zones: all)

The zone-level outdoor airflows and the system-level intake airflow should be determined based on the current version of ASHRAE Standard 62.1, but should not be less than the values required by local code unless approved by the authority with jurisdiction. The number of people used in computing the breathing zone ventilation rates should be based on known occupancy, local code, or the default values listed in ASHRAE Standard 62.1.

Caution: The occupant load, or exit population, for egress design to comply with the fire code is typically much higher than the zone population used for ventilation system design. Using occupant load rather than zone population to calculate ventilation requirements can result in significant overventilation, oversized HVAC equipment, and excess energy use.

For all zones, time-of-day schedules in the building automation system (BAS) should be used to introduce ventilation air only when a zone is expected to be occupied.

HV11 *Cooling and Heating Equipment Efficiencies* (Climate Zones: all)

The cooling and heating equipment should meet or exceed the efficiency levels listed in the climate-specific tables in Chapter 4. The cooling equipment should also meet or exceed the part-load efficiency level where shown.

- Efficiency levels listed in the Chapter 4 tables are based on the equipment-specific rating standards listed in ASHRAE/IES Standard 90.1.
- Efficiency levels listed for ground-source heat pumps are based on "ground loop" test conditions according to ASHRAE/ARI/ISO Standard 13256-1 (ASHRAE 1998). GSHPs should be provided with two-stage or variable-speed compressors to increase part-load efficiency. Digital scroll compressors are generally capacity control devices and may not reduce energy use. If these compressors are being considered, the part-load efficiency should be comparable to a two-stage or variable-speed compressor.
- At the time of publication, no industry rating standard exists for packaged, direct expansion (DX) dedicated outdoor-air equipment. The energy simulations used for this Guide assumed that the dedicated OA unit was served by a chiller with an efficiency listed in the Chapter 4 tables. If a different type of equipment is considered, the efficiency should be comparable to this.
- A few individual zones in a school building may be served by single-zone equipment (such as packaged or split DX units). In this case, this equipment should meet the more stringent of either the requirements of local code or the current version of ASHRAE/IES Standard 90.1.

Rating and certification by industry organizations is available for various types of HVAC equipment. In general, certification is provided by industry-wide bodies that develop specific procedures to test the equipment to verify performance. ASHRAE/IES Standard 90.1 contains minimum efficiency requirements for equipment that is covered by a rating standard or certification program. Certification that incorporates published testing procedures and transparency of results is much more reliable for predicting actual performance than certification that is less transparent.

For types of equipment for which certification is available, select products that have been certified. Examples of such equipment include packaged heat pumps, packaged air-conditioning units, water chillers, gas furnaces, hot-water boilers, cooling towers, air-to-air energy recovery devices, and water heaters.

For types of equipment for which certification is not available, rigorously research performance claims made by the supplier. The project team should determine what testing procedures were used to develop the performance data and identify limitations or differences between the testing procedures and intended use of the equipment.

HV12 *Fan Power and Motor Efficiencies* (Climate Zones: all)

Fan systems should meet the efficiency levels listed in the climate-specific tables in Chapter 4, which are expressed in terms of a maximum power (watts) per cfm of supply air.

Motors for fans 1 hp or larger should meet National Electrical Manufacturers Association (NEMA) premium efficiency motor guidelines, where available.

HV13   *Part-Load Dehumidification* (Climate Zones: all)

Most basic, constant-volume systems (small packaged rooftop units, DX split systems, fan coils, WSHPs, etc.) supply a zone with a constant amount of air regardless of the cooling load. The system must deliver warmer air under part-load conditions to avoid overcooling the space. In a typical chilled-water application, a modulating valve reduces system capacity by throttling the water flow rate through the cooling coil. The warmer coil surface that results provides less sensible cooling (raising the supply-air dry-bulb temperature), but it also removes less moisture from the passing airstream (raising the supply-air dew point). In a typical DX application (such as a WSHP with a single-stage compressor and constant-speed fan), the compressor cycles off regularly to avoid overcooling. As the compressor operates for a smaller percentage of the hour, dehumidification capacity decreases significantly. The compressor does not run long enough for the accumulated condensate to fall into the drain pan, and it stays off for longer periods of time, allowing the remaining moisture on the coil surface to re-evaporate while the fan continues to run.

Briefly stated, a basic constant-volume system matches sensible capacity to the sensible load; dehumidification capacity is coincidental. As the load diminishes, the system delivers ever-warmer supply air. Some dehumidification may occur, but only if the sensible load is high enough. As a result, the space relative humidity will tend to increase under part-load conditions. Therefore, select systems that minimize the number of hours that the space relative humidity remains above 60%.

Following are some (but not all) of the possible methods for improving part-load dehumidification:

GSHPs (see HV1) or Fan-Coil Units (see HV2). The dedicated OA system (see HV4) should be designed to dehumidify the OA so that it is dry enough (low enough dew point) to offset the latent loads in the spaces. This helps avoid high indoor humidity levels without additional dehumidification enhancements in the GSHP or fan-coil units.

Alternatively, some GSHPs can be equipped with a multiple-speed fan and a two-stage or variable-capacity compressor for improved part-load dehumidification, which can reduce the dehumidification load on the dedicated OA unit. Or, some fan coils can be equipped with multiple-speed fans for improved part-load dehumidification, which can reduce the dehumidification load on the dedicated OA unit.

Multiple-Zone, VAV Air Handlers (see HV3). VAV systems typically dehumidify effectively over a wide range of indoor loads, as long as the VAV air-handling unit continues to provide cool, dry air at part-load conditions. Use caution when resetting the supply air temperature (SAT) or CHW temperature during the cooling season. Warmer supply air (or water) means less dehumidification at the coil and higher humidity in the space. If SAT or CHW reset is used in a climate with humid seasons, include one or more zone humidity sensors to disable reset if the relative humidity within the space exceeds 60%.

HV14   *Economizer* (Climate Zones: ❷ ❸ ❹ ❺ ❻ ❼ ❽)

Economizers, when recommended, help save energy by providing free cooling when ambient conditions are suitable to meet all or part of the cooling load. In humid climates, consider using enthalpy-based controls (versus dry-bulb temperature controls) with air-side economizer to help ensure that unwanted moisture is not introduced into the space. Economizers, whether air side or water side, should meet the requirements of ASHRAE/IESNA Standard 90.1.

A motorized outdoor air damper should be used instead of a gravity damper to prevent unwanted OA from entering during the unoccupied periods when the unit may recirculate air to maintain setback or setup temperatures. The motorized OA damper for all climate zones should be closed during the entire unoccupied period, except when it may open in conjunction with an unoccupied economizer or pre-occupancy purge cycle.

Periodic maintenance is important with economizers, as dysfunctional economizers can cause substantial excess energy use because of malfunctioning dampers or sensors (see HV28).

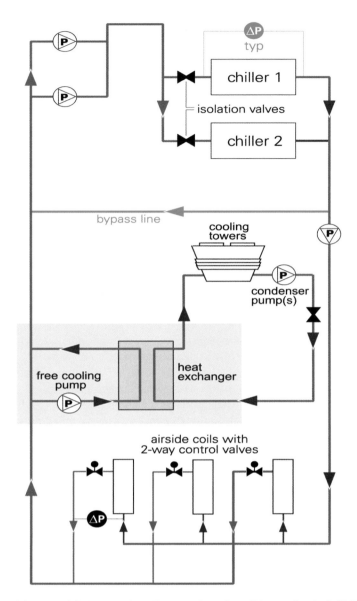

Figure 5-29 (HV14) Waterside Economizer in a Water-Cooled Chiller System
Source: Trane (2008)

An HVAC system that uses a dedicated outdoor air system (see HV4) presents a challenge for incorporating an air-side economizer. Because the dedicated OA unit and ductwork is typically sized based on the minimum ventilation rates required, rather than zone heating or cooling, the capacity of the system for providing air-side economizing is smaller than in a mixed air system. In moderate climates, oversizing of the dedicated OA system may increase economizer capacity, thereby reducing the need to operate the cooling plant during mild weather.

An analysis of the annual cooling loads can help determine the maximum cooling load of the system when the weather would allow for economizing to be used. Oversizing of the dedicated OA system should correspond to this maximum cooling load.

A water-side economizer is particularly well suited for a chilled-water fan-coil system (see HV2). When a water-cooled chiller is used, a separate plate-and-frame heat exchanger is installed between the chilled-water and condenser-water piping. An example of a water-side economizer in a water-cooled chiller system is shown in Figure 5-29. When outdoor conditions permit, the cooling tower provides cold water to the heat exchanger, which transfers heat from the warmer water returning from the fan coils, thereby reducing or eliminating the load on the water chiller. In cool or dry climates, the cooling energy saved exceeds the added energy use for operating the cooling tower fans at high speeds.

When an air-cooled chiller is used, a separate dry cooler or fluid cooler (closed-circuit cooling tower) may be installed in series with the air-cooled chiller to provide water-side economizing. Alternatively, some air-cooled chillers can be equipped with water-side economizer coils located upstream of the air-cooled condenser coils

HV15   *Demand-Controlled Ventilation* (**Climate Zones: all**)

Demand-controlled ventilation (DCV) can reduce the energy required to condition OA for ventilation. To address indoor air quality (IAQ), the setpoints (limits) and control sequence must comply with ASHRAE Standard 62.1 (ASHRAE 2010b). (Refer to the *Standard 62.1 User's Manual* [ASHRAE 2011c] for specific guidance.)

When the climate-specific tables in Chapter 4 recommend DCV, the controls should vary the amount of OA in response to the need in a zone. The amount of OA could be controlled by (1) a time-of-day schedule in the building automation system (BAS); (2) an occupancy sensor (such as a motion detector) that indicates when a zone is occupied or unoccupied; or (3) a CO_2 sensor, as a proxy for ventilation airflow per person, which measures the change in CO_2 levels in a zone. Employing DCV in a DOAS requires an automatic damper and sensor for each DCV zone. A controller will then modulate the damper to maintain proper ventilation.

CO_2 sensing should be used in zones that are densely occupied and have highly variable occupancy patterns during the occupied period, such as gymnasiums, auditoriums, multipurpose rooms, cafeterias, and some classrooms. For the other zones, occupancy sensors can be used to reduce ventilation when a zone is temporarily unoccupied. For all zones, time-of-day schedules in the BAS should be used to introduce ventilation air only when a zone is expected to be occupied.

There are two primary approaches for CO_2 sensing: distributed sensors and centralized sensors. The distributed approach involves installing a CO_2 sensor in each zone where DCV is desired. The centralized approach involves sampling points in each zone but relies on a centralized set of sensors. Both approaches require scheduled maintenance and calibration, otherwise IAQ or energy efficiency may be compromised.

A CO_2 sensor should be installed in the breathing zone of the room. Ventilation is controlled by comparing the measured zone CO_2 concentration to the outdoor CO_2 concentration (measured or assumed) and then modulating the ventilation control damper for that zone. (Refer to the *Standard 62.1 User's Manual* [2011c] for specific guidance on controls and setpoints.)

Selection of the CO_2 sensors is critical in both accuracy and response ranges. Inaccurate CO_2 sensors can cause excessive energy use or poor IAQ, so they need to be calibrated as recommended by the manufacturer (see HV28).

Finally, when DCV is used, the system controls should prevent negative building pressure. If the amount of air exhausted remains constant while the intake airflow decreases, the building may be under a negative pressure relative to outdoors. When air is exhausted directly from the zone (art or vocational classrooms, science laboratories, kitchens, locker rooms, or even a classroom with a restroom connected to it), the DCV control strategy must avoid reducing intake airflow below the amount required to replace the air being exhausted.

HV16   *System-Level Control Strategies* (**Climate Zones: all**)

Control strategies can be designed to help reduce energy. Having a setback temperature for unoccupied periods during the heating season or a setup temperature during the cooling season can help to save energy by avoiding the need to operate heating, cooling, and ventilation equipment. Programmable thermostats allow each zone to vary the temperature setpoint based on time of day and day of the week. But they also allow occupants to override these setpoints or ignore the schedule altogether (by using the "hold" feature), which thwarts any potential for energy savings. Another approach is to equip each zone with a zone temperature sensor and

Demand-Controlled Ventilation

Outdoor Air-Handling Units

Demand-controlled ventilation (DCV) can be an effective strategy to reduce the dedicated outside air system's (DOAS) energy consumption. ASHRAE Standard 62.1-2010 allows dynamic reset of outdoor airflow based on CO_2, occupancy sensors, or room occupancy schedules. Dynamic reset acknowledges that all spaces in an education facility will not be at maximum occupancy simultaneously. The actual diversity is very significant. The students move between the classrooms and other spaces throughout the day. The delivery of outdoor air is most efficient if it matches the student movement.

Turkey Foot Middle School, a 130,000 ft^2 facility completed in 2010, utilizes two variable-volume DOAS units. The project's goal was to provide outdoor air to spaces only when occupied and to regulate the airflow to the minimum that matches room population. The air is preconditioned to 68°F through the use of a heat recovery energy wheel and a combination chilled/hot-water coil. Outdoor air is then ducted to each room and the airflow is regulated using a VAV box for each room. The air is distributed within the classroom by a ceiling-mounted diffuser. The direct-digital-control (DDC) system in Turkey Foot utilizes measured CO_2 PPM data and then modulates the damper in the VAV box as required to meet the outdoor airflow requirement for each room. Each room has a CO_2 sensing port that samples the air at a centralized CO_2 sensor panel via a pneumatic air system.

then use a BAS to coordinate the operation of all components of the system. The BAS contains time-of-day schedules that define when different areas of the building are expected to be unoccupied. During these times, the system is shut off and the temperature is allowed to drift away from the occupied setpoint.

Optimal start uses a system-level controller to determine the length of time required to bring each zone from the current temperature to the occupied setpoint temperature. Then the controller waits as long as possible before starting the system so that the temperature in each zone reaches occupied setpoint just in time for occupancy. This strategy reduces the number of hours that the system needs to operate and saves energy by avoiding the need to maintain the indoor temperature at occupied setpoint even though the building is unoccupied.

A pre-occupancy ventilation period can help purge the building of contaminants that build up overnight from the off-gassing of furnishings or materials. When it is cool at night, it can also help precool the building. In climates with humid seasons, however, care should be taken to avoid bringing in humid OA during unoccupied periods.

In a VAV system, SAT reset should be implemented to minimize overall system energy use. This requires considering the trade off between compressor, heat, and fan energy, as well as the impact on space humidity levels. If SAT reset is used in a climate with humid seasons, include one or more zone humidity sensors to disable reset if the humidity level in the space exceeds a desired upper limit.

While a dedicated OA unit (see HV4) should deliver the conditioned OA at a cool temperature whenever possible, there are times when the discharge air temperature should be reset upward to minimize overall system energy use or avoid discomfort (Murphy 2006). Some possible strategies include resetting based on the temperature in the coldest zone (to avoid activating the boiler in a fan-coil system), resetting based on the temperature in the water loop (for a GSHP system), resetting based on the position of the furthest-closed VAV damper (in a VAV system), or resetting based on the outdoor temperature.

HV17   *Thermal Zoning* (Climate Zones: all)

K-12 school buildings should be divided into thermal zones based on building size, orientation, space layout and function, and after-hours use requirements.

Zoning can also be accomplished with multiple HVAC units or a central system that provides independent control for multiple zones. The temperature sensor for each zone should be installed in a location that is representative of that entire zone.

When using a multiple-zone VAV system or a dedicated outdoor air system, avoid using a single air-handling unit to serve zones that have significantly different occupancy patterns. Using multiple air-handling units allows those units serving unused areas of the building to be shut off, even when another area of the building is still in use. An alternate approach is to use the BAS to define separate operating schedules for these areas of the building, thus shutting off airflow to the unused areas while continuing to provide comfort and ventilation to areas of the building that are still in use.

HV18   *Ductwork Design and Construction* (Climate Zones: all)

Good duct design practices result in lower energy use. Low pressure loss and low air leakage in duct systems are critical to lowering the overall fan energy. Lowering the pressure needed to overcome dynamic pressure and friction losses will decrease the fan motor size and the needed fan energy. Refer to the "Duct Design" chapter of the 2009 *ASHRAE Handbook—Fundamentals* (ASHRAE 2009) for detailed data and practices.

Dynamic losses result from flow disturbances, including changes in direction, duct-mounted equipment, and duct fittings or transitions. Designers should reevaluate fitting selection practices using the ASHRAE Duct Fitting Database (ASHRAE 2008b), a program that contains more than 220 fittings. For example, using a round, smooth radius elbow instead of a mitered elbow with turning vanes can often significantly lower the pressure loss. Elbows should not be placed directly at the outlet of the fan. To achieve low loss coefficients from fittings, the flow needs to be fully developed, which is not the case at the outlet of a fan. To minimize the system effect, straight duct should be placed between the fan outlet and the elbow.

Be sure to specify 45° entry branch tees for both supply and return/exhaust junctions. The total angle of a reduction transition is recommended to be no more 45°. The total angle of an expansion transition is recommended to be 20° or less.

Poor fan performance is most commonly caused by improper outlet connections, nonuniform inlet flow, and/or swirl at the fan inlet. Look for ways to minimize the fan/duct system interface losses, referred to as *system effect losses*. Be sure the fan outlet fittings and transitions follow good duct design and low pressure loss practices. Project teams must address space requirements for good, low-pressure duct design in the early programming and schematic design phases. Allow enough space for low-pressure drop fittings and locate air-handling units that result in short, straight duct layouts. Avoid the use of close-coupled fittings.

The use of flexible duct should be limited because these ducts will use more fan energy than a metal duct system. Recent research has shown that flexible duct must be installed with less than 4% compression to achieve less than two times the pressure loss of equivalent-sized metal ductwork (Abushakra et al. 2004; Culp and Cantrill 2009). If the compression is more than 30%, the pressure loss can exceed nine times the pressure loss of metal ductwork. In addition, Lawrence Berkeley National Laboratory (LBNL) has shown that the loss coefficients for bends in flexible ductwork have a high variability from condition to condition, with no uniform trends (Abushakra et al. 2002). Loss coefficients ranged from a low of 0.87 to a high of 3.3 (for comparison purposes, a die-stamped elbow has a loss coefficient of 0.11). If a project team decides to use flexible duct, the following is advised:

- Limit the use of flexible duct to connections between duct branches and diffusers or VAV terminal units.
- Flexible sections should not exceed 5 ft in length (fully stretched).
- Install the flexible duct without any radial compression (kinks).
- Do not use flexible duct in lieu of fittings.

Where permissible, consider using plenum return systems with lower pressure loss. Whenever using a plenum return system, design and construct the exterior walls to prevent uncontrolled infiltration of humid air from outdoors (Harriman et al. 2001).

HV19   *Duct Insulation* (Climate Zones: all)

The following ductwork should be insulated:

- All supply air ductwork
- All outdoor air ductwork
- All exhaust and relief air ductwork between the motor-operated damper and penetration of the building exterior
- All ductwork located in unconditioned spaces or outside the building envelope
- All ductwork located in attics, whether ventilated or unventilated
- All ductwork buried either outside the building or below floors

In addition, all airstream surfaces should be resistant to mold growth and resist erosion, according to the requirements of ASHRAE Standard 62.1.

While return and exhaust ductwork above a top floor ceiling (with a roof above) or in an unventilated attic may seem like it doesn't need insulation, there is a real possibility that air removed from the space can have moisture condensation if the duct is located in a cold space. This condensation could cause physical damage and be a source of mold growth.

HV20   *Duct Sealing and Leakage Testing* (Climate Zones: all)

The ductwork should be sealed in accordance with ASHRAE/IES Standard 90.1. All duct joints should be inspected to ensure they are properly sealed and insulated, and the ductwork should be leak tested at the rated pressure. The leakage should not exceed the allowable cfm/100 ft^2 of duct area for the seal and leakage class of the system's air quantity apportioned to each section tested. See HV22 for guidance on ensuring the air system performance.

HV21   *Exhaust Air Systems* (Climate Zones: all)

Zone exhaust airflows (for restrooms, janitorial closets, science laboratories, kitchens, art and vocational classrooms, locker rooms, etc.) should be determined based on the current version of ASHRAE Standard 62.1, but should not be less than the values required by local code unless approved by the authority having jurisdiction.

Central exhaust systems for restrooms, janitorial closets, and locker rooms should be interlocked to operate with the air-conditioning system, except during unoccupied periods. Such a system should have a motorized damper that opens and closes with the operation of the fan. The damper should be located as close as possible to the duct penetration of the building envelope to minimize conductive heat transfer through the duct wall and avoid having to insulate the entire duct. During unoccupied periods, it should remain closed and the exhaust fan turned off. Consider designing exhaust ductwork to facilitate recovery of energy (see HV5) from Class 1 and Class 2 (e.g., restrooms) exhaust air, per the requirements of ASHRAE Standard 62.1.

Kitchens will generally have separate exhaust and make-up air systems according to the use of the kitchen and to the equipment manufacturers' suggestions (see KE1–7 for more discussion of kitchen equipment). If showers are provided in locker rooms, exhaust must be increased during use and will generally require separate air intakes (intake hood or make-up air unit). Science laboratories should have exhaust systems if noxious chemicals or preservatives are used. Make-up air will be necessary to prevent room pressure from becoming negative with respect to the outside.

HV22   *Testing, Adjusting, and Balancing* (Climate Zones: all)

After the system has been installed, cleaned, and placed in operation, the system should be tested, adjusted, and balanced (TAB) in accordance with ASHRAE Standard 111 (ASHRAE 2008a) or SMACNA's TAB manual (SMACNA 2002).

This will help to ensure that the correctly sized diffusers, registers, and grilles have been installed, that each space receives the required airflow, and that the fans meet the intended performance. The balancing subcontractor should certify that the instruments used in the measurement have been calibrated within 12 months before use. A written report should be submitted for inclusion in the operations and maintenance (O&M) manuals.

HV23   *Air Cleaning* (Climate Zones: all)

Another requirement of the HVAC system is to ensure that the air delivered to the conditioned space is relatively clean. This improves system performance (by keeping the coils cleaner, for example) and keeps the air-distribution system relatively clean. Some of the contaminants that affect IAQ can be classified as particulates, gases, or biologicals. The methods and technologies for effectively controlling these contaminants differ, so it is important to define the contaminants of concern for a given facility.

Comply with, at least, the minimum requirements for particulate filtration and air cleaning defined by ASHRAE Standard 62.1. For more information on using air cleaning to improve the indoor environment beyond minimum requirements, refer to the *Indoor Air Quality Guide: Best Practices for Design, Construction, and Commissioning* (ASHRAE 2009b).

Use a filter differential pressure gauge to monitor the pressure drop across the filters and send an alarm if the predetermined pressure drop is exceeded. Filters should be replaced when the pressure drop exceeds the filter manufacturer's recommendations for replacement or when visual inspection indicates the need for replacement. The gauge should be checked and the filter should be visually inspected at least once every three months.

HV24   *Relief versus Return Fans* (Climate Zones: all)

Relief (rather than return) fans should be used when necessary to maintain building pressurization during economizer operation. Relief fans reduce overall fan energy use in most cases, as long as return dampers are sized correctly. However, if return duct static pressure drop exceeds 1.0 in. of water, return fans may be needed.

HV25   *Zone Temperature Control* (Climate Zones: all)

The number of spaces in a zone and the location of the temperature sensor (thermostat) will affect the control of temperature in the various spaces of a zone. Locating the thermostat in one room of a zone with multiple spaces provides feedback based only on the conditions in that room. Locating a single thermostat in a large open area may provide a better response to the conditions of the zone with multiple spaces. Selecting the room or space that will best represent the thermal characteristics of the space due to both external and internal loads will provide the greatest comfort level.

To prevent misreading of the space temperature, zone thermostats should not be mounted on an exterior wall. Where this is unavoidable, use an insulated sub-base for the thermostat.

In spaces with high ceilings, consider using ceiling fans or high/low air distribution to reduce temperature stratification during the heating season.

Six primary factors must be addressed when defining conditions for thermal comfort: metabolic rate, clothing insulation, air temperature, radiant temperature, air speed, and humidity. Appropriate levels of clothing, the cooling effect of air motion, and radiant cooling or heating systems, for example, can increase occupant comfort energy efficiently.

Note: The analysis for this Guide assumed an occupied heating setpoint of 71°F, an unoccupied heating setpoint of 60°F, an occupied cooling setpoint of 74°F, and an unoccupied cooling setpoint of 81°F.

HV26   *Heating Sources* (Climate Zones: all)

Many factors, including availability of service, utility costs, operator familiarity, and the impact of source energy use, come into play in deciding whether to use gas or electricity for heating.

Forced-air electric resistance and gas-fired heaters require a minimum airflow rate to operate safely. These systems, whether stand alone or incorporated into an air-conditioning or heat-pump unit, should include factory-installed controls to shut down the heater when there is inadequate airflow that can result in high temperatures.

Ducts and supply air diffusers should be selected based on discharge air temperatures and airflow rates.

HV27   *Noise Control* (Climate Zones: all)

Being able to communicate is essential if learning is to take place in a classroom. Proper acoustics is especially important for children because their ability to hear and listen is different than that of adults. Providing good acoustics reduces barriers to education for people with non-native language skills, those with learning disabilities, and people with impaired hearing. The need for clear communication in classrooms has been recognized for many years and has been addressed by ASA S12.60-2010 (ASA 2010).

When noise from sources other than students and teachers is too high, the ability to communicate is reduced. Examples of sound sources that are of frequent concern include aircraft, traffic on nearby roads, HVAC equipment, and activities in other spaces. Excessive reverberation also impacts communication. Addressing proper acoustics during the design stage of a project will likely minimize the impact on costs. The criteria found in ASA S12.60-2010 (part 1) should be followed. The ASA standard provides guidance on wall types and performance to effectively block noise from other spaces. It also recommends acoustical analysis of the HVAC system to determine the resulting sound levels. This analysis process starts with having reliable and accurate information about the expected sound power levels produced by the selected equipment. The sound power levels depend on the actual operating conditions of the equipment. Furthermore, the sound emitted from the equipment is different for the various sound components, such as ducted discharge, ducted inlet, or casing radiated sound. To acquire accurate sound data, require the supplier of the HVAC equipment to provide sound data based on the appropriate standard (such as AHRI 260 for ducted equipment, AHRI 350 for unducted equipment, or AHRI 270 for outdoor equipment).

Once accurate sound power levels are available, the various paths that the sound can travel from the equipment to the classroom need to be considered. The *ASHRAE Handbook—HVAC Applications* (ASHRAE 2011b) describes methods for estimating sound levels in the occupied space. This acoustical analysis allows the designer to evaluate the attenuation along each sound path, estimate the noise generated as air travels through the ductwork, account for room effects, and finally add the contributions from each of the paths to determine the sound level in the space.

Avoid installation of the HVAC equipment (including heat pumps, fan-coil units, and VAV terminals) within or directly above classrooms. Consider placing equipment in locations above less critical spaces (such as storage areas, restrooms, and corridors) or in acoustically treated closets adjacent to the space. The acoustical analysis should indicate the amount of attenuation required for the noise associated with the supply air, return air, or noise radiated from the HVAC equipment. Short, direct runs of ductwork between the fan and supply or return outlet will rarely provide sufficient attenuation to meet the desired acoustic goals. Figure 5-30 shows a recommended installation for floor-mounted heat pumps.

Take care when selecting and installing diffusers. As noted in the *ASHRAE Handbook—HVAC Applications*, diffusers need to be installed with a long enough section of straight duct on the inlet to prevent or reduce aerodynamic noise generation.

Refer to ASHRAE's *Practical Guide to Noise and Vibration Control for HVAC Systems* (ASHRAE 2005) for specific guidance by system type.

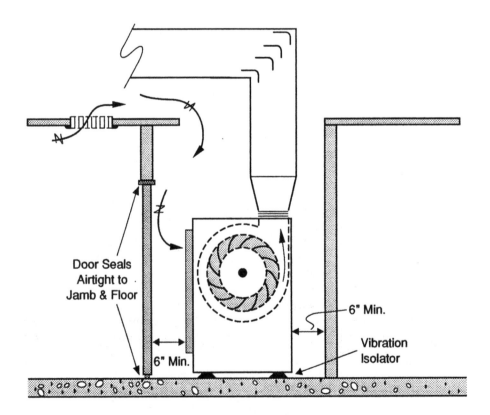

Figure 5-30 (HV27) Floor-Mounted Heat Pumps Installation
Source: ASHRAE (2005)

HV28   *Proper Maintenance* (Climate Zones: all)

Regularly scheduled maintenance is an important part of keeping the HVAC system in optimum working condition. Neglecting preventive maintenance practices can quickly negate any energy savings expected from the system design.

Filters should be replaced regularly (see HV23). Dampers, valves, louvers, and sensors must all be periodically inspected and calibrated to ensure proper operation. This is especially important for OA dampers and CO_2 sensors. Inaccurate CO_2 sensors can cause excessive energy use or poor IAQ, so they need to be calibrated as recommended by the manufacturer.

A BAS can be used to notify O&M staff when preventive maintenance procedures should be performed. This notification can be triggered by calendar dates, run-time hours, the number of times a piece of equipment has started, or sensors installed in the system (such as a pressure switch that indicates when an air filter needs to be replaced).

REFERENCES AND RESOURCES

Abushakra, B., I.S. Walker, and M.H. Sherman. 2002. A study of pressure losses in residential air distribution systems. Proceedings of the ACEEE Summer Study 2002, American Council for an Energy Efficient Economy, Washington, D.C. Lawrence Berkeley National Laboratory Report 49700.

Abushakra, B., I.S. Walker, and M.H. Sherman. 2004. Compression effects on pressure loss in flexible HVAC ducts. *International Journal of HVAC&R Research* 10(3):275–89.

AHRI. 2001. AHRI Standard 260-2001, *Sound Rating of Ducted Air Moving and Conditioning Equipment*. Arlington, VA: Air-Conditioning, Heating, and Refrigeration Institute.

AHRI. 2008. AHRI Standard 270-2008, *Sound Rating of Outdoor Unitary Equipment*. Arlington, VA: Air-Conditioning, Heating, and Refrigeration Institute.

AHRI. 2008. AHRI Standard 350-2008, *Sound Rating of Non-Ducted Indoor Air-Conditioning Equipment*. Arlington, VA: Air-Conditioning, Heating, and Refrigeration Institute.

ASA. 2010. ANSI/ASA S12.60-2010, *Acoustical Performance Criteria, Design Requirements, and Guidelines for Schools*. Melville, NY: Acoustical Society of America, Inc. http://asastore.aip.org.

ASHRAE. 1997. *Ground-Source Heat Pumps: Design of Geothermal Systems for Commercial and Institutional Buildings*. Atlanta: American Society of Heating, Refrigerating and Air-Conditioning Engineers.

ASHRAE. 1998. ANSI/ASHRAE/ARI/ISO Standard 13256-1-1998, *Water-Source Heat Pumps Testing and Rating for Performance*. Atlanta: American Society of Heating, Refrigerating and Air-Conditioning Engineers.

ASHRAE. 2005. *Practical Guide to Noise and Vibration Control for HVAC Systems I-P*, 2nd Edition. Atlanta: American Society of Heating, Refrigerating and Air-Conditioning Engineers.

ASHRAE. 2007a. ANSI/ASHRAE Standard 52.2-2007, *Method of Testing General Ventilation Air-Cleaning Devices for Removal Efficiency by Particle Size*. Atlanta: American Society of Heating, Refrigerating and Air-Conditioning Engineers.

ASHRAE. 2007b. ANSI/ASHRAE/ACCA Standard 183-2007 (RA2011), *Peak Cooling and Heating Load Calculations in Buildings Except Low-Rise Residential Buildings*. Atlanta: American Society of Heating, Refrigerating and Air-Conditioning Engineers.

ASHRAE. 2008a. ANSI/ASHRAE Standard 111-2008, *Measurement, Testing, Adjusting, and Balancing of Building HVAC Systems*. Atlanta: American Society of Heating, Refrigerating and Air-Conditioning Engineers.

ASHRAE. 2008b. ASHRAE Duct fitting database 5.00.00. Atlanta: American Society of Heating, Refrigerating and Air-Conditioning Engineers.

ASHRAE. 2008c. *ASHRAE Handbook—HVAC Systems and Equipment*. Atlanta: American Society of Heating, Refrigerating and Air-Conditioning Engineers.

ASHRAE. 2009a. *ASHRAE Handbook—Fundamentals*. Atlanta: American Society of Heating, Refrigerating and Air-Conditioning Engineers.

ASHRAE. 2009b. *Indoor Air Quality Guide: Best Practices for Design, Construction and Commissioning.* Atlanta: American Society of Heating, Refrigerating and Air-Conditioning Engineers.

ASHRAE. 2010a. ANSI/ASHRAE Standard 55-2010, *Thermal Environmental Conditions for Human Occupancy.* Atlanta: American Society of Heating, Refrigerating and Air-Conditioning Engineers.

ASHRAE. 2010b. ANSI/ASHRAE Standard 62.1-2010, *Ventilation for Acceptable Indoor Air Quality.* Atlanta: American Society of Heating, Refrigerating and Air-Conditioning Engineers.

ASHRAE. 2010c. ANSI/ASHRAE/IES Standard 90.1-2010, *Energy Standard for Buildings Except Low-Rise Residential Building*s. Atlanta: American Society of Heating, Refrigerating and Air-Conditioning Engineers.

ASHRAE. 2010d. *ASHRAE GreenGuide: The Design, Construction, and Operation of Sustainable Buildings,* 3rd Ed. Atlanta: American Society of Heating, Refrigerating and Air-Conditioning Engineers.

ASHRAE. 2011a. ASHRAE Guideline 10-2011, *Interactions Affecting the Achievement of Acceptable Indoor Environments.* Atlanta: American Society of Heating, Refrigerating and Air-Conditioning Engineers.

ASHRAE. 2011b. *ASHRAE Handbook—HVAC Applications.* Atlanta: American Society of Heating, Refrigerating and Air-Conditioning Engineers.

ASHRAE. 2011c. *Standard 62.1 User's Manual.* Atlanta: American Society of Heating, Refrigerating and Air-Conditioning Engineers.

ASHRAE. 2011d. *Standard 90.1 User's Manual.* Atlanta: American Society of Heating, Refrigerating and Air-Conditioning Engineers.

Bonnema, E., Leach, M., and S. Pless. 2011. Technical support document: Development of the *Advanced Energy Design Guide for K-12 Schools—50% Energy Savings.* NREL/TP-5500-51437. National Renewable Energy Laboratory, Golden, CO. www.nrel.gov/docs/fy11osti/51437.pdf.

Culp, C., and D. Cantrill. 2009. Pressure losses in 12", 14", and 16" non-metallic flexible ducts with compression and sag. *ASHRAE Transactions* 115(1).

Harriman, L., G. Brundett, and R. Kittler. 2001. *Humidity Control Design Guide for Commercial and Institutional Buildings.* Atlanta: American Society of Heating, Refrigerating and Air-Conditioning Engineers, Inc.

Morris, W. 2003. The ABCs of DOAS: Dedicated Outdoor Air Systems. *ASHRAE Journal* 45(5).

Mumma, S., and K. Shank. 2001. Selecting the supply air conditions for a dedicated outdoor air system working in parallel with distributed sensible cooling terminal equipment. *ASHRAE Transactions* 107(1).

Mumma, S. 2001. Designing dedicated outdoor air systems. *ASHRAE Journal* 43(5).

Mumma, S. 2008. Terminal equipment with DOAS: Series vs. parallel. *Engineered Systems* 45(5).

Murphy, J. 2006. Smart dedicated outdoor air systems. *ASHRAE Journal* 48(7).

National Electrical Manufacturers Association, www.nema.org, Standards and Publications section.

Schaffer, Mark. 2011. *Practical Guide to Noise and Vibration Control for HVAC Systems.* Atlanta: American Society of Heating, Refrigerating and Air-Conditioning Engineers, Inc.

SMACNA. 2002. *HVAC Systems—Testing, Adjusting and Balancing.* Chantilly, VA: Sheet Metal and Air Conditioning Contractors' National Association, Inc.

Trane. 2008. "Free" cooling using water economizer. *Engineers Newsletter* 37(3):4.

Warden, D. 1996. "Dual Fan Dual Duct: Better Performance at Lower Cost." *ASHRAE Journal* 38(1).

Warden, D. 2004. "Dual Fan, Dual Duct Goes to School." *ASHRAE Journal* 46(5).

QUALITY ASSURANCE

Quality assurance (QA), including commissioning (Cx), will help ensure a building functions in accordance with its design intent and meets the performance goals established for it. Quality assurance, including a robust measurement and verification (M&V) program, should be an integral part of the design and construction process and of the continued operation of the facility. The objective of an M&V process is to ensure that new equipment in a facility is performing as originally specified and that projected savings are being realized. Benchmarking and M&V can be most effective during your warranty period to address building systems and components that are not operating as intended.

You can use M&V to determine savings from the following:

• Energy management
• Energy conservation
• An energy efficiency project or program

Compare measured use before and after a project is implemented and be sure to make adjustments for weather and other conditions.

After the building is commissioned, establish M&V procedures for actual building performance to identify corrective actions and repairs. Monitor and record utility consumption and its attending factors to establish building performance during the first year of operation.

General Information on quality assurance and commissioning is included in Chapter 2, and Appendix C provides examples for the commissioning process.

COMMISSIONING

QA1   Design and Construction Team (Climate Zones: all)

Selection of the design and construction team members is critical to a project's success. Owners need to understand how team dynamics can play a role in the building's performance. Owners should evaluate qualifications of candidates, past performance, cost of services, and availability of the candidates in making their selection. Owners need to be clear in their expectations of how team members should interact. It should be clear that all members should work together to further team goals. The first step is to define members' roles and responsibilities. This includes defining deliverables at each phase during the design and commissioning processes.

QA2   Owner's Project Requirements and Basis of Design (Climate Zones: all)

The Owner's Project Requirements (OPR) details the functional requirements of a project and the expectations of how the facility will be used and operated. This includes strategies and recommendations selected from this Guide (see Chapter 4) that will be incorporated into the project, anticipated hours of operation provided by the owner, a measurement and verification plan, and Basis of Design assumptions.

The OPR forms the foundation of the team's tasks by defining project and design goals, measurable performance criteria, owner directives, budgets, schedules, and supporting information in a single, concise document. The QA process depends on a clear, concise, and comprehensive OPR. Development of the OPR document requires input from all key facility users and operators. It is critical to align the complexity of the systems with the capacity and capability of the facility staff.

The next step is for the design team members to document how their design responds to the OPR information. This document is the Basis of Design (BoD). It records the standards and regulations, calculations, design criteria, decisions and assumptions, and the system descriptions. The narrative must clearly articulate the specific operating parameters required for the systems to form the correct basis for later quality measurements. Essentially, it is the engineering background information that is not provided in the construction documents that map out how the architect and engineering firm end up with their designs. For example, it would state key criteria such as future expansion and redundancy considerations. It should include important criteria such as what code, standard, or guideline is being followed for the various engineered systems, including ventilation and energy. It provides a good place to document owner input necessary for engineered systems, such as identifying what electrical loads are to be on emergency power.

QA3 *Selection of Quality Assurance Provider* (Climate Zones: all)

QA is a systematic process of verifying the OPR, operational needs, and BoD and ensuring that the building performs in accordance with these defined needs. The selection of a QA provider should include the same evaluation process the owner would use to select other team members. Qualifications in providing QA services, past performance of projects, cost of services, and availability of the candidate are some of the parameters an owner should investigate and consider when making a selection. Owners may select a member of the design or construction team as the QA provider. While there are exceptions, in general most designers are not comfortable operating and testing assemblies and equipment and most contractors do not have the technical background necessary to evaluate performance. Commissioning requires in-depth technical knowledge of the building envelope and the mechanical, electrical, and plumbing systems and operational and construction experience. This function is best performed by a third party responsible to the owner because political issues often inhibit a member of the design or construction organizations from fulfilling this responsibility.

QA4 *Design and Construction Schedule* (Climate Zones: all)

The inclusion of QA activities in the construction schedule fulfills a critical part of delivering a successful project. Identify the activities and time required for design review and performance verification to minimize time and effort needed to accomplish activities and correct deficiencies.

QA5 *Design Review* (Climate Zones: all)

A second pair of eyes provided by the commissioning authority (CxA) or QA provider gives a fresh perspective that allows identification of issues and opportunities to improve the quality of the construction documents with verification that the OPR is being met. Issues identified can be more easily corrected early in the project, providing potential savings in construction costs and reducing risk to the team.

QA6 *Defining Quality Assurance at Pre-Bid* (Climate Zones: all)

The building industry has traditionally delivered buildings without using a verification process. Changes in traditional design and construction procedures and practices require educating the construction team about how the QA process will affect the various trades bidding on the project. It is extremely important that the QA process be reviewed with the bidding contractors to facilitate understanding of and to help minimize fear associated with new practices. Teams who have participated in the Cx process typically appreciate the process because they are able to resolve problems while their manpower and materials are still on the project, significantly reducing delays, callbacks, and associated costs while enhancing their delivery capacity.

These requirements can be reviewed by the architect and engineer of record at the pre-bid meeting, as defined in the specifications.

QA7 *Verifying Building Envelope Construction* (Climate Zones: all)

The building envelope is a key element of an energy-efficient design. Compromises in assembly performance are common and are caused by a variety of factors that can easily be avoided. Improper placement of insulation, improper sealing or lack of sealing at air barriers, wrong or poorly performing glazing and fenestration systems, incorrect placement of shading devices, misplacement of daylighting shelves, and misinterpretation of assembly details can significantly compromise the energy performance of the building (see cautions in EN20–23 and daylighting information in DL12).

QA8   *Verifying Lighting Construction* (Climate Zones: all)

Lighting plays a significant role in the energy consumption of the building. Lighting for all of the space types should be reviewed against anticipated schedule of use throughout the day. Refer to EL13–19 for specific space type lighting information.

QA9   *Verifying Electrical and HVAC Systems Construction* (Climate Zones: all)

Performance of electrical and HVAC systems are key elements of this Guide. How systems are designed as well as installed affect how efficiently they will perform. Collaboration between the entire design team is needed to optimize the energy efficiency of the facility. Natural daylight and electric lighting will impact the heating and cooling loads from both a systems capacity and hourly operation mode. This area should be paid close attention in design reviews. Proper installation is just as important as proper design. Making sure the installing contractor's foremen understand the owner's goals, the QA process, and the installation details is key to system performance success. A significant part of this process is a careful and thorough review of product submittals to ensure compliance with the design. It is in everyone's best interest to install the components correctly and completely the first time. Trying to inspect quality in the middle of a project is time consuming, costly, and usually doesn't work. It's much better to ensure all team members are aligned with the QA process and goals. Certainly, observations and inspections during construction are necessary. The timing is critical to ensure that problems are identified at the beginning of each system installation. This minimizes the number of changes (time and cost) and leaves time for corrections.

QA10   *Functional Performance Testing* (Climate Zones: all)

Functional performance testing of systems is essential to ensure that all the commissioned systems are functioning properly in all modes of operation. This is a prerequisite for the owner to realize the energy savings that can be expected from the strategies and recommendations contained in this Guide. Unlike most appliances these days, none of the mechanical/electrical systems in a new facility are "plug and play." If the team has executed the Cx plan and is aligned with the QA goals, the performance testing will occur quickly, and only minor issues will need to be resolved. Owners with O&M personnel can use the functional testing process as a training tool to educate their staff on how the systems operate as well as for system orientation prior to training.

QA11   *Substantial Completion* (Climate Zones: all)

Substantial completion generally indicates the completion and acceptance of the life safety systems and that the facility is ready to be occupied. All of the systems should be operating as intended. Expected performance can only be accomplished when all systems operate interactively to provide the desired results. As contractors finish their work, they will identify and resolve many performance problems. The CxA/QA provider verifies that the contractor maintained a quality control process by directing and witnessing testing and then helps to resolve remaining issues.

QA12   *Final Acceptance* (Climate Zones: all)

Final acceptance generally occurs after the Cx/QA issues in the issues log have been resolved, except for minor issues the owner is comfortable with resolving during the warranty period.

QA13   *Establish Building Operation and Maintenance Program* (Climate Zones: all)

Continued performance and control of O&M require a maintenance program. Detailed O&M system manual and training requirements are defined in the OPR and executed by the project team to ensure the O&M staff has the tools and skills necessary to provide ongoing maintenance for the building. The O&M manuals can be used by the O&M staff to develop a maintenance program.

The level of expertise typically associated with O&M staff for buildings covered by this Guide is generally much lower than that of a degreed or licensed engineer, and they typically need assistance with development of a preventive maintenance program. The CxA/QA provider can help bridge knowledge gaps and assist in developing programs that help ensure continued high performance. The benefits associated with energy-efficient buildings are realized when systems perform as intended through proper design, construction, and O&M.

MEASUREMENT AND VERIFICATION (M&V)

QA14   *Monitor Post-Occupancy Performance* (Climate Zones: all)

Establishing M&V procedures for actual building performance after commissioning occurs can help identify when corrective action and/or repair is required to maintain energy performance.

Energy consumption and factors that affect it should be monitored and recorded to establish building performance during the first year of operation using submetered data and utility bills (See QA15). Collecting submetered data within the first year is recommended to allow for issues to be diagnosed and addressed while the necessary materials and labor are still covered under warranty. At a minimum, the submetering system should be designed to measure each energy end use at the system level (lighting, HVAC, general 120V, renewables, etc.).

Submetering can be used to ensure that building energy profiles match occupancy schedules and that miscellaneous electric loads are being turned off at night. If submetered data show a reduction in lighting energy on sunny days, you can demonstrate that your daylighting system is working. Submetered data can also be used to verify that renewable energy systems are functioning properly. Variations in energy usage can often be attributed to changes in weather, occupancy, operational schedule, and maintenance procedures; submetering at the system level and tracking these variation-inducing parameters allows data to be reviewed in an efficient manner that results in definitive conclusions. CxA/QA providers can help owners and facility staff to understand when operational tolerances are exceeded and can provide assistance in defining what actions may be required to return the building to peak performance.

Another important function of submetered data is to document real-world energy savings of low-energy buildings and compare measured data to design goals. School districts and design teams can use this data to inform and improve future school designs and operations. In addition, designers can demonstrate to clients that they can achieve real world energy performance. The post-occupancy evaluations provide lessons learned in the design, technologies, operation, and analysis techniques to ensure these and future buildings operate at a high level of performance over time. For additional details on this process, along with case studies and lessons learned from real life examples, refer to NREL's published report (Torcellini et al. 2006).

QA15   *M&V Electrical Panel Guidance* (Climate Zones: all)

Designing the electrical distribution system to be submetered reduces complexity, minimizes the number of meters, shortens installation time, and minimizes rewiring. Install separate meters for each major end use including lighting, HVAC, general 120V, and renewables. To help facilitate submetering, disaggregate your electrical panels (put lights together on one panel, HVAC on another, miscellaneous loads on a third, etc.), and repeat for emergency circuits. When possible, install submeters at the main distribution panel (and repeat for emergency circuits) to minimize installation and wiring costs. Consider using electrical panels with integral submeters to reduce capital costs. Integrate testing of the meters into your commissioning plan to ensure that the submetering system is operating correctly.

QA16   *M&V Data Management and Access* (Climate Zones: all)

Detailed M&V systems can results in an overwhelming amount of data. The success of an M&V system depends on proper management of this data. Collect submetered data at resolutions appropriate for the intended use. For example: save 1-minute data for one day to aid with equipment troubleshooting and identify failures, save data at 5-minute intervals for one week to help analyze the building schedules and save 15-minute data for at least one year to help with benchmarking, to determine annual energy performance, to compare to the original energy model (weather variance removed), and to compare end-use benchmarks. In general, make sure you have sufficient data resolution to determine electricity demand information and equipment failures.

To ensure ease of interoperability and consistency with other submetering efforts in your district, comply with your district's metering standard. If one does not exist, consider developing a metering standard that documents interoperability and accessibility requirements. In addition, allow for external consultants and design team members to easily access the metered data remotely.

QA17 *M&V Benchmarking* (Climate Zones: all)

An owner should benchmark utility bills and submetered data to ensure energy performance targets are met and should be prepared to repeat this exercise monthly. Commissioning agents and quality assurance providers can typically help owners and facility staff to understand when operational tolerances are exceeded and can help determine actions to return the building to peak performance.

Benchmarking the energy usage of a building facilitates the identification of poor performance. Monthly energy performance should be benchmarked against historic performance and other facilities in the district. Annual energy performance should be benchmarked using ENERGYSTAR Portfolio Manager and the energy targets provided in this guide (see Chapter 3). Training should be provided to facility operators to help use the benchmarking data to diagnose operational issues.

TEACHING TOOLS

QA18 *The Building as a Teaching Tool* (Climate Zones: all)

Designing and operating an energy efficient school is a great opportunity to integrate the building features into the curriculum. Schools that incorporate energy efficiency and renewable energy technologies as part of the core curriculum standards make a strong statement about the importance of protecting the environment. In addition, the building is used as a tool to enhance student achievement by relating the subjects and building features as project-based learning experience.

One way to achieve this hands-on approach to teaching is by exposing portions of the building systems through see-through display cut outs of the interior finishes such as walls, floors or ceiling to allow students to see and learn from the building systems. These building elements become teaching aids and create opportunities for student-guided tours that galvanize core curriculum skills for science, engineering, technology, and math (STEM); English language arts (ELA); social studies; and arts education. For example, students could be reading a book on how energy is produced while observing their schools' energy performance through measurements or energy dashboard information that reinforces statistics, math, and research skills. Students could also participate in energy competitions among classrooms, which help promote awareness and develop leadership skills.

Photovoltaic (PV) systems are a common alternative-energy teaching tool. PV systems allow for the use of real-time information that can be integrated into the school curriculum. The students can take a tour of the installation, monitor real-time system performance, and observe how their school impacts the environment individually and in the community. The monitoring programs are available as dashboards, kiosks, or Web interfaces. See RE1 in the "Additional Bonus Savings" section for more information on PV systems.

Wind turbine systems are another alternative energy teaching tool. Wind Powering America, a U.S. Department of Energy (DOE) initiative, sponsors the Wind for Schools project to

Teaching Tools

Exposed Wall Insulation with Information Sign
Photo source: Mike Rogers, ME Group

Building systems can be used to provide teaching tools for students and allow for the incorporation of energy efficiency and renewable energy technologies into the core curriculum standards. Examples include photovoltaic (PV) systems and see-through display cut-outs of interior building systems such as wall insulation. Real-time information displays and information signs explaining the technology and what is shown assist with guided tours for students and visitors.

Photovoltaic System with Information Sign
Photo source: Mike Nicklas, Innovative Design

Table 5-15   Teaching Tools Resources

Energy Dashboard Examples
Desert Edge High School, Green Touchscreen Web site, http://desertedge.greentouchscreen.com/

Educational Resources
EnergyHog website, Educators Web site: www.energyhog.org/adult/educators.htm
The Green Schools Alliance website, Green Cup Challenge Web site: www.greencupchallenge.net
Junior Energy Web site: www.juniorenergy.org

Renewable Energy Resources
SolarOne (S[1]) website, Green Design Lab Web site: http://solar1.org/education/greendesignlab/
Kid Wind Project website: http://learn.kidwind.org/

Government Resources
National Energy Education Development Project website: www.need.org
New York City Schools Sustainability website, Green Curriculum Web site: http://schools.nyc.gov/sustainability
U.S. Department of Energy, Energy Efficiency & Renewable Energy website, Energy Education & Workforce Development, K-12 Lesson Plans & Activities Web site: www1.eere.energy.gov/education/lessonplans/default.aspx
U.S. Department of Energy, Energy Efficiency & Renewable Energy website, Wind Powering America, Wind for Schools Web site: www.windpoweringamerica.gov/schools_wfs_project.asp
U.S. Energy Information Administration Energy Kids Web site: www.eia.doe.gov/kids/
U.S. Environmental Protection Agency website, Region 5 Pollution Prevention Web site: www.epa.gov/reg5rcra/wptdiv/p2pages/toolbox.htm
U.S. Environmental Protection Agency, ENERGY STAR Kids Web site: www.energystar.gov/index.cfm?c=kids.kids_index
U.S. Environmental Protection Agency website, Region 2 Sustainability Web site: www.epa.gov/region02/sustainability/greencommunities/vampire_ed_tool.html
U.S. Environmental Protection Agency, A Student's Guide to Global Warming Web site: www.epa.gov/climatechange/students/index.html

International Resources
Engaging Places from United Kingdom Web site: www.engagingplaces.org.uk/home

raise awareness about the benefits of wind energy while simultaneously developing a wind energy knowledge base for future leaders of our communities, states, and nation. Teaching materials and informational resources about the Wind for Schools project, including where school wind projects are located across the United States, can be found on the Wind Powering America Web page on the DOE Energy Efficiency and Renewable Energy (EERE) Wind and Water Power Web site (DOE 2011c). This and other resources for teaching tools are listed in Table 5-15. See RE2 in the "Additional Bonus Savings" section for more information on wind turbine systems.

REFERENCES AND RESOURCES

ASHRAE. 2002. ASHRAE Guideline 14, *Measurement of Energy and Demand Savings*. Atlanta: American Society of Heating, Refrigerating and Air-Conditioning Engineers.

ASHRAE. 2005. ASHRAE Guideline 0-2005, *The Commissioning Process*. Atlanta: American Society of Heating, Refrigerating and Air-Conditioning Engineers.

ASHRAE. 2007. ASHRAE Guideline 1.1-2007, *HVAC&R Technical Requirements for The Commissioning Process*. Atlanta: American Society of Heating, Refrigerating and Air-Conditioning Engineers.

DOE. 2002. International performance measurement & verification protocol: Concepts and options for determining energy and water savings Volume I. DOE/GO-102002-1554, U.S. Department of Energy, Washington, DC. http://www.nrel.gov/docs/fy02osti/31505.pdf.

DOE. 2008. M&V guidelines: Measurement and verification for federal energy projects, version 3.0. U.S. Department of Energy, Federal Energy Management Program, Washington, DC. http://www1.eere.energy.gov/femp/pdfs/mv_guidelines.pdf

DOE. 2011a. Energy savings performance contracts. Federal Energy Management Program, U.S Department of Energy. http://www1.eere.energy.gov/femp/financing/espcs.html.

DOE. 2011b. ENERGY STAR Portfolio manager overview. Department of Energy, Washington, DC. http://www.energystar.gov/index.cfm?c=evaluate_performance.bus_portfoliomanager.

DOE. 2011c. Wind powering America. U.S. Department of Energy, Energy Efficiency and Renewable Energy, Washington, DC. http://www.windpoweringamerica.gov/schools/projects.asp.

Torcellini, S. Pless, M. Deru, B. Griffith, N. Long, and R. Judkoff. 2006. Lessons learned from case studies of six high-performance buildings. NRETL/TP-55-037542, National Renewable National Laboratory, Golden, CO.

ADDITIONAL BONUS SAVINGS

OTHER HVAC STRATEGIES

HV29   *Natural Ventilation and Naturally Conditioned Spaces*
(Climate Zones: ❷B ❸B ❸C ❹C ❺B and as appropriate elsewhere in a mixed-mode approach)

Compared to buildings with fixed-position windows, buildings with properly applied and properly used operable windows can provide advantages in schools, including energy conservation and energy conservation education.

Natural ventilation involves the use of operable elements in the façade of a building to bring in OA. ASHRAE Standard 62.1-2010 (ASHRAE 2010b) requires either engineering analysis to confirm adequate ventilation or compliance with prescriptive requirements that govern the size and spacing of the openings, as well as the permanent accessibility of the controls by the occupants.

Occupant-controlled naturally conditioned spaces, as defined by ASHRAE Standard 55 (ASHRAE 2010a), are "those spaces where the thermal conditions of the space are regulated primarily by the opening and closing of windows by the occupants." ASHRAE Standard 55 allows an adaptive comfort standard to be used under a limited set of conditions.

When considering either natural ventilation or naturally conditioned spaces, one must first consider the climate and the number of hours when an occupant might want to open the windows and evaluate whether a natural scheme is possible for the range of outdoor temperature and humidity. If the climate supports natural ventilation/conditioning, then the design team should also investigate the outdoor air quality (to determine the acceptability of introducing it directly into the occupied spaces); noise impacts from adjacent streets, railways, or airports; and building security concerns.

A mixed-mode (or hybrid) approach uses a combination of natural ventilation from operable windows (either manually or automatically controlled) and a mechanical system that includes air-distribution equipment. A mixed-mode system usually falls into one of three categories:

- *Zoned use:* Some areas of the building are provided with natural ventilation and a mechanical ventilation/conditioning system for times when natural ventilation is not effective. The remainder of the building is served by only a mechanical ventilation system.
- *Change-over use:* An area of the building is naturally ventilated/conditioned for part of the year, but is fully heated or cooled during extreme weather.
- *Concurrent use:* An area of the building is naturally ventilated but artificially cooled (often via a passive radiant system).

It is important to evaluate the frequency of natural ventilation use because in mixed-mode systems, the owner is often purchasing two systems: a mechanical air-conditioning system and the operable windows in the façade.

In mixed-mode systems, the mechanical ventilation system should be shut off when windows are opened. Operable window systems can be controlled manually or by electrical interlock. Manual control provides the opportunity for curriculum on energy efficiency, but automatic controls (such as interlocks) may save more energy.

HV30   *Thermal Storage* (**Climate Zones: all**)

Adding thermal storage to an HVAC system can reduce the utility costs associated with cooling by shifting operation of the cooling equipment from times of high-cost electricity (daytime) to times of low-cost electricity (nighttime). This avoids or reduces the electricity required to operate the cooling equipment during the daytime hours. Operation of the cooling equipment is shifted to the off-peak period, during which the cost of electricity and the demand charge are lower. The cooling equipment is used during that period to cool or freeze water inside storage tanks, storing the thermal energy until the on-peak period.

During the nighttime hours, the outdoor dry-bulb and wet-bulb temperatures are typically several degrees lower than during the day. This lowers the condensing pressure, allowing the cooling equipment to regain some of the capacity and efficiency it loses by producing colder fluid temperatures to recharge the storage tanks.

Another potential benefit of thermal storage is a reduction in the size and capacity of the cooling equipment. When thermal storage is used to satisfy all or part of the design cooling load, the cooling equipment may be able to be downsized as long as it has enough time to recharge the storage tanks.

HV31   *Thermal Mass* (**Climate Zones: all**)

Another approach to reducing peak cooling demand is to take advantage of the building's thermal mass. Many school buildings are constructed of concrete or masonry walls. The thermal mass of these materials can absorb excess solar heat and stabilize indoor temperatures.

In locations with large diurnal swings and low humidity levels, night precooling is an effective strategy. The principle is to precool the building during the nighttime (or morning off-peak) hours with cool outdoor air. This cools the building's thermal mass and reduces the cooling load during on-peak hours. When implemented effectively, many zones can maintain comfortable space temperatures for several hours without supplemental cooling, thereby reducing energy use.

Incorporating thermal mass as an energy-saving strategy involves locating insulation on the outside of the wall mass (see EN5). This allows the wall to absorb excess heat from inside the building, and the insulation minimizes heat transfer to the outdoors. This approach also benefits passive solar heating strategies (see EN32).

Thermal mass is particularly valuable as an energy-saving strategy in zones that allow for greater variability in space temperatures. Examples may include gymnasiums, auditoriums, and cafeterias. A greater (wider) allowable temperature range results in more annual hours when precooling is effective.

HV32   *Thermal Displacement Ventilation* (**Climate Zones: all**)

Thermal displacement ventilation (TDV) systems are different from conventional overhead air delivery systems. TDV systems deliver air near the floor, at a low velocity, and at a temperature of about 65°F (compared to around 55°F with overhead air delivery). The goal of TDV systems is to cool the occupants, not the space. Cool air flows along the floor until it finds warm bodies. As the air is warmed, it rises around occupants, bathing them in cool fresh air.

Air quality improves because contaminants from occupants and other sources tend to rise out of the breathing zone rather than being mixed in the space. Similarly, cooling loads decrease because much of the heat generated by occupants, lights, and computer equipment

Thermal Energy Storage

Ice Storage Tanks and Air-Cooled Chiller

The Fossil Ridge High School in Fort Collins, CO, uses thermal energy storage to lower operating costs associated with cooling the building. The system consists of eight ice storage tanks and a 140 ton air-cooled chiller. The chiller is operated at night when the cost of electricity is lower, to freeze water inside the storage tanks.

Adding thermal storage to the chilled-water system reduces utility costs by shifting the operation of the chiller from periods when the cost of electricity is high (e.g., daytime) to periods when the cost of electricity is lower (e.g., nighttime). During the nighttime hours, the outdoor dry-bulb temperature is typically lower than during the day. This allows the chiller to operate at a lower condensing pressure and regain some of the capacity and efficiency lost by producing the colder fluid temperatures needed to freeze the storage tanks.

Due to the high-performance envelope and lighting system designs, the peak cooling load is only 250 tons (1050 ft^2/ton). For this project, the thermal energy storage was sized to offset a portion of peak cooling load, allowing for the installation of a downsized chiller (140 tons, or almost 1900 ft^2/ton of chiller capacity).

rises directly out of the occupied zone and is exhausted from the space. (This is especially true in classrooms designed for 100% OA.)

TDV is most appropriate for spaces with ceilings higher than 10 ft to permit temperature stratification. However, heating performance may be worse than with systems that deliver air at greater velocities, since mixing (not stratification) is desirable for heating. In non-arid climates,

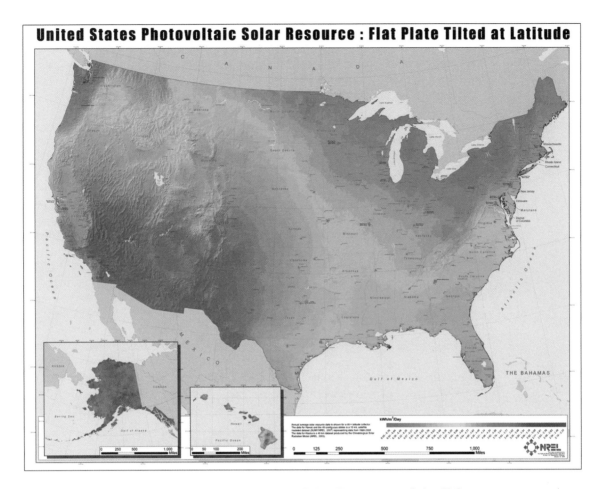

Figure 5-31 Photovoltaic Solar Resources of the U.S.
Source: National Renewable Energy Laboratory (NREL)

the supply air must be sufficiently dehumidified before it is reheated, or mixed with warm return air to achieve the desired 65°F SAT.

HV33   *ASHRAE Standard 62.1 IAQ Procedure* **(Climate Zones: all)**

Additional energy savings can be provided through the use of ASHRAE Standard 62.1 (ASHRAE 2010). The Ventilation Rate Procedure is a widely-used, prescriptive procedure used to determine the amount of outdoor air that must be introduced based on occupancy, space type, room size, and zone air-distribution effectiveness. It assumes contaminant sources and strengths based on typical room types.

The IAQ Procedure is an alternative approach provided by ASHRAE Standard 62.1. It bases building outdoor airflow rates on an analysis of project-specific contaminant sources. The designer must identify all contaminants of concern, find acceptable levels for the contaminants, identify contaminant generation sources and rates, and determine that the resultant contaminant levels are below the acceptable levels. This must occur both at design and during system operation.

This procedure may allow the designer to reduce the amount of outdoor air introduced (below the rates prescribed by the Ventilation Rate Procedure) by applying various design strategies to reduce contaminants from indoor and outdoor sources. These strategies may include air-cleaning devices, selecting materials with lower source strengths, and specific contaminant monitoring to demonstrate performance results better than those achieved with the Ventilation Rate Procedure.

HV34   *Evaporative Cooling* (Climate Zones: all)

Evaporative cooling can reduce the energy use associated with traditional air-cooled refrigeration equipment. The increased density and heat transfer coefficient of water compared to air can result in increased energy efficiency ratios, particularly in dry climates.

There are two primary forms of evaporative cooling:

- *Direct evaporative cooling:* This equipment introduces moisture into the outdoor airstream and relies on the evaporation of the water to produce moist, cooler air. This moist and cool air is supplied to zones that require cooling. Because this method introduces humidity into the occupied zone, direct evaporative cooling work best in hot, dry climates such as those found in the Southwest region of the United States.
- *Indirect evaporative cooling:* This strategy relies on a heat exchanger to prevent the introduction of moist air into the conditioned space. Common examples of indirect evaporative cooling include cooling towers as well as energy recovery ventilators (ERV) with an evaporative cooler in the exhaust airstream.

While direct evaporative cooling may be limited to use in hot, dry climates, indirect evaporative cooling has more widespread application. Cooling towers are an indirect evaporative cooling technology that increases the energy efficiency of a system when coupled with a water-cooled chiller.

Many school projects have installed energy recovery ventilators to precool incoming air when in cooling mode (see HV5). An ERV equipped with a sensible energy recovery device and an evaporative cooling module in the exhaust airstream provides additional cooling capacity without introducing moisture into the building. This operates by cooling the exhaust airstream, which increases the temperature differential between the cool exhaust air and warm outdoor air.

The maintenance aspects of evaporative cooling equipment can vary, but common factors include chemical treatment, water quality and availability, cooling tower maintenance, evaporative media replacement, and seasonal shutdown. These, and other factors, should be considered with the operations and maintenance plan for the project.

REFERENCES AND RESOURCES

ASHRAE. 2010a. ANSI/ASHRAE Standard 55-2010, *Thermal Environmental Conditions for Human Occupancy.* Atlanta: American Society of Heating, Refrigerating and Air-Conditioning Engineers.

ASHRAE. 2010b. ANSI/ASHRAE Standard 62.1-2010, *Ventilation for Acceptable Indoor Air Quality.* Atlanta: American Society of Heating, Refrigerating and Air-Conditioning Engineers.

RENEWABLE ENERGY

RE1   *Photovoltaic (PV) Systems* (Climate Zones: all)

Photovoltaic (PV) systems have become an increasingly popular option for on-site electric energy production for both energy cost savings and as a teaching opportunity in schools. These systems require very little maintenance and have long lifetimes but are often difficult to cost justify without alternative financing and leveraging available incentives. However, the average cost of PV systems has declined significantly in recent years. PV systems can be effectively used in schools in almost all climate zones in the U.S. Figure 5-31 shows the PV solar energy resources in the U.S.

Options for installing PV systems include rooftop (including collectors integrated with the roofing membrane), ground-mounted, or as the top of a covered parking system. Unshaded south facing standing seam metal roofs or flat membrane roofs offer the simplest and most cost-effective mounting surfaces for roof top PV systems. Ensure roof structures are adequate for the added weight of the PV system and be aware of any roof-top warranty implications from adding PV systems. Roof mounting systems that do not penetrate the continuous insulation of the roof deck, such as a self ballasted racking system, should be used. To allow for easy installation of PV systems on the roofs of schools, provide extra conduit from the roof to the inverters, typically located either in an electrical room or a secure outdoor location. Also ensure the main electrical distribution system, from the main distribution panel to the building transformer, has the capability of carrying additional PV wiring.

Smaller systems are typically used mostly as teaching devices. They are usually installed in plain view to make them visible to the students, teachers, and the surrounding community, thereby helping to inform the public of the importance of renewable energy sources and the technology involved. See QA18 for teaching tool strategies that use PV systems.

There are many unique funding opportunities for PV systems in schools. In addition to the many rebate programs offered by state and local utility companies, there are often significant incentives, loans, grants, and buyback programs for PV systems in K-12 schools. The Database for State Incentives for Renewables & Efficiency (NREL 2011a) shows some of the opportunities available to schools in various states.

There are numerous tools available for modeling energy production from PV systems. One such tool is National Renewable Energy Laboratory's (NREL) PVWatts™ calculator available on the NREL Web site as part of their Renewable Data Resource Center (NREL 2011b). The tool determines the energy production and cost savings of grid-connected PV energy systems throughout the world. It allows school designers, installers, manufacturers, and students to easily develop estimates of the performance of PV installations.

RE2   *Wind Turbine Power* (Climate Zones: all)

Wind energy is one of the lowest-priced renewable energy technologies available today, costing between \$0.05–\$0.11 per kilowatt-hour, depending on the wind resource and project financing of the particular project. For K-12 school buildings, small-to-medium-sized wind turbines are typically considered. These turbines range from 4 to 200 kW and are typically mounted on towers from 50 to 100 ft and connected to the utility grid through the building's electrical distribution system.

One of the first steps to developing a wind energy project is to assess the area's wind resources and estimate the available energy. From wind resource maps, you can determine if your area of interest should be further explored. Note that the wind resource at a micro level can vary significantly; therefore, you should get a professional evaluation of your specific area of interest.

The map in Figure 5-32 shows the annual average wind power estimates at 50 m above ground. It combines high- and low-resolution data sets that have been screened to eliminate land-based areas unlikely to be developed due to land use or environmental issues. In many states, the wind resource has been visually enhanced to better show the distribution on ridge crests and other features. Estimates of the wind resource are expressed in wind power classes ranging from Class 1 (lowest) to Class 7 (highest), with each class representing a range of mean wind power density or equivalent mean speed at specified heights above the ground. This map does not show Classes 1 and 2, as Class 2 areas are marginal and Class 1 areas are unsuitable for wind energy development. In general, at 50 m, wind power Class 4 or higher can be useful for generating wind power. More detailed state wind maps are available at the Wind Powering America website (DOE 2011).

Although the wind turbines themselves do not take up a significant amount of space, they need to be installed an adequate distance from the nearest building for several reasons, including turbulence reduction (which affects efficiency), noise control, and safety. It is essential that coordination occurs between the owner, design team, and site planner to establish the optimal wind turbine location relative to the other facilities on the site.

The three largest complaints about wind turbines are noise, hazard to birds, and aesthetic appearance. Most of these problems have been resolved or greatly reduced through technological

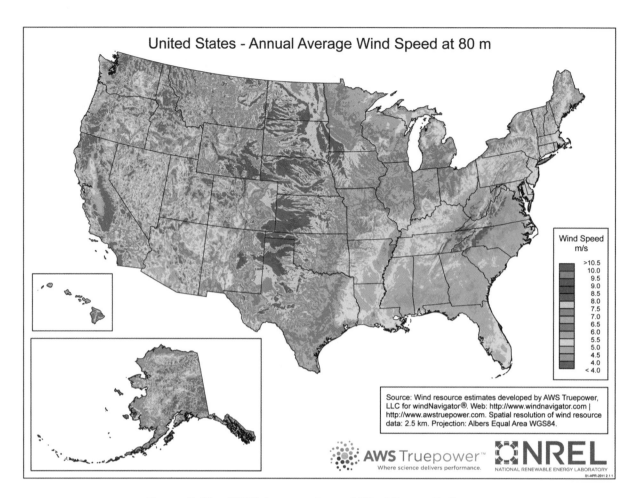

Figure 5-32 (RE2) Average Annual Wind Power Estimates
Source: National Renewable Energy Laboratory (NREL)

development or by properly siting wind turbines. Most small wind turbines today have an excellent safety record. An important factor is to consider how the wind turbine controls itself and shuts itself down. Can operators shut it off and stop the turbine when they want or need to do so? This is extremely important and, unfortunately, there are very few small turbines that have reliable means to stop the rotor on command. The few that do may require you to do so from the base of the tower—not exactly where you want to be if the turbine is out of control in a wind storm. Look for a system that offers one or more means to shut down and preferably stop the rotor remotely.

Using energy modeling, the electric energy consumption of a building can be estimated. Using this data in conjunction with the financial detail of the project including the rebates, the owner and designer must then chose the correct size turbine that meets their needs. Note that the closer the match of the turbine energy output to the demand, the more cost-effective the system will be. Make sure that all costs are listed to give a total cost of ownership for the wind turbine. This includes the wind turbine, tower, electrical interconnection, controls, installation, maintenance, concrete footings, guy wires, and cabling.

In addition to evaluating the initial cost of the turbine, it is extremely important to consider the federal and state policies and incentive programs that are available. The Database for State Incentives for Renewables & Efficiency (NREL 2011a) provides a list of available incentives, grants, and rebates. Also critical to the financial success of a wind turbine project is a favorable net metering agreement with the utility.

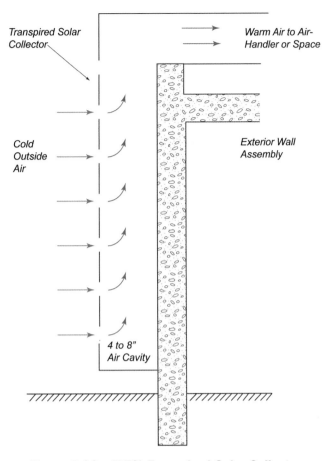

Figure 5-33   (RE3) Transpired Solar Collector

RE3   *Transpired Solar Collector* (Climate Zones: ❸ ❹ ❺ ❻ ❼)

A transpired solar collector is a renewable energy technology that, when coupled with a mechanical system, provides free heating of the air. As illustrated in Figure 5-33, the system is composed of a perforated metal panel with an air cavity between the panel and the exterior wall. As the panel absorbs solar radiation, air is drawn into the cavity. As the air passes over the surface of the wall, the air is warmed.

Warm air is drawn into the mechanical system during heating mode. The free heating of the air can significantly reduce the demand for electric or fossil fuel heating. When heated air is not desired, a bypass damper allows the system to relieve the warm air out of the cavity. Equally important, a separate outside air location is required at these times to provide ventilation air using ambient temperature air rather than the warm air in the transpired solar collector.

Since buildings often go through a morning warm up, east- and south-facing walls are most suitable for transpired solar collector installations. In very cold climates, a west-facing wall may also be suitable. Due to the surface area typically available, gymnasiums are the most common installation locations for schools.

RE4   *Power Purchase Agreements* (Climate Zones: all)

A primary barrier to the use of various on-site renewable energy strategies is the high initial capital investment cost. One way to finance and implement such a strategy is through a power purchase agreement. School systems have successfully implemented renewable energy systems, such as photovoltaic, wind, and solar hot-water, using these financing programs.

Power purchase agreements involve a third-party who will design, install, own, operate, and maintain the power generation asset. The school facility then contracts to purchase the energy produced by the generation system, usually for a long period of time. This arrangement allows the school to avoid the high first cost and keeps the balance sheet clear of obligation. It also locks in an energy price, thus hedging the cost of energy over time from fluctuations in the prices of other energy sources. These agreements are especially attractive to non-tax-paying entities that cannot access tax-based incentives that help to offset the cost of renewable systems. The agreements are complicated, with many considerations, and require negotiation by people familiar with the complexities, both from an engineering perspective as well as from a legal and financial perspective.

REFERENCES AND RESOURCES

DOE. 2011. Wind & water program. Wind Powering America, U.S. Department of Energy, Washington, DC. http://www.windpoweringamerica.gov/wind_maps.asp.

NREL. 2011a. Database of state incentives for renewables & efficiency. Subcontract XEU-0-99515-01, National Renewable Energy Laboratory, U.S. Department of Energy. http://www.dsireusa.org/.

NREL. 2011b. PVWatts site specific data calculator, V1.0. National Renewable Energy Laboratory, U.S. Department of Energy, Washington, DC. www.nrel.gov/rredc/pvwatts/site_specific.html.

Appendix A— Envelope Thermal Performance Factors

A

Each recommendation table in Chapter 4 presents a prescriptive construction option for each opaque envelope measure. Table A-1 presents U-factors for above-grade components, C-factors for below-grade walls, and F-factors for slab-on-grade floors that correspond to each prescriptive construction option. Alternative constructions would be equivalent methods for meeting the recommendations of this Guide provided they are less than or equal to the thermal performance factors listed in Table A-1.

Table A-1 Opaque Construction Options

Roof Assemblies		Walls, Above Grade		Floors	
R	**U**	**R**	**U**	**R**	**C**
Insulation Above Deck		**Mass Walls**		**Mass**	
20	0.048	5.7	0.151	4.2 c.i.	0.137
25	0.039	7.6	0.123	10.4 c.i.	0.074
30	0.032	11.4	0.090	12.5 c.i.	0.064
35	0.028	13.3	0.080	14.6 c.i.	0.056
Attic and Other		19.5	0.062	16.7 c.i.	0.051
38	0.027	**Steel Framed**		20.9 c.i.	0.042
49	0.021	13 + 7.5 c.i.	0.064	23.0 c.i.	0.038
60	0.017	13 + 15.6 c.i.	0.042	**Steel Framed**	
Metal Building		13 + 18.8 c.i.	0.037	19	0.052
19 + 10 FC	0.057	**Wood Framed and Other**		30	0.038
19 + 11 Ls	0.035	13	0.089	38	0.032
25 + 11 Ls	0.031	13 + 3.8 c.i.	0.064	49	0.027
30 + 11 Ls	0.029	13 + 7.5 c.i.	0.051	60	0.024
25+11+11 Ls	0.026	13 + 10.0 c.i.	0.045	**Wood Framed and Other**	
		13 + 12.5 c.i.	0.040	19	0.051
Slabs		13 + 15.0 c.i.	0.037	30	0.033
R - in.	**F**	13 + 18.8 c.i.	0.032	38	0.027
Unheated		**Metal Building**		49	0.022
10 - 24	0.54	0 + 9.8 c.i.	0.094	60	0.018
20 - 24	0.51	0 + 13.0 c.i.	0.072		
Heated		0 + 19.0 c.i.	0.050		
7.5 - 12	0.60	0 + 22.1 c.i.	0.044		
10 - 24	0.90	0 + 25.0 c.i.	0.039		
15 - 24	0.86				
20 - 24	0.843	**Walls, Below Grade**			
20 - 48	0.688	**R**	**C**		
25 - 48	0.671	7.5 c.i.	0.119		
20 full slab	0.373	10.0 c.i.	0.092		
		15.0 c.i.	0.067		

C = thermal conductance, Btu/h·ft^2·°F
c.i. = continuous insulation
F = slab edge heat loss coefficient per foot of perimeter, Btu/h·ft·°F
FC = filled cavity
Ls = liner system
R = thermal resistance, h·ft^2·°F/Btu
R - in. = R-value followed by the depth of insulation in inches
U = thermal transmittance, Btu/h·ft^2·°F

Appendix B—International Climatic Zone Definitions

Table B-1 shows the climate zone definitions that are applicable to any location. The information is from ASHRAE/IESNA Standard 90.1-2007, Normative Appendix B, Table B-4 (ASHRAE 2007). Climate zone information for specific cities in Canada, Mexico, and other international cities can be found in the same appendix and is also available on the AEDG Web page (www.ashrae.org/aedg) in the "Additional Information" section. Weather data is needed in order to use the climate zone definitions for a particular city. Weather data by city is available for a large number of international cities in 2009 *ASHRAE Handbook—Fundamentals* (ASHRAE 2009).

Table B-1 International Climatic Zone Definitions

Climate Zone Number	Name	Thermal Criteria*
1A and 1B	Very Hot–Humid (1A) Dry (1B)	9000 < CDD50°F
2A and 2B	Hot–Humid (2A) Dry (2B)	6300 < CDD50°F ≤ 9000
3A and 3B	Warm–Humid (3A) Dry (3B)	4500 < CDD50°F ≤ 6300
3C	Warm–Marine (3C)	CDD50°F ≤ 4500 AND HDD65°F ≤ 3600
4A and 4B	Mixed–Humid (4A) Dry (4B)	CDD50°F ≤ 4500 AND 3600 < HDD65°F ≤ 5400
4C	Mixed–Marine (4C)	3600 < HDD65°F ≤ 5400
5A, 5B, and 5C	Cool–Humid (5A) Dry (5B) Marine (5C)	5400 < HDD65°F ≤ 7200
6A and 6B	Cold–Humid (6A) Dry (6B)	7200 < HDD65°F ≤ 9000
7	Very Cold	9000 < HDD65°F ≤ 12600
8	Subarctic	12600 < HDD65°F

*CDD = cooling degree day, HDD = heating degree-day.

DEFINITIONS

Marine (C) Definition—Locations meeting all four of the following criteria:

- Mean temperature of coldest month between 27°F and 65°F
- Warmest month mean < 72°F
- At least four months with mean temperatures over 50°F
- Dry season in summer. The month with the heaviest precipitation in the cold season has at least three times as much precipitation as the month with the least precipitation in the rest of the year. The cold season is October through March in the Northern Hemisphere and April through September in the Southern Hemisphere.

Dry (B) Definition—Locations meeting the following criterion:

- Not marine and $P < 0.44 \times (T - 19.5)$
  where
  P = annual precipitation, in.
  T = annual mean temperature, °F

Moist (A) Definition—Locations that are not marine and not dry.

REFERENCES

ASHRAE. 2007. ANSI/ASHRAE/IESNA Standard 90.1-2007, *Energy Standard for Buildings Except Low-Rise Residential Buildings*. Atlanta: American Society of Heating, Refrigerating and Air-Conditioning Engineers.

ASHRAE. 2009. *ASHRAE Handbook—Fundamentals*. Atlanta: American Society of Heating, Refrigerating and Air-Conditioning Engineers. [Available in print form and on CD-ROM.]

Appendix C— Commissioning Information and Examples

Following are examples of what a commissioning scope of services and a responsibility matrix (Table C-1) might include. Project teams should adjust these to meet the needs of the owner and project scope, budget, and expectations.

COMMISSIONING SCOPE OF SERVICES

INTRODUCTION

Commissioning (Cx) is a quality assurance (QA) process with four main elements. First, the architectural and engineering team must clearly understand the building owner's goals and requirements for the project. Next the architectural and engineering team must design systems that support or respond to those requirements. The construction team must understand how the components of the system must come together to ensure that the system is installed correctly and performs as intended. Last, the operators of the system must also understand how the system is intended to function and have access to information that allows them to maintain it as such. This process requires more coordination, collaboration, and documentation between project team members than traditionally has been provided.

The intent of this appendix is to help provide an understanding of the tasks, deliverables, and costs involved. An independent commissioning authority (CxA), one that is contracted directly with the building owner, will be the building owner's representative to facilitate the Cx process and all of its associated tasks. The CxA will lead the team to ensure everyone understands the various tasks, the roles they play, and the desired outcome or benefit for following the Cx process. The systems required to be commissioned are those that impact the use of energy. Project team members responsible for the design or installation of those systems will have the majority of the Cx work. The majority of the field work will be the responsibility of the mechanical, electrical, and control contractors.

Cx of a new building will ultimately enhance the operation of the building. Reduced utility bills, lower maintenance costs, and a more comfortable and healthier indoor environment will result. Cx focuses on creating buildings that are as close to the owners' and users' objectives (as delineated in the Owner's Project Requirements) as possible. Early detection and resolution of potential issues are the keys to achieving a high-quality building without increasing the total effort and cost to the team members. Resolving design issues early will significantly reduce efforts during construction. Finding mistakes after installation or during start-up are costly to everyone. Checklists will assist the contractors during installation, and installation issues will be detected early. Early detection will reduce the amount of rework required compared to late detection at final inspection. This will also benefit the owner and occupants since the building will work as intended from day one of operation.

SYSTEMS

The systems under this scope of services include the following.

- The entire heating, ventilating, and air-conditioning (HVAC) system (boilers, chillers, pumps, piping, and air distribution systems).
- The building automation system (BAS) for the HVAC system.
- The domestic hot-water system.
- The electrical systems (lighting and receptacle systems, electrical panels, transformers, motor control centers, electrical motors, and other electrical items excluding emergency power systems).
- The building envelope as it relates to energy efficiency (insulation, wall framing—thermal bridging, air leakage, glazing solar and thermal characteristics, and fenestration framing— thermal bridging).

These listed systems will be commissioned by the tasks described in the "Commissioning Tasks" section of this chapter.

DELIVERABLES

The following deliverables are part of the Cx scope of services.

- Commissioning Plan
- Owner's Project Requirements (OPR)
- CxA's design review
- Construction installation checklists
- CxA's site visit reports
- System functional performance tests
- Systems manual
- Owner training
- Cx report
- Systems warranty review
- Final Cx report

SCHEDULE

Cx begins in the early stage of design and continues through building operation. The following sections detail the specific step-by-step activities that owners, designers, and construction team members need to follow in each phase of the project's delivery.

Planning Phase

- Document OPR (project intent)
- Develop Commissioning Plan
- Specify architect/engineer Cx requirements
- Assist with the architect/engineer selection process

Design Phase

- Verify that the design meets the OPR
- Write Cx specifications

Construction Phase

- Verify that the submittals meet OPR
- Verify that the installation meets OPR
- Verify that the components function as required
- Facilitate training of building operators

Acceptance Phase

- Verify that the systems work as required and meets OPR
- Verify that the OPR are met throughout the building
- Develop systems manual
- Review contractors' operation and maintenance and systems manuals

Operational Phase

- Warranty review
- Verify that the operation of the building is optimal

COMMISSIONING TASKS

Commissioning Plan

The CxA will write the Commissioning Plan and detail the Cx tasks and schedule for executing the Commissioning Plan tasks. In addition, the communication channels will be listed and samples of all forms, procedures, and checklists used for the project will be provided. The Cx responsibilities of each of the project team members will be listed. The Commissioning Plan will be updated as the project progresses and as forms, procedures, checklists, schedules, agendas, reports, etc., are finalized or revised. These updates will be distributed at major milestones to all project team members.

Owner's Project Requirements (OPR)

The OPR document describes the main expectations the owner wants the project to meet. As the owner usually wants to meet most of the expectations of all stakeholders, input from a representative of each stakeholder is beneficiary.

For the referenced project the CxA will facilitate and write the OPR with input from the owner.

Commissioning Specifications

The Cx specifications will clearly state what will be expected from the contractors. This will include activities the contractor needs to participate in and documentation procedures required throughout the construction period. Sample forms and procedures will be provided to show the contractors visuals of what they will need to complete in the construction and acceptance phases. The Cx specifications will also include the training requirements as well as the documentation needed to develop the systems manual.

The CxA will provide the requirements for Cx in the construction phase to be integrated into the specifications.

Basis of Design (BoD)

The Basis of Design (BoD) includes all engineering and architectural calculations and assumptions on how to design the systems such that the OPR are met. This document will be written by the architect and engineers and will be reviewed by the CxA for completeness and quality. Comments will be provided if any pertinent information is missing or if more details are needed. The BoD will need to be updated if any changes occur during the project. This is needed to inform all project team members about revised assumptions and new directions the project is heading in.

Design Review

During the design review the CxA will focus on verifying that the OPR will be met. In addition, the design documents will be reviewed for constructability, operability, and maintainability. The review will take place at 70% completion and be back-checked for resolution of issues at 95% and design completion. Effort will be made to resolve all design issues throughout the remaining design phase and verify that they have been resolved in the later design submittals and the construction documents (CDs).

The design review will also focus on the selection, evaluation, and choice of the main systems. Review the design documents against the OPR to verify that the project will meet the intent of the owner. Any choices, conclusions, or design details that deviate from the OPR will be brought to the attention of the owner and the general contractor. Additional information will be requested when documentation is insufficient to support the conclusions and choices or when required design assumptions or calculations have not been provided.

Energy efficiency is achieved by verifying the design and operation of the systems and by making the building owner aware of alternative building systems and equipment options.

Examples of building systems that will be evaluated include the following:

- Building envelope
- Building ventilation
- Lighting
- Office equipment
- HVAC equipment
- Control systems and strategies
- HVAC distribution systems
- Domestic hot-water systems
- Water use
- Occupancy schedules
- Utility rate structures

Installation Checklist Database

A checklist database will be established for all components included in the commissioned systems. The checklists will focus on providing the contractor guidance about critical requirements during installation to clearly establish the expectations of the installations.

The CxA will design these checklists to minimize the paperwork for the contractors but at the same time to cover the critical installation issues.

Construction Verification

The CxA will facilitate monthly on-site construction meetings to ensure all design, construction, and building owner representatives understand the process, the desired outcomes, and the roles/responsibilities of the various team members. The CxA will focus on training and on the Cx process during construction while at these site visits. During the construction review, the CxA will focus on verifying that the Cx process is being followed by statistical sampling and verifying that the construction checklists are completed and submitted as required. The CxA will also verify that the record drawings are on site and are being updated with any deviations in installations compared to the construction drawings. In addition, the construction progress will be evaluated against the established OPR. The CxA will verify that the Cx process is proceeding as intended during the construction phase and will review the site visit reports and Cx meeting minutes. The CxA will notify the building owner and general contractor if the Cx process is not progressing as intended by identifying and resolving issues. The day-to-day follow-up will be the responsibility of the general contractor and the subcontractors.

Review Submittals

The CxA will review the submittals concurrently with the architect and engineers. Any observed deviations from the OPR will be noted and submitted to the architect and engineers to be evaluated and submitted with their comments back to the contractor. The architect and engineers' submittal review process will also be evaluated. A selection of the architect and engineers' submittals responses will be reviewed to verify that any deviations from the design documents are properly addressed. The CxA must understand the general contractor's project delivery process and its impact on the submittal review step.

Training

The training agenda format will be submitted by the engineers to the general contractor and owner to schedule the required training sessions. The CxA will review this training agenda and attend a key training session. Each training session will be evaluated after completion of the training. Any deviations from the expected competence level of the operation and maintenance (O&M) staff will be discussed with the owner and contractors, and the remaining training agendas will be revised to accommodate any lacking knowledge.

Systems Performance

The systems performance tests will be completed as soon as all submittals for the systems manual have been received and all installation checklists have been completed. These systems performance tests will focus on the installed systems' capabilities to meet the design intent. The CxA will document the procedures required for these tests and submit these test procedures to general contractor for the project team's and general contractor's review. The subcontractors are responsible for ensuring that all systems can meet the specified requirements and for demonstrating that the systems are able to perform all procedures successfully. The CxA will witness a representative number of systems performance tests to verify that all systems work as intended. If any of the systems performance tests are unsatisfactory, these systems and a representative number of other similar systems will be required to be retested at the contractors' expense.

Review Systems Manual

The general contractor will generate the systems manual based on the subcontractor submittals for the installed equipment and the test and start-up results. The CxA will review this systems manual and provide any comments to general contractor.

Commissioning Report

The Cx report will summarize the results of Cx activities for the project. This Cx report will essentially be the Commissioning Plan with all the results of the Cx activities. The initial Cx report will be submitted two weeks after substantial completion, and the final report will be submitted one year after substantial completion. This is the responsibility of the CxA.

Operation and Warranty Review

The operation and warranty review will be completed at ten months after completion. The review will focus on the experiences of the O&M staff with the building operation and evaluate the systems performance and operation relative to the OPR. Any deviations from the original operational intent and any component failures will be noted and addressed with the owner's representative. A report will be issued to the owner with suggested actions to take.

Table C-1 Sample Commissioning Scope Matrix—Responsibilities and Schedule

Responsibility						Project Phase				Commissioning Task
Architect	Engineer	General Contractor / Construction Manager	Subcontractors	CxA	Owner	Predesign	Design	Construction	Construction	
						X				**Designate CxA (qualifications apply)**
										Provide name, firm, and experience information for the CxA
						X				**Develop the OPR; include:**
										Primary purpose, program, and use of proposed project
										Project history
										Program needs, future expansion, flexibility, quality of materials, and construction and operational cost goals
										Environmental and sustainability goals
										Energy efficiency goals
										Indoor environmental quality requirements
										Equipment and system expectations
										Building occupant and O&M personnel requirements
							X				**Develop a Commissioning Plan**
										Cx program overview
										Goals and objectives
										General project information
										Systems to be commissioned
										Cx team
										Team members, roles, and responsibilities
										Communication protocol, coordination, meetings, and management
										Description of Cx process
							X				**Implement a Commissioning Plan**
										Document the OPR
										Prepare the BoD
										Document the Cx review process
										Develop systems functional test procedures
										Review contractor submittals
										Verify systems performance
										Report deficiencies and resolution processes
										Develop the systems manual
										Verify the training of operations
										Accept the building systems at substantial completion
										Review building operation after final acceptance

Table C-1 Sample Commissioning Scope Matrix—Responsibilities and Schedule *(Continued)*

Responsibility						Project Phase				Commissioning Task
Architect	Engineer	General Contractor / Construction Manager	Subcontractors	CxA	Owner	Predesign	Design	Construction	Construction	
							X			**BoD**
										Include narrative of systems to be commissioned
										Document design assumptions
										Reference applicable standards and codes
							X			**Cx requirements in CDs (include in specifications)**
										Specify Cx team involvement
										Specify contractors' responsibilities
										Specify submittals and submittal review procedures for Cx process/systems
										Specify O&M documentation requirements
										Specify meetings documentation process and responsibilities
										Specify construction verification procedures and responsibilities
										Specify start-up plan development and implementation
										Specify responsibilities and scope for functional performance testing
										Specify criteria for acceptance and closeout
										Specify rigor and requirements for training
										Specify scope for warranty review site visit
							X			**Conduct Cx Design Review**
										Review and update OPR for clarity, completeness, and adequacy
										Review BoD for all issues identified in OPR
										Review design documents for coordination
										Review design documents for compliance with OPR and BoD
										If multiple reviews are performed, check compliance with previous review comments
							X			**Review of Contractor Submittals**
										Review all product submittals to make sure they meet BoD, OPR, and O&M requirements
										Evaluate submittals for facilitating performance testing
										Review all contractor submittals for compliance with design intent and CDs

Table C-1 Sample Commissioning Scope Matrix—Responsibilities and Schedule *(Continued)*

Architect	Engineer	General Contractor / Construction Manager	Subcontractors	CxA	Owner	Predesign	Design	Construction	Construction	Commissioning Task
								X		**Verify Installation and Performance of the Systems to be Commissioned**
										Perform installation inspection (pre-functional checklist)
										Perform system performance testing (functional test)
										Evaluate results compared to OPR and BoD
								X		**Complete Summary Cx Report**
										Executive summary
										Document history of system deficiencies/issues
										Record system performance test results
								X		**Develop Systems Manual**
										Develop systems manual in addition to O&M manuals submitted by contractor
										Include in systems manual:
										Final version of BoD
										System single-line diagrams
										As-built sequence of operations, control drawings, and original setpoints
										Operating instructions for integrated building systems
										Recommended schedule of maintenance requirements and frequency
										Recommended schedule for retesting of commissioned systems
										Blank testing forms from original Commissioning Plan for retesting
										Recommended schedule for calibrating sensors and actuators
					X			X	X	**Project Training Requirements**
										Create project training requirements document with owner
										Participate in project training session
										Ensure O&M staff and occupants receive required training and orientation
										Create and document post-training survey
										Verify and document that training requirements are met
					X				X	**8–10 Month Warranty Walkthrough**
										Perform a warranty systems review within ten months after substantial completion
										Resolve any issues found
										Create a plan for resolution of outstanding Cx-related issues